For Yen Lu, a
new dear friend.
Hope you enjoy

TALES
OF
WO-CHI-CA

~ne Levine + *June Gordon*

TALES
OF
WO-CHI-CA

*Blacks, Whites and Reds
at Camp*

BY
June Levine and Gene Gordon

Page Layout and Design by Jos Sances
Jacket Design by Jos Sances and the authors

Library of Congress Cataloging-in-Publication Data

Levine/Gordon
Tales of Wo-Chi-Ca: Blacks, Whites and Reds at Camp

1. Radical Summer Camps, 2. Paul Robeson, 3. American History, I. Title

PCN 2002100142
ISBN 0-9717435-0-9

Printed on acid free paper in the United States of America

"Merry-go-round" and "Let America Be America Again" from THE COL-
LECTED POEMS OF LANGSTON HUGHES by Langston Hughes, copyright
© 1994 by The Estate of Langston Hughes. Used by permission of Alfred A.
Knopf, a division of Random House, Inc.

"If We Must Die" and "To A Dark Girl" courtesy of the Literary Representative
for the Works of Claude McCay and the Works of Gwendolyn Bennett,
Schomburg Center for Research in Black Culture, The New York Public
Library, Astor, Lenox and Tilden Foundations.

Additional copies may be ordered from
Avon Springs Press
1548 Golden Rain Rd.#12
Walnut Creek, CA 94595
(925) 934-3204
june.gene@yahoo.com

Dedicated to the memory of

Eve Levine

Secretary and Registrar
of
Camp Wo-Chi-Ca

Mother of two
Wo-Chi-Ca girls

ACKNOWLEDGMENTS

Wholehearted thanks to...

Jos Sances of Alliance Graphics in Berkeley for kind, expert and indispensable assistance

Jane Rollins for loving financial aid

Seth Rick and the Chester Rick Foundation

Bonnie Weiss for painstaking proofreading (but still, we are accountable for any errors that remain)

Sue Weinstock Gould for providing *the Diary of Marian Cuca*, and Fred Jerome for a photograph of Marian Cuca

Irwin Silber for generous help with songs

Bob Friedman who maintains the Wo-Chi-Ca web site

Anne Barry, Helen Garvey, Ann Lieberman, Ann and Al Wasserman for advice and assistance

Barbara Spielberg for Peekskill material

McNaughton & Gunn Printers with whom it is a pleasure to work

Lloyd Brown and Martin Duberman on whose Robeson biographies we draw heavily

Tamiment Library of New York

Phyllis Hersh, Carol and Fred Rosenthal, Barbara and Peter Sciaky, Marion and Lloyd "Mustard" Stempel, Mary Zimmerman and others too many to mention, for hospitality on our trips

And countless Wo-Chi-Cans who submitted anecdotes, memoirs, and read early drafts of the manuscript

FOREWORD

I was almost eleven and beginning to understand that there was a harsh world out there – Hitler, Mussolini, Father Coughlin, Ethiopia, Spain – when my mother joined the International Workers Order and sent me to their children's sleep-away camp, turning me into a proper little Bolshevik. Which is to say that Camp Wo-Chi-Ca was about something more than warehousing a bunch of kids pleasantly for a few summer weeks.

Behind the facade of providing swimming and games and braiding lanyards and nature study and square dancing and chorus and drama and so forth, what those commies did to us innocent children was fill us full of dangerous ideas, i.e., no fights, talk it over! treat your bunkmates as you would yourself! consider what's best for the group as well as yourself; respect the dignity of the kitchen worker and the kitchen worker's work! in union there is strength! hate racism! if you have a little extra, help the camper who hasn't enough; wash your hands before entering the dining room! Not to speak of all those communistic songs about love for all humankind that we had to learn! No wonder so many of us turned out the way we did: social workers, for heaven's sake, Harvard professors, God knows what else... folksingers!

Yes, here we are in the book, many soft-headed, brainwashed Wo-Chi-Canites (to the end, I fear) our awful left-wing principles intact, we petition signers, we anti-war demonstrators, we pick-eters, women's rights advocates, immigration counselors – ripe for picking off by the next un-Patriotic Enough Committee. Also included are a few who managed to resist all that wicked influence. Clever Davey Horowitz, summer of 1951, for instance, and Prof. Ron Radosh, summer of – oh, wait, Ron didn't actually go to Wo-Chi-Ca, he just knows it was bad. Well, good for them anyway – you'll never catch THEM having to answer questions on the stand about THEIR principles. Whew!

June Levine and Gene Gordon's book will of course wake up wonderfully happy memories for those of us who were there at Wo-Chi-Ca, and some that are very sad, like the camp's unsuccessful struggle to survive McCarthyism. It's altogether a fine story. I couldn't put it down. For others who never had the Wo-Chi-Ca experience, it will be a glimpse of a time and place when hundreds of youngsters each summer discovered that even as children we could think as individuals and also be part of a community, could participate in a life of ideas along with sports and games.

The contributors of memoirs appear to have done well with that indoctrination, even through deeply disappointing times and distressing events. They seem to have escaped the crippling bitterness that turned others against their own hearts. Wo-Chi-Ca must have been doing something right. Not only that, but the book is a fine example of the camp ideal: Who says serious can't be fun!

Ronnie Gilbert
Berkeley, California

CONTENTS

INTRODUCTION

Once, long ago, on the gentle slopes of a mountain, there flourished a summer camp for kids. In that secluded spot, the warm sun of July and August smiled on hundreds of children hiking, swimming, dancing, singing... They explored nature; they fashioned arts and crafts. Their camp they called Wo-Chi-Ca.

Nearby farmers assumed the camp with the Indian name was a place where feather-bedecked children chanted, danced, and sat cross-legged to make beaded wallets.

But like an arrow gone wildly astray, these images veered far off the mark. The name Wo-Chi-Ca was a contraction of Workers Children's Camp. Red indeed was the color, but not of Indian war paint. These children of workers would, in the early years, raise a red flag and sing the "Internationale."

In addition to blazing red, the camp gleamed a proud black. Many Negroes were seen at Wo-Chi-Ca; they comprised nearly twenty percent of camper enrollment and fully a quarter of the staff. Moreover, the camp was host to many Jews as well as a number of Asians, Puerto Ricans, and Italians. These strange city slickers looked, to the natives of surrounding small towns, as if they came off slave ships and Ellis Island freighters – certainly not the Mayflower!

Well, wasn't this the American idea – the true American melting pot? Locals did observe Camp Wo-Chi-Ca to be a patriotic place, always big on Fourth of July celebrations. And well they knew that in the grim war against the Germans and Japanese, some of those camp people died fighting for their country. So the neighbors, while they reckoned the camp to be pretty peculiar, allowed that Wo-Chi-Cans were American enough to meet on the diamond in many a friendly baseball game. That is until 1950. Then, seething with hate from the Cold War and Red Scare, local 'patriots' converted their playful bats to lethal clubs. They assailed campers verbally and physically. "Wo-Chi-Ca stands for integration, integration means Communism, and Communism is un-American!" They invaded the grounds demanding removal of the PAUL ROBESON sign from the Playhouse. In the end the camp had to shut down.

Only twenty summers – a brief existence of a small camp in a back-water of New Jersey. Half a century has flown since Wo-Chi-Ca folded its tents forever. And yet Wo-Chi-Ca lives on, not only as a long-lost utopia or childhood dream, but in life-long principles and progressive ideals.

True, many similar camps existed at the time. Twenty-seven "Communist camps" operated in New York State alone, according to a government inquisition. But all agree – friend or foe – that Wo-Chi-Ca was utterly unique. How did this short-lived, this evanes-cent children's camp grow to such legendary proportions? Come with us down the old trails, and hear these Tales of Wo-Chi-Ca.

June Levine and Gene Gordon
Franklin Lake Hot Springs, California
April, 2002

Oh camp so fine, Wo-Chi-Ca mine,
There's not another camp like mine!

TEMPEST BORN

I n summer, don't we long to leave behind the heat, the crowds, the noise of the city? We want to hike in the woods instead, to swim or read, relax in the sun, watch the stars. The good old summertime should be *nitgedaigit* time, a time "not to worry."

Early in the last century, poor working people especially wanted to get their children out of the city. Hot and humid streets – sooty and smelly, dirty and dangerous – was this where kids should spend their summer vacation?

Butchers, painters, garment workers would scrimp and save all year for two care-free weeks in the country. By the 1920's they could find low-cost summer retreats just a short train ride from New York. Fanning out in all directions, families thronged to the woods. American Communists also joined this great exodus, and in fact, Party members at this time had sufficient numbers to maintain their very own vacation spots.

With hammers and sickles painted on its bungalow doors, a camp actually named Nitgedaigit was one such haven where comrades went to spend their vacation and not to worry. Though primarily a resort for adults, enough parents brought their kids to Nitgedaigit that a program for them became necessary. They asked a young woman named Julia Gaberman to organize children's activities.

Today, in her nineties, Julia Gaberman Davis recalls these early years.

I loved art in college. But I was afraid I wouldn't be able to earn a living as an artist, so I took a degree in chemistry. But in the Depression I couldn't find work even as a scientist. The only jobs open were Home Relief, so I went to work for the New York City Welfare Department.

I worked in Welfare for many years, and I rose to high administrative positions. I married a pharmacist, Leon Davis. In 1932, Leon started a small union of drugstore workers and built it into the largest organiztion of health care workers in the country. For fifty years my husband was the leader of Local 1199. He was legendary!

In the 1920s I was in the Young Pioneers, the youth group of the Communist Party. But I didn't lecture the Nitgedaigit kids on Communism; that was not my way. I preferred games, nature studies and even sex education. I wondered whether to give up on the sex business after I overheard a boy saying "My father planted an egg in my mother."

When a group from Nitgedaigit left to open another camp in nearby Wingdale, New York, I organized the children's program at this new camp as well. But at Camp Unity it was difficult for both children and adults to share the lake, playing fields, and especially the dining room. Someday, we hoped, there would be a separate summer camp just for kids. Where the land would come from, we didn't know. But we already had a name for our dream: Workers Children's Camp. That was my idea. I said, "For short we can call it Wo-Chi-Ca!"

Meanwhile, in a neighboring state, a progressive farmer and his wife found it increasingly difficult to make a go of their farm. In the Depression year of 1934, it failed completely, and the Lanz family donated the 127-acre property to Camp Unity. Here was the land! And so, conceived in rural New York and delivered in agrarian New Jersey, Wo-Chi-Ca, a true Depression Baby was born.

The infant's cradle would rock in the turbulent winds of a country in dire economic collapse. Over thirteen percent of America's population was without work – millions let go, hundreds of thousands on strike, tens of thousands forced off their land. In 1934, the very year of Wo-Chi-Ca's birth, terrible storms ruined 300 million acres of cropland in the 'Dust Bowl' of Kansas, Texas, Colorado, and Oklahoma. John Steinbeck saw impoverished farmers "...streaming over the mountains, hungry and restless – restless as ants, scurrying to find work to do – to lift, to push, to pull, to pick, to cut – anything, any burden to bear, for food."

In that same year, the 'Big Strike' of seamen and dock workers closed down all ports from Seattle to San Diego. San Francisco workers – 100,000 strong – paralyzed the city in a general strike. And in Southern mills, half a million textile workers walked off their jobs during 'The Great Uprising.'

Wasn't it odd that in such tumultuous times a group of New York laboring people would devote themselves to a new summer camp for kids? No, not so strange. These men and women of the Depression who laid the foundation for Wo-Chi-Ca were working class fighters on the cutting edge of struggle. It was they who organized the unions and led the strikes. They fought the tenement evictions, agitated for home relief, for unemployment insurance. They marched to free the Scottsboro defendants.

But why establish a Wo-Chi-Ca when they might send their children to other radical summer camps where they would also absorb and appreciate the politics of their parents? There were a number of reasons. Some radical camps provided a cultural experience with a pronounced Jewish emphasis; some stressed the local folklore. Few of the children's camps of the time served both boys and girls. And almost none of the camps would be as dirt cheap as Wo-Chi-Ca.

Most of all, the idealists who would found Wo-Chi-Ca wanted their children to experience 'The World of the Future' today, through shared living with those of different racial and ethnic backgrounds. They especially wanted to welcome Negro children at their new camp. Labor-based, co-educational, affordable, inter-racial – for a children's camp in 1934, a revolutionary concept.

And so, in the spring of that year, an advance party arrived at the wooded farm in New Jersey. The scene they beheld dismayed them: a peeling, plastered farm-house dating back to Colonial days, an abandoned farm workers' bunkhouse taken over by a dozen straggling chickens, a ravaged red barn, a dirty, damp mess hall. Rank and gross poison ivy possessed it entirely. Could they fix the place up? Money was scarcer than hens' teeth. A call for help went out to the unions. "Brother, Can You Spare a Dime?" Scores of volunteers came up from the city – office workers, unemployed, construction workers hauling salvaged building material – all navigating the winding dirt roads to the foot of the Schooleys Mountains. "Life is Just a Bowl of Cherries," they sang as they uprooted the poi-son ivy. Then, itching from head to foot, they took up hammers and saws.

The first priority was to pump fresh water from the old well and store it. A water tower became the initial construction feat: steel girders anchored in cement sup-porting a wooden barrel.

The volunteers rebuilt the mess hall and covered its peeling walls with knotty pine. They constructed a large wash house with showers and flush toilets. They scrubbed chicken manure from the farm worker shacks, partitioning them into spaces for painting, photography, clay modeling, arts and crafts. The old barn, now fitted with benches and a stage, would serve as theater and assembly hall. A summer camp was taking shape.

Vaino Hill, a Finnish master builder, came to help and never left; he stayed on as year-round caretaker. In snowy winter months he carved benches and cabinets as well as eighteen round tables of oak for the mess hall.

Bronx stonemason Angelo Calabrese, who had worked on the great cathedral of Saint John the Divine, laid down flagstone walkways to replace dirt paths. Along each walk he fashioned graceful stone drinking fountains cleverly designed to hold blocks of ice. The Calabrese children – Primo, Mickey and Billy – dug clay from the creek to help their father construct an incinerator. All three kids stayed on as campers, their own labor paying their way.

"Yukon" Bares, Eddie Silverberg, Nick Caggiano and their crews constructed eight wooden bunkhouses, each holding ten or twelve cots. Screens across the upper half of the bunks let in air. If it rained, the campers could lower large wooden panels over the screens. Sunlight streamed in by day, but at night, with no money for electricity, the bunks were dark. The campers would have to grope their way to bed by flashlight and starlight.

The shining star in Camp Wo-Chi-Ca's sky turned out to be the crumbling old farmhouse. Work crews, stripping the peeling plaster, discovered hand-cut stone walls now glowing in the sun.

The crowning touch to their labors the workers placed at the camp entrance. Now, when the first busloads of children tumbled out, they would behold an elegant hand-carved wooden sign:

So many children passed that sign that it wasn't long before the camp needed more sleeping space. Again volunteers went to work, assembling wooden platforms to support well-patched canvas tents. The side of each tent bore large stenciled letters: "I&C." What could they stand for, the young campers wondered – "Ice Cream and Cookies?" No, someone joked – "Immigrants and Communists!" No one dreamed these were discarded army tents and that I&C meant "Inspected and Condemned."

Each dome-shaped tent, with cots for eight campers and a counselor, had a 'glory hole' at the top for ventilation. The lower part of the tent rolled up to let in more air, but often mosquitoes came along too. At the first sign of rain, four campers would rush outside, grab the hanging ropes and run around the tent to close the glory hole flap. Meanwhile, the other four unrolled the side flaps, then jumped inside to join their tent mates in the damp khaki twilight.

Later, larger rectangular tents arrived which could sleep twelve. These, too, had sides to let down for rain, but no glory hole. Instead, the entire front could be opened up like the flap on old-fashioned long johns. Campers especially coveted the two front beds, for on starry nights they might hope to see a shooting star before they fell asleep.

Wo-Chi-Ca's season started at the end of June when the public schools closed, and it ran through Labor Day – five periods of two weeks each. The camp had room for only two hundred children at one time; there were always more applicants than spaces. How to allocate those spaces?

Wo-Chi-Ca's directors aimed, above all, for ethnic diversity and racial integration. Since so many campers came from union families, the former came naturally. The Irish, Italian, Polish, Slavic and Jewish streams formed the pool from which Wo-Chi-Ca drew its constituency. But racial integration – how could that be achieved? Where would Negro kids come from? Most Black families, barred from unions and segregated in ghettos, would not know of Camp Wo-Chi-Ca. They had to be recruited.

Organizers reached out to Black neighborhoods. They visited the Harlem Children's Fresh Air Fund, the Harlem Children's Camp Fund, the Harlem YMCA, inviting them to send their children to Camp Wo-Chi-Ca where integration and equality would be guaranteed.

So successful were these pioneers of affirmative action that by 1943 (when most of the big city was lily-white and Harlem chiefly black), Wo-Chi-Ca could count one Black child in every group of five campers.

Sheila Walkov Newman reflects on this:

I remember a song we sang. It was one of the most beautiful songs I had ever heard. My favorite lines were:

> **Where the children of the workers**
> **Live as one big family,**
> **Black and white we are united**
> **In a true democracy.**

I found my first boyfriend that summer. He was bright, adorable, and Black. We shared the same interest in animals and nature study. He was also nine but somewhat shorter than I. We spent a lot of time touching each other's hair. He liked to feel my long silky strands and I enjoyed rubbing his thick wool.

Yes, integration did become a reality. However, black or white, many working class families could not afford even Camp Wo-Chi-Ca's low rates. In the opening year of 1935, the camp charged eight dollars a week. That same eight dollars could feed a family of four for a week. But the fully employed production worker earned only $16.00 a week. If the parents sent their child to camp, how would they buy shoes and pay the rent? Only through finacial aid could many children attend camp. The Amalgmated Clothing Workers' Union, the Butchers' Union, the Carpenters, Furriers, Painters, and other unions all assisted the children of needy members.

But what of children from non-union families, or from families unemployed or on strike? To provide for them, the camp secured grants from the Greater New York Fund, the Welfare Council of New York City, and the Fresh Air Fund. Wo-Chi-Ca could now offer needy children full 'camperships.'

In addition, the International Workers Order, a progressive insurance company, supported Wo-Chi-Ca solidly. Its members organized benefit concerts, rummage sales, and reached deep into Depression pockets to pull out nickels and dimes. No child would be turned away from camp for lack of funds. Of course, there were parents able to pay their children's way, if only for two weeks. A few, even in Depression days, could manage four or six weeks – perhaps the entire summer. But these more fortunate children were not favored with a rate reduction for staying longer. On the contrary, discounts were given to those staying the shortest time. Their parents had greater need, felt the directors, and lesser ability to pay.

Those who could afford a full summer were charged a rate close to actual operating expenses. For example, a camper enjoying a ten-week stay would pay two hundred dollars, or twenty dollars a week. Her tent-mate in the next bed, however, who stayed two weeks, paid only ten dollars a week. Thus did Wo-Chi-Ca cast aside commercial practice and turn rate schedules upside down.

Unfair? Few parents objected. Most saw the greater fairness in favoring the poor rather than rewarding the well-to-do with a discount for the 'large economy size.' Whether Communists, radicals or staunch liberals, all accepted the principle "From each according to his ability; to each according to his needs."

Wo-Chi-Ca's radicalism was far from unique in the Thirties. Americans were eating in bread lines and soup kitchens while their government burned vast acres of wheat, poured millions of gallons of milk down sewers, and dumped tons of butter in the sea. At a time when multitudes of workers took over factories in sit-down strikes, and thousands marched off to fight fascism in Spain, when legions of people questioned the very validity of capitalism itself – a little left-wing camp in New Jersey hardly raised an eyebrow.

In fact, as we have seen, Wo-Chi-Ca enjoyed the support of local and state agencies. A government bureau administering New Jersey's commodity program qualified Wo-Chi-Ca for assistance. Into the camp's kitchen flowed fruits, vegetables, milk, butter and cheese – 'surplus' food the farmers could not sell, the campers' parents could not buy, and the state would otherwise destroy.

And yet, with all the assistance from unions, government bodies, neighborhood and fraternal organizations, the camp still ran in the red. It was a constant struggle to pay the staff, hire the blue school buses, gas up the old wooden station wagon...

In 1939 a gentle giant would return from long self-exile overseas, and in August of 1940 make his first visit to Camp. Very quickly he would become Wo-Chi-Ca's faithful champion and chief fund-raiser. In the meantime, Wo-Chi-Ca managed somehow. The newly founded camp survived its infancy and grew with every year more strong and sound. The workers' children, away from the hazards of the city, found haven in the country. A Wo-Chi-Ca spirit had emerged, a camaraderie, an excitement, the shared society of black and white and red in the green woods. Wo-Chi-Cans surveyed their house of solid stone, the whispering trees, their swimming hole with running brook, and found good in everything.

SWEET SORROW

Only by way of dirt roads could Camp Wo-Chi-Ca be reached. Horse-drawn wagons would lug ice to Camp over dusty country lanes. Three-hundred-pound blocks of ice, melting in the hot Jersey sun, were needed to refrigerate all the food Wo-Chi-Ca's kitchen prepared. For ten weeks, the camp had to feed two hundred children three times a day. Not until the end of World War II were refrigerators mass-produced, and so ice and more ice. But if some food did go bad, the local farmers profited, for this small spoilage and the much larger quantity of corncobs, vegetable peelings, and garbage from the mess hall went to feed their pigs.

Wo-Chi-Ca did open its gates to others besides icemen and pig farmers; as a matter of fact, the camp was quite cosmopolitan. From their visiting parents, Wo-Chi-Cans heard the latest reports of the fight to save the 'Scottsboro Boys.' Their mothers and fathers told exciting stories of mass protests in New York to free the nine Alabama Negroes unjustly accused of rape. But even more thrilling, a key figure in the Scottsboro case actually worked at Camp. Those nine guys riding the rails looking for work? Lester Carter was on that same train with them. Carter, a white man from Knoxville, Tennessee, maintained the innocence of the Negroes in the railroad car and testified for them in the trials. Now he came to live and work at interracial Camp Wo-Chi-Ca.

The minds of the campers never strayed far from the civil war in Spain. They sang "Viva La Quince Brigada" and other songs of the International Brigades. They applauded when two Wo-Chi-Cans enlisted in the Abraham Lincoln Battalion to fight for the Spanish Republic. They wept to hear that one of these two – Ralph Wardlaw, their Camp Director – was missing in action. Wo-Chi-Ca roared with rage at the German bombers that killed civilians in Guernica, and mourned when Madrid fell to the fascists.

In America too, revolutionary events were occurring. The mass effort to organize industrial unions inspired many Wo-Chi-Cans; they wanted to be involved. Senior campers piled into a bus and crossed the state line to Easton, a grimy industrial town in Pennsylvania. There the Wo-Chi-Cans joined the picket line of striking workers at the C.K. Williams Paint Company. Then, to cheers from the strikers, the campers put on a performance of song and dance. As they rode through Easton, Wo-Chi-Cans expressed surprise at how different the drab streets seemed from their own colorful neighborhoods in New York.

Young Wo-Chi-Ca applauded the creation of the Works Progress Administration (WPA). This federal program put millions of unemployed to work constructing highways and government buildings, erecting dams and bridges, and creating public parks. The WPA also hired artists, writers, musicians and actors.

Wo-Chi-Cans acclaimed the passage of the 'radical' Social Security Act that instituted unemployment insurance and old-age pensions. At the same time, the New Jersey campers grew alarmed at the rise of German fascism; they expressed horror at *'Kristallnacht,'* the 'Night of Broken Glass,' a hideous rampage in which Nazi gangs destroyed Jewish shops, smashed synagogues, murdered Jews in the streets, and rounded up thousands for concentration camps.

In occupied Europe, with its murderous racism, a Jewish girl – hiding from the Nazis in an Amsterdam attic – keeps a diary. Safe in America, a Jewish girl from the Bronx – almost the same age as Anne Frank – writes of her summertime adventures at a workers children's camp. Here at Wo-Chi-Ca, one could be a proud Jewish girl with Negro friends.

I just got back from two weeks at Camp Wo-Chi-Ca. It was my first time. What a two weeks! Both my parents work, so my grandmother took me down from the Bronx to Washington Square. The bus driver in Manhattan got out of his seat to come down to the sidewalk and pick up my suitcase. We had already dragged it three blocks from the subway to the bus stop.

Then I climbed into the big blue Wo-Chi-Ca bus and I was so excited! I rushed to a window seat to wave good-bye to my grandmother. She had a worried look on her face and I felt tears in my eyes. But just then there was a thump on my side: a boy sat down next to me. I didn't want him to see me crying, so I blew my nose.

He smiled at me and asked, "Do you have hay fever too?" His voice was very soft, and his skin a deep chocolate brown. So this is what my granmother calls a "schvartze." My mother and father tell me they're supposed to be called "Negroes." But the idea of one with hay fever flabbergasted me. I had no time to think about this, for another Negro – this one a tall teenage girl – was standing in the aisle, and as the bus started moving, she led us in a song. It was new to me, but had an easy-to-learn chorus. Soon I was singing along with all the other kids.

> **You are the best, I love you best,**
> **Your name is known from East to West.**
> **Oh camp so fine, Wo-Chi-Ca mine –**
> **There's not another camp like mine.**

My new friend told me this was his second time at Wo-Chi-Ca, and he promised to show me around when we got there. We sang all the way, a two-hour ride. Then the singing died down when the buses turned into a gravel driveway. The kids who had been to Camp before told us newcomers about the Wo-Chi-Ca sign, and now we were all eager to be the first ones to spot it.

"There it is," someone yells. "We're here!"

A mad scramble now begins, with everyone wanting to be first off the bus. But the doors stay shut. What are the drivers waiting for? Suddenly, we see campers outside. A crowd of boys and girls smiling, waving and singing. Now the bus doors open.

> **We welcome you to Wo-Chi-Ca,**
> **We're mighty glad you're here.**
> **We'll set the earth reverberating**
> **With a mighty cheer – RAH RAH!**
> **We'll sing you in; we'll sing you out,**
> **Your mighty praises we will shout:**
> **Hail, hail, the gang's all here**
> **And you're welcome to Wo-Chi-Ca!**

We all rush out of the buses. It seems like a madhouse at first, getting our suitcases and finding out which bunk we would be in. I was assigned to bunk 16 with nine other girls, and my new friend was right next door in Bunk 17, only it was a tent!

*My counselor was Bernice, but we called her "Bunny." She goes to Brooklyn College in the winter. She was also the swim instructor, and you could go swimming every afternoon, unless you signed up for baseball or volleyball. Or you might want to go back to the 'shacks' to continue your morning activities – clay maybe, or drawing and painting. You might help put out the camp newspaper, **The Daily Wo-Chi-Can**, or join the drama group to put on a play. You could browse through the books in the library, or listen to records in the music room, or even play the old piano. Whew! We could choose whatever we wanted, but who could possibly do even half these things in two weeks?*

But one thing we all had to do and that was rest an hour after lunch. The first half-hour you were supposed to stay on your bed. Of course we griped about that, but to tell the truth it was kind of nice to lie down and hear Mozart and Beethoven playing over loudspeakers. Sometimes I even fell asleep!

The second half of rest hour we had discussions. The first thing we did was elect a bunk president to chair our meetings. Then we had to decide what to name our bunk. Some of the bunk names were "Walt Whitman," "President Roosevelt," and "Frederick Douglass." There was "The Abraham Lincoln Brigade," "The Daily Worker," and there was even one bunk called "Lenin." Our bunk had a tie vote between "Harriet Tubman" and "Madame Curie."

One rest period, we discussed comic books – some of the girls bring them from home. Bunny showed us how they were full of ugly racial and ethnic stereotypes. We also talked about respect for the workers who clean our bathrooms, and why we shouldn't mark up the walls. And we planned what to wear for 'Big Day.'

Big Day was the last Sunday, which was also visitors' day. Mommy came up by bus, but Daddy had to work in the city. My bunk did a skit about slavery. I played a mean overseer. Last period (before I got to camp) they did "Italians in America." Next period, the theme will be the contribution of Jews to our country.

After our skit, the chorus sang "No More Auction Block for Me" and then the dance group performed an African dance.

We made a big banner in the Art Shack, with Charlie White. I helped him work on a mural, which won't be done till the end of the summer, so I guess I'll see it next year. I hope Charlie is at Camp next summer. I think Art was my most favorite activity because Charlie is so wonderful.

While we worked on the mural, Charlie told us stories about his fascinating life. I don't want to forget any of it, so I am putting it all in my diary. Some day when I'm an old lady, I'll be able to say I knew the famous artist Charles White when I was a young girl!

Charlie is pretty famous already. A lot of his murals that he did for the WPA are in post offices and libraries. He paints portraits of famous Negroes like Sojourner Truth, Booker T. Washington and Frederick Douglass. Charlie told us that when he was growing up in Chicago he never learned anything in school about these heroes.

He had his work on exhibit in a big university in Washington DC. And he won an award so he and his wife could travel around the South. He painted lots of scenes of poor families in the country. His wife is Elizabeth Catlett – we call her Betty. She's the one with the very long braids. She is a painter too, and also does sculpture.

Charlie likes teaching art to kids because he had a big struggle to become an artist. He was born in the middle of a race riot in Chicago and raised

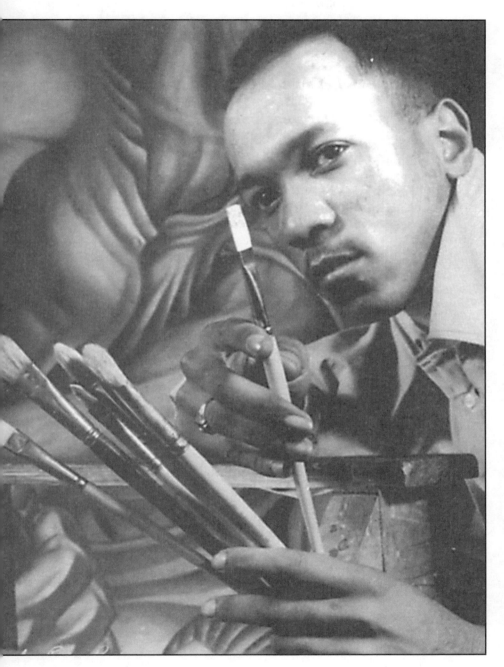

Charles White in Chicago at work on a WPA mural

by his mother. She worked cleaning houses for people. They were very poor. Charlie started to draw when he was only six years old. He begged his mother for oil paints, and she finally bought him some. But she didn't have money to buy canvas. One day when he was home alone, Charlie took down a living room window shade and painted on it. His mother spanked him and took away his paints for a month. But later, she framed the picture and treasured it all her life.

As a senior in high school, Charles won scholarships to two different art schools. But both times he showed up for class, the schools claimed a mistake had been made and refused to accept him. He had to win a statewide competition before the Chicago Art Institute finally let him in.

Charlie says he is a graphic artist, because he prefers to draw in black and white. Here is a clipping of a review of one of his exhibits I saved from the **New York Telegram:**

> **He is a mature, powerful, articulate talent.**
> **He paints Negroes, modeling their figures**
> **in blocky masses that might have been**
> **cut from granite. He works with tremendous**
> **intensity. His subjects are militant, fiery,**
> **strong, they are symbols rather than people –**
> **symbols of his race's unending battle for equality.**

Besides all his wonderful artwork, Charlie is something my parents will be happy to hear – a socialist. He believes deeply in the Wo-Chi-Ca way of life, with liberty and justice for all.

But oh, Dear Diary! Getting back to the story of my life at Wo-Chi-Ca. After those two weeks I feel as if I have changed forever. The wonderful counselors, the exciting programs, the famous visitors. Wo-Chi-Ca is such a special place, and I feel like I also am very special because I went there. I want to go back again and again.

How I hated to leave when my two weeks were up. We were all crying when we got on the bus to take us home. We sang sad songs all the way back to the city. Now I will be counting the days till next summer.

Finally, Dear Diary, I must tell you that when we got off the bus at Washington Square, I put my arms around the Negro boy who first made friends with me. "So long, Tommy," I whispered. "Parting is such... – see you next summer?"

Our young Wo-Chi-Can gave us an inspiring but all-too-brief account of Charles White's life. She looked forward to seeing him the following year at Camp, but Charlie was drafted into the army, a very different kind of camp.

The still-segregated army assigned artist Charles White to a camouflage unit. He was directed to paint the barracks green – over and over again. Charlie's division was sent in 1944 to fight not fascists but floodwaters. Weakened from standing waist-deep in the icy waters of the Ohio and Mississippi Rivers, Charlie contracted tuberculosis. He spent three years in a VA hospital. Finally discharged, Charles and his wife, artist Elizabeth Catlett, moved to Mexico to study print-making. The marriage collapsed, however, and they divorced in 1947.

Charles returned to New York to paint, but his tubercular lungs put him back in the hospital. At this point, Wo-Chi-Ca re-entered his life in the person of a lovely young woman.

Charles had met Frances Barrett in 1942 when he was art director at Camp. She was then a sixteen-year-old counselor who had lately lost both parents. Charles was very kind to the orphaned girl, and Frances, touched by his compassion, took a great interest in his career. She collected reviews of his exhibits, pasting them in a scrapbook.

Now, six years after their meeting at Camp, Fran learned that Charles was again flat on his back in a TB ward. She rushed to see him. In spite of warnings about contagion that kept other visitors hovering at the foot of the bed, Frances spontaneously ran directly to Charlie's side and hugged him.

When he was strong enough to leave the hospital, a welcome home party for Charlie was arranged by his Wo-Chi-Ca friend Margie Goss. Charlie urged her to invite Frances: "I've developed the worst crush on Frances Barrett," he wrote. "Really, Margaret, this is serious. I must see her again."

Frances did attend the party and their eight-year acquaintance now blossomed into love. In just six weeks, the interracial couple married – an act of great courage in 1950. Both knew what would lie ahead. Frances was the child of a 'mixed marriage.' Her father, a Catholic priest, was excommunicated for leaving his order to be with his beloved. The child Frances was five years old before her parents could find a minister willing to marry them. As for Charlie, he had been badly beaten outside a Manhattan nightclub for mingling with a group that included white women.

Fran and Charles could not even hold hands in public. Yet, sustained by their mutual experience at Wo-Chi-Ca, they determined to build a life together. Charlie's letter to Fran reveals the depths of his convictions: "I have a deep and tremendous faith in love," he wrote, "in people and in Marxism."

They later moved to California for Charlie's health. There, they adopted two beautiful interracial children. Their circle of close friends included Harry Belafonte, Sidney Poitier, Aldous Huxley, Dalton Trumbo, Miriam Makeba, Gordon Parks...

In Altadena, Charlie painted, taught art classes, and exhibited his work. The German Democratic Republic included Charles White in its first show of American art and welcomed him as a guest of honor. Governor Jerry Brown appointed Charles a Commissioner of the California Afro-American Museum.

But in 1976, tuberculosis finally killed him. Today, in Altadena, a Los Angeles suburb noted for its racially mixed character, a lovely county park named for Charles White keeps his memory green.

Charlie lives also in *Reaches of the Heart*, his wife's moving account of their life together. Frances Barrett White, after a long struggle with breast cancer, died in July of 2000.

In the life and work of his students, Charlie's influence also endures. Accomplished painter Betty LaDuke, for example, cites the beloved Wo-Chi-Ca art director as her role model and inspiration when she was little Betty Bernstein from the Bronx.

Charles White gave to the world an extraordinary body of work: drawings and paintings treasured by museums, collectors and ordinary people everywhere. And yet this illustrious artist was only one of many on the staff of Camp Wo-Chi-Ca.

BLACK GALAXY

Margaret Taylor Goss and Elizabeth Catlett – one a dear friend of Charles White, the other his first wife – both these women shared their art with Wo-Chi-Ca children.

Margie, an art teacher from Chicago, supervised a number of counselors. Before coming to Camp she had already made a name for herself in the art world. She worked in many media as writer and poet, painter and printmaker. Her children's book, *Jasper, the Drummin' Boy*, was staged as a hilarious play by the Wo-Chi-Ca Drama Group. Many a camper in the Art Shack learned block printing under the guidance of Margie. She especially liked to create linoleum prints, Margie explained to the kids. "They can be sold affordably, so that everyone can appreciate art."

Margie Goss modified her name soon after she met Wo-Chi-Ca's new night watchman. Charles Burroughs came to Camp from the USSR. Though born in the States, Charlie was taken to the Soviet Union at the age of two. His mother, Black Communist Williana Burroughs, wanted her son to grow up free from discrimination. Charlie became an artist – a trapeze artist with the Moscow Circus! Speaking English with a Slavic accent, singing folk songs in soulful Russian, the tall handsome Black man was an appealing exotic presence at Camp. "I heard him singing under my bunk window," Margie sighed, "and decided I didn't want to be single any more."

A shared passion for their heritage took Margie and Charlie on frequent trips to Africa. Often, they brought back works of art. A museum they started in their Chicago living room soon outgrew the space and required its own building. Today, the Du Sable Museum of African American History is ranked foremost of its kind in the world.

Charlie Burroughs died in 1994. But Margaret, now in her eighties, still teaches, writes and creates works of art. In 1998, she led the campaign demanding that the U.S. Post Office issue a stamp in honor of Paul Robeson. Truly a Renaissance woman, Margaret Taylor Goss Burroughs has been named one of the ten outstanding Black artists in America.

The path leading Elizabeth Catlett to Camp Wo-Chi-Ca wound through the Howard University School of Art, the State University of Iowa, and the Chicago Art Institute. At the 1940 American Negro Exposition in Chicago her limestone sculpture, "Mother and Child" took first prize.

It was there that she met Charles White. Before long, the two young artists married. Relocating to New York, they were soon drawn into the circle of Black radical artists in the Harlem Renaissance. They became friends with Jacob and Gwendolyn Lawrence, with Paul Robeson, with Ernest Critchlow...

They also met poet Gwendolyn Bennett, a founder of Harlem's George Washington Carver School. Elizabeth Catlett joined the teaching staff of this progressive labor school. No wonder that with this group of friends, Betty and Charles found their way to New Jersey's left wing children's camp.

Strolling with the children around Wo-Chi-Ca grounds, Betty paused to reflect that the very land on which they stood was once home to Native Americans. The campers learned that the English dubbed these first inhabitants "Delaware Indians." The Indians, however, called themselves Lenape, which meant "genuine people." The peaceful tribe once cultivated corn, beans, squash, and pumpkin on this land now occupied by Camp Wo-Chi-Ca.

These original people greeted European settlers with "delight and shouts of admiration." English Quakers, for their part, were conscientious and insisted upon buying title to Indian lands. But communistic natives could no more understand private ownership of land than individual ownership of air or sunlight. In the end, the Lenape lost land, air and sunlight. They were forced off their land and – carrying their worthless treaty signed by William Penn – they walked a trail of tears.

To honor the Leni-Lenape, Betty and the campers created a totem pole. During the course of the project hundreds of children learned woodcarving, painting and the importance of careful research in accurately depicting the Indian designs. On a grassy slope near the camp's newly built log cabin, Wo-Chi-Cans erected their colorful totem pole. It stood almost as high as the topmost beam of the cabin. The totem pole would endure for fifty years, long outlasting the camp itself. Elizabeth would later move to Mexico City, terminate her marriage to Charles White and marry Francisco Mora, a radical painter and muralist. Elizabeth joined Mora in the printmaking collective Taller de Grafica Popular. This collective included such artists as Diego Rivera, Frida Kahlo, Rufino Tamayo, Jose Clemente Orozco and David Alfaro Siqueiros. Most were members of the Mexican Communist Party.

At the National School of Fine Arts, "Maestra" Catlett was the first woman director of the Sculpture Department. Her work expresses deep social and political concerns: celebration of motherhood, struggles of working women of color. She is one of the leading Black artists of the 20th century.

Only museums and wealthy collectors can purchase Elizabeth Catlett's magnificent sculpture. But her prints from woodcuts and lithographs are sold throughout the world at prices affordable to working people. It was at Camp Wo-Chi-Ca that Betty first realized the possibility of making art accessible to all.

"Sharecropper" by Elizabeth Catlett

Ernest Crichlow was another Wo-Chi-Ca artist who came from the same Harlem milieu as his friends the Whites and the Lawrences.

Ernest Critchlow at Wo-Chi-Ca

As Camp art director, Ernie outlined his philosophy...

The function of art at camp should be to further the self-expression of the camper. Art should not be approached as the special gift of a few but as the means of expression for the many. Every effort must be made to encourage campers to discuss their work and the work of fellow campers. This will aid them in understanding and appreciating each other's ideas and differences. This working together lays the basis for our democratic way of life.

A founder of New York's Cinque Gallery, showcase for African American artists, Ernie has received dozens of awards and honorary degrees. His gentle guidance opened the doors of art to many Wo-Chi-Ca children.

Dramatics also played a vital part in the life of Wo-Chi-Ca. Campers performed improvisations, original skits, and full-length works ranging from Gilbert and Sullivan to Clifford Odets. Often, the amateur players would benefit from the professional direction of a theater artist such as Vinette J. Carroll.

Before coming to Camp, Vinnie had been a trailblazer, playing George Bernard Shaw roles never previously performed by a Black woman. She went on to teach and direct at the High School of Performing Arts in New York City. She took on numerous roles in film and television, acted on Broadway, and directed in both London and New York. In fact, Vinette J. Carroll became, in 1976, the first Black woman to direct a Broadway musical, her own creation, *Your Arm's Too Short to Box with God*.

Vinette Carroll founded the interracial Urban Arts Corps in 1967: "If we can all get to be a part of a more universal experience, we will get to see our similarities more than we see our differences."

After fifty years in theater, Vinette J. Carroll now directs her own repertory company in Fort Lauderdale, Florida where she stages the work of Black playwrights. Many of the plays she produces and directs have a religious theme, quite fitting for their setting in a renovated church.

Wo-Chi-Ca children were fortunate to have as dance instructor the magnificent Pearl Primus. Born in Trinidad, Pearl became a leading interpreter of African dance in the United States.

Pearl had studied biology in college, intending to be a doctor. But as a Black woman in the Depression she could not even get a laboratory job. A champion sprinter and broad jumper in school, Pearl turned to dance. Ballet was out, for Negroes were routinely barred. Anyway, Pearl liked modern dance more. "My body," she declared, "is built for heavy stomping."

The first Black student admitted to the New Dance School, Pearl won entry on a scholarship, cleaning the studio in exchange for extra lessons.

In 1943, Pearl made her debut as a choreographer. She created a dance piece to "The Negro Speaks of Rivers," a Langston Hughes poem. She composed for Alvin Ailey. No one who ever saw it can forget Pearl's heartrending dance to Billie Holiday's song "Strange Fruit."

The dancing of Pearl Primus was notable for its intensity. The critics raved about her "primitive panther-like power and grace. Everything about her was directed downward with terrible force." But when she taught dance at Wo-Chi-Ca, she was gently encouraging, calling the youngest children "my cherubs." Her example inspired a number of Wo-Chi-Cans to become dancers themselves.

Pearl Primus instructing campers at Wo-Chi-Ca

Before her death in 1994, Pearl Primus received the National Medal of Arts, and from the Liberian government the Star of Africa.

Pearl danced, she asserted, "to protest bigotry and hate." She performed at benefits in IWO lodges to raise funds for Camp Wo-Chi-Ca. The love many alumni still have for modern dance, the appreciation of its African roots, they owe to Pearl Primus.

Wo-Chi-Ca, rich in husband/wife teams, rejoiced in the artistic couple Jacob Lawrence and Gwendolyn Knight. Jake, painting along with campers on sheets of brown wrapping paper, would recount tales of his Harlem childhood.

Harlem was a dangerous place for kids. Half the men were unemployed, hanging around on street corners. My mother was worried, me being alone and all while she was out working. She enrolled me in a WPA arts program that met in the basement of the public library. There, I fell in love with painting. I spent lots of time in the great art museums studying the Botticellis, the Goyas, and the Egyptian wall paintings. And I read all the books about Negro history – that Schomburg Library had such a good collection. Pretty soon I was spending so much time reading and painting that I just dropped out of school altogether. But I didn't hang out on the streets. I took art lessons from Charles Alston for seven years, just like the old apprentice days.

Charles took me to meet writers like Langston Hughes and Claude McKay, painters like Aaron Douglas and Ben Shahn. Harlem was full of wonderful artists, and I never wanted to be anything but a painter myself. I made up my mind that someday I would tell the story of my people with my paintbrush.

I was very lucky; so many older artists helped me get started. Augusta Savage, a wonderful sculptor, let me have a space to work in her studio. She took me under her wing – in fact she helped me get my first paid job, on a WPA project when I was only eighteen. Gwen and I met at Augusta's studio. We got married just before the war began.

I was drafted into the Coast Guard, and assigned to the first integrated ship in America. They put me to work as a combat artist. But it sure was different from Harlem. Most of the guys on board never heard of the great Negro heroes and not much about our people's history either. My parents were part of the great migration from the South to the northern cities, and I've tried to tell that story in my paintings. I also like to honor our great leaders.

These narrative paintings, many-paneled works on subjects such as Frederick Douglass, Harriet Tubman, and John Brown, attracted attention while Jacob Lawrence was still very young. The Baltimore Museum of Art devoted an entire room to the forty-one panels of the Toussaint L'Ouverture series. Jacob Lawrence was the first Black artist to be represented by a New York gallery.

Lawrence was awarded the NAACP's Spingarn Medal, the National Medal of Art, and over two dozen honorary degrees. He taught at Pratt Institute,

"Graduation" by Jacob Lawrence

Brandeis University, the New School and the University of Washington. He created immense murals such as the one adorning Seattle's Kingdome Stadium and a seventy-two-foot mural recently installed at New York's Times Square subway station.

He has produced over a thousand artworks, including book illustrations for John Hershey's *Hiroshima, Aesop's Fables*, and the Bible. Both African travel and the U.S. civil rights movement influenced Lawrence's art. Visible in all his work is compassion for those who suffer as well as the celebration of individual dignity. For fifty years, until his death in June of 2000, Jacob Lawrence was the foremost Black artist in the United States.

Though married to such a preeminent artist, Gwendolyn Knight created her own distinct reputation. Born in the West Indies, she began to paint at age eight, and by the time she met her future husband Jacob in Harlem, Gwen was a serious artist: a lover of painting, photography, sculpture, architecture and all the visual arts.

Theater art, however, and especially dance, provided her greatest inspiration. A deep love and genuine knowledge of modern dance permeates all Gwen's art. "Dance is the way I draw, the way I work." Her paintings are admired for their line and movement. Oil is Gwen's favorite medium; portraits and still life comprise the main body of her work.

Educated at Howard University, painter in the WPA Mural Project, recipient of honorary doctorate degrees from Seattle University and the University of Minnesota, noted art historian, life-long painter, Gwendolyn Knight is completing eighty full years of artistic activity. She continues to create, and in addition – since the death of her husband – Gwen travels around the country to discuss the legacy of Jacob Lawrence's art. Gwendolyn Knight, Wo-Chi-Ca art counselor of the 1940's, is still going strong in the 21st century.

Those brown-paper pictures the campers painted with Jake and Gwen seldom survived the summer. But on the walls of the Barn, Wo-Chi-Cans painted murals intended to last forever: heroic workers both black and white as well as a splendid portrait of Paul Robeson. For the new Playhouse, John Wilson – still another African American serving as art director at Camp – designed a huge kaleidoscopic panel.

John too, after Wo-Chi-Ca, would go on to a brilliant career. He would illustrate many books for children, including a biography of Malcom X. His powerful monument to Dr. Martin Luther King Jr. would grace the nation's capital. The painting and sculpture of John Wilson would be exhibited on college campuses and in museums throughout the world. Before these great accomplishments, John, a young artist in the summer of 1949, helped the Wo-Chi-Ca kids paint a vivid forty-foot mural on the proscenium arch above the stage of the Paul Robeson Playhouse.

Both Barn and Playhouse still stand after all these years, but the Wo-Chi-Ca murals no longer adorn their walls. If a work of art is meant to exist for eternity, then those murals, it might be said, lived no longer than the flash of a camera; they remain today only as photographs, faded black and white images in old yearbooks. How and when did the wall paintings vanish? Were they scraped off, painted over, or... – what did happen to Charles White's mural art, and that of Jacob Lawrence and Ernest Critchlow and John Wilson? We question in vain, for blank walls, alas, tell no tales.

Wo-Chi-Ca walls may remain mute in regard to murals, but with respect to poetry, the walls fairly sing. Today, in the old Barn, stanzas heard at Camp sixty years ago echo still. They say if you put your ear to a certain corner of the Paul Robeson Playhouse, you can hear a poem of Langston Hughes.

> **Where is the Jim Crow section**
> **On this merry-go-round,**
> **Mister, cause I want to ride?**
> **Down South where I come from**
> **White and colored**
> **Can't sit side by side.**
> **Down South on the train**
> **There's a Jim Crow car.**
> **On the bus we're put in the back –**
> **But there ain't no back**
> **To a merry-go-round!**
> **Where's the horse**
> **For a kid that's black?**

Yes, a great deal of verse can still be heard here if one listens carefully in the Playhouse and the old Barn. Perhaps a couplet full of wonder by Countee Cullen...

> **Yet do I marvel at this curious thing:**
> **To make a poet black, and bid him sing!**

...or a Claude McKay sonnet, Shakespearean in form, in content, revolutionary.

> **If we must die, let it not be like hogs**
> **Hunted and penned in an inglorious spot,**
> **While round us bark the mad and hungry dogs,**
> **Making their mock at our accursed lot.**
> **If we must die, O let us nobly die,**
> **So that our precious blood may not be shed**

In vain; then even the monsters we defy
Shall be constrained to honor us though dead!
O kinsmen! We must meet the common foe!
Though far outnumbered let us show us brave,
And for their thousand blows deal one deathblow!
What though before us lies the open grave?
Like men we'll face the murderous, cowardly pack,
Pressed to the wall, dying, but fighting back!

Imagine our little plot in the New Jersey woods replete with poets. Picture, if you will, the Stone House, and on its wide lawn a whole host of black bards and troubadours – artists of the Harlem Renaissance all sitting at Camp Wo-Chi-Ca! And at the very center of this circle, hear Wo-Chi-Ca's own Gwendolyn Bennett:

I love you for your brownness,
And the rounded darkness of your breast;
I love you for the breaking sadness in your voice
And shadows where your wayward eyelids rest.
Something of old forgotten queens
Lurks in the lithe abandon of your walk,
And something of the shackled slave
Sobs in the rhythm of your talk.
Oh, little brown girl, born for sorrow's mate,
Keep all you have of queenliness,
Forgetting that you once were slave,
And let your full lips laugh at Fate!

The New Negro poets revered Gwen Bennett, for she sang of racial pride, she celebrated blackness and the rediscovery of Africa. She gave all her devotion, for more than twenty years, to Harlem and to art. Gwen energized and in many ways personified the Harlem Renaissance.

An active member of the Harlem Artists Guild, Gwen also directed the Harlem Community Art Center and served on the board of the Negro Playwright's Guild. Gwendolyn Bennett designed covers for poetry and art magazines, composed dozens of poems, stories, articles, and reviewed the work of other Black artists. She wrote and illustrated for *Opportunity,* the organ of the National Urban League as well as for *The Crisis*, the publication of the NAACP.

Gwen's background was unusual. Her childhood playmates were Paiute Indians on the Nevada reservation where her mother and father both taught school. When the Bennett marriage dissolved, Gwendolyn's mother was awarded custody of the couple's only child. But Gwendolyn's father kidnapped her and took her to

Gwen Bennett

live with him in New York. At Brooklyn Girls High, Gwen's talent led to her election to the Dramatic Society, the first 'colored girl' ever so honored.

She went on to Columbia University, studied at the Pratt Institute, and won an art fellowship to Paris. Gwen taught fine arts, design, watercolor and crafts at Howard University in the nation's capitol. In Harlem too, Gwen nurtured countless young artists.

But all the affection and respect Gwen enjoyed could not save her. She was forced to quit her post as director of the Harlem Community Art Center. **"Miss Gwen Bennett Suspended in Red Probe!"** screamed the *Amsterdam News*. The witch hunters had found her.

Gwen then took a teaching and administrative post at the Jefferson School for Democracy, a Marxist educational institution. In this same period, she helped organize a labor school stressing political action – the George Washington Carver Community School. Both schools were 'investigated' by the Dies Committee, a forerunner of the McCarthy Committee. Again and again, Gwen Bennett was persecuted for her Communist sympathies.

She came to Camp on weekends to escape her demanding life in the City; at Wo-Chi-Ca Gwen could breathe free. She refreshed her spirit in reading poetry aloud to appreciative campers. One young camper, Robert Nemiroff, was so inspired by Gwen's love of poetry that he became a poet himself.

Something else about Gwen Bennett inspired Robert Nemiroff. And Gwen, in fact, had a reason more precious even than poetry – love! – to spend weekends at Wo-Chi-Ca. Gwen had risen above racial barriers and married a Caucasian; her husband was Dick Crosscup, head counselor and educational director at Wo-Chi-Ca. The couple would often be seen holding hands as they walked Wo-Chi-Ca grounds. Robert Nemiroff would later marry Black poet and playwright Lorraine Hansberry, devoting his life to her brilliant career.

Clearly, the campers were deeply impressed by the devotion of Gwen Bennett and Dick Crosscup to each other. Their visible love embodied the black/white unity that was the Wo-Chi-Ca ideal.

STAFF OF HONOR

The Bennett/Crosscup marriage was a Wo-Chi-Ca union of artist and administrator: Gwen the camp poet, and Dick its educational director. Dick's work began even before Camp opened. Each spring weekend in the city, he would train counselors, teaching them basic child psychology and methods to ensure that every youngster had a happy camp experience. It was Dick who instituted the 'Camper's Progress Report,' sent home to parents. Unlike a school report card, it centered on the personality traits of the child. The emphasis was on getting along with other campers.

1942
CAMP WO-CHI-CA

Port Murray, N.J.   80 Fifth Av. NYC
                                     Al 4-7037

CAMPER'S PROGRESS REPORT

CAMPER _June Levine_   BUNK _22_   PERIODS _Second_

To further the wholesome growth and development of your child, here are our judgements and recommendations, based on our experience at camp. We trust you will accept this in the same spirit of helpfulness with which we intend it.

Personality and development: *June got along very well with the others, although she exibited a slight crankiness on one or two occasions. She is very cooperative, and was valuable in the various bunk duties. Her mother is to be congratulated for the fact that June did not take advantage of her allergies to act like a "privileged character." She is a poor eater, and must be watched carefully. Also, she should be pushed as much as possible towards participation in athletics.*

Activities and interests: *Very interested in Dramatics. Played a speaking role in Big Day Show. Served as Bunk Librarian.*

Health: *June fully enjoyed the first week. During the second week, her hayfever got more troublesome, but I think she had a good time anyway. She was always ready for camp activities with an enthusiastic response.*

If you wish further to discuss your child's progress, please do not hesitate to communicate with us. We would appreciate you returning to us the enclosed brief questionaire, which may help us in improving our camp.

Yours for the children,
Richard B. Crosscup

Richard B. Crosscup
Educational Director

Ruth Towber
Counselor

Dick Crosscup, in winter months, taught English at a New York private school with a program of child-centered progressive education. At Camp, he had the uncanny ability to learn – within a day of the opening of each period – the names of all the new arrivals. As he strolled around camp he greeted by name each child he encountered. Dick was the one you would turn to if you were homesick, if you thought some rule was unfair, or if you had a great idea for a new project.

Dick Crosscup with campers

Arty Bolton recalls that when he and Dick Loring were only ten they drew up plans for a cable car that would operate from the swimming hole. It would eliminate the long sweaty uphill climb back to the bunks. They presented their drawings to Dick Crosscup, who examined them carefully, promising to look into the idea. Even though nothing ever came of their Rube Goldberg contraption, Arty still remembers how proud they felt that an adult took them so seriously.

The kids adored Dick, both for his reassuring quiet manner and something quite contrary – his telling of hair-raising ghost stories. Dick's "Rominy Gruen" was always in demand at evening campfires. In a dry quiet style Dick spun out his tale about a crying little girl who disappeared behind the mess hall, dropping her handkerchief and vanishing into the woods. Everyone searched for her, but she was never found. It turned out that the girl had never come to Camp at all, but had died a week before she was due to arrive. Today's alumni still get goose bumps recalling Dick Crosscup's voice fading into the night, whispering "Ro-mi-ny, Rominy Gru-u-en..."

V for Victory

Dick never criticized directly, but he knew how to put an egotistical staff member in his place. Irwin Silber, then a somewhat brash teenage journalism instructor, remembers to this day a Crosscup joke at his expense. At a staff meeting, Dick quietly told a story about a big problem in heaven. It seems God was suffering from a delusion: He thought He was Irwin Silber!

Kalman "Butch" Lasky started as head of Camp Maintenance and eventually became Wo-Chi-Ca's executive director. An electrician in the winter, Butch was the dynamo that kept Wo-Chi-Ca humming all summer. He saw to it that groceries were delivered on time; he made sure the young counselors got to bed by eleven; he handled the never-ending crises in a camp where every two weeks a new batch of kids – as many as a hundred – piled out of the buses.

At staff meetings Butch might shout and bluster, but after listening to the others he always concluded with "Let's do what's best for the kids."

Besides his official duties, Butch often appeared in the Barn to lead folk songs and spirituals, of which he seemed to have an inexhaustible supply. His enthusiasm was infectious, whether singing with the children or batting for the counselors' baseball team. Butch took his turn at the plate in every camper-staff baseball game, and, along with the kids, yelled at the umpire.

Butch Lasky

At evening programs, the campers would beg Butch for his special rendition of "Lil' Liza Jane." The Camp Director often obliged, racing up and down the tiny stage, flailing his arms like a mustachioed windmill.

One summer a young girl sneaked up on stage behind Butch to imitate his every move. The audience roared. Finally, Butch turned around and discovered his 'shadow.' He laughed as hard as anyone did. From that night on, Butch would insist that the shadow join him whenever he performed. A Wo-Chi-Ca tradition was born.

Long after the bunk counselors and their young charges went to sleep, Butch sat up reading reports: Woody, the rickety old station wagon, needs a new clutch... two bad cases of poison ivy in the infirmary... Vaino needs lumber to repair fences... two counselors have been observed holding hands and "demonstrating an obvious attachment" – not a good example for the younger campers.

This would call forth Butch's dreaded lecture to the staff entitled "Respect for Each Other." For some time he skirted the actual subject, but finally concluded with the pointed injunction: "NO SEX ON CAMP GROUNDS!"

The cooks were highly admired workers, for they prepared three meals each day for two hundred campers. Assisting the cooks, a teenage crew of dishwashers, waitresses and pot wallopers. Especially memorable was head cook Joe Wallace, a Black man originally from Alabama. Joe worked winters in the city as an assistant cook at a restaurant, but at Camp he had full responsibility for the entire kitchen.

Joe Wallace was an inspired cook who, with practiced ease, turned out delicious soups, stews, pancakes, and southern fried chicken. Joe alternated between calm efficiency and outbursts of temper directed against his bumbling amateur helpers. The teen-aged kitchen staff regarded Joe with equal parts of adoration and fear.

Bernice Bickle Meltzer remembers cleaning up a spill on the kitchen floor. "I dipped a mop in a big pot of water on the stove. I didn't realize it was water Joe was heating for spaghetti! He roared at me like a mad bull and chased me out of the kitchen with a broom."

"Another time," Bunny writes, "I tried to open one of those giant mayonnaise jars by banging on it with a metal serving spoon. Of course the jar cracked in two. I looked up and there was Joe staring at me. This time he just shook his head and walked away. I guess he thought I was completely hopeless."

Joe usually went to sleep very early, for he was hard at work in the mess hall by six in the morning. But now and then he would drop by one of the evening gatherings and be prevailed upon to sing. Almost invariably he would croon "Are You

From Dixie?" with an encore of "Polly Wolly Doodle All the Day." For some progressive kids who sneered at the South as a place of bigotry and race hatred, it was a revelation to hear a Black man sing lovingly about his homeland.

When Joe Wallace retired, a Black woman, Ada B. Jackson, took his place. She had run for Congress in 1948 on the American Labor Party ticket. Ada's soft-spoken, laid-back manner was in sharp contrast to Joe's bellowing style. Ada too inspired loyalty and devotion. Sometimes, after an especially delicious meal, the campers would burst into applause and demand that Ada come out of the kitchen and take a bow. Ada and her husband Clarence, who worked on outside maintenance, celebrated their 20th wedding anniversary at Camp, cutting a cake lovingly made by the kitchen staff.

Ada often spoke of "those who have accepted the challenge to live and work for what we believe." She loved to see "the happy faces of children of different races, nationalities and creeds, playing, working and living together in peace and harmony." Wo-Chi-Ca, she wrote in the Camp Yearbook, was "the hope and dream of those who struggle for peace, security, and freedom for all." Ada believed her work and that of other staff members "tied human beings in the one common bond that promotes real brotherhood."

As important as was good nutrition, so too was expert health care. The camp infirmary always had a staff of professionals. Grace Horowitz came to Wo-Chi-Ca in 1946, straight out of nursing school, "three years of a stuffy, strict medical establishment."

Prior to Wo-Chi-Ca, Grace had attended the progressive Yiddish camps Boiberek and Kinderland. But in Wo-Chi-Ca's broader ethnic and racial diversity, Grace saw her ideals come to life.

Grace and a second nurse shared a bedroom in the infirmary and were available twenty-four hours a day. Each morning the nurses treated a myriad of minor complaints – bruises, cuts, sprains, rashes, mosquito bites... Most of the children were in and out in a few minutes, but a young camper with a severe cold, or poison ivy from head-to-foot, might be put to bed and seen by the town doctor.

What if the patient were ill enough to miss the Big Day Parade – what could be more awful? But a procession of bunkmates and counselors, groups of visiting dignitaries, perhaps even a booming hello from Paul Robeson himself would provide consolation. After a hardy handshake from Wo-Chi-Ca's hero, one young patient refused to wash his hands for two whole days.

The infirmary, in spite of its antiseptic odor, was often as lively as a theater. Musicians played their banjos and guitars, while poets dropped in to recite their latest work. One rainy afternoon, Angie Lebowitz, a nurse in the summer of '43, taught the campers how to make origami birds with flapping wings. These paper cranes were the selfsame birds later made by Japanese children – victims of the atomic bomb at Hiroshima – and sent round the world.

Grace became a Brooklyn Public Health Nurse as well as a school nurse, an outreach coordinator in mental health, and finally, a family counselor. She campaigned for nuclear disarmament and women's rights. In 1964 she joined a medical team in Mississippi, treating Southern Blacks injured while trying to vote.

More than fifty years later, Grace Horowitz Chawes still cherishes her memories of Camp. "Wo-Chi-Ca was a summer of freedom and joy."

Camp Wo-Chi-Ca's reputation attracted staff members from as far away as California. To teachers, social workers, office workers, manual laborers – whoever who could get the time off from a regular job – a summer at Wo-Chi-Ca meant a chance to make a real and lasting difference in a child's life. It was a chance to reside in a community of people who lived and breathed freedom and equality. Though it offered hard work and low pay (beginners earned only $50 to $75 for the whole season), the utopian camp in New Jersey could choose from the best to fill its staff.

Even the youngest camper looked forward to the day he or she would be old enough to scrub pots in the kitchen, wait tables, or be a bunk counselor. "Imagine actually getting paid to work at Wo-Chi-Ca!" High school and college students vied for the opportunity to be a substitute parent to a dozen exuberant youngsters, even with the nightly bathroom runs for the kids who wet their beds – 'Marines' as they were called.

More than anything else, Wo-Chi-Ca was a singing camp: everyone, without exception, sang. The busiest and perhaps the most popular staff member was the music director. One memorable person to hold this position was Naomi Feld Bassuk.

I was a student at Brooklyn College and I desperately needed a summer job. Matt Hall, Wo-Chi-Ca's director, asked if I could lead a children's chorus. I had never done that, but I'd been around music all my life: I started composing at the age of five. "Yes, I can do it," I said. And so I came to Camp in 1942 as a bunk counselor/music specialist.

For three summers I was Education Assistant and Music Director. I stayed up late every night planning programs, but I always got up early in the morning. In fact, I was the one who woke the bugler for reveille!

The Chorus did everything: folk songs, topical songs, union songs, work songs, Dust Bowl ballads, and Negro spirituals. We did classical music, even produced a full-scale opera by Mozart – "Bastien and Bastienne."

Everyone pitched in to make costumes and sets, and the dance group created original dances. Two twelve-year olds, Peggy Mair and Ernie Lieberman sang the lead roles.

We performed pieces by Villa-Lobos and Bach. We sang in Italian, Spanish and French – in German, Hebrew and Yiddish. We did Earl Robinson's "Lonesome Train." We did a cantata by Herbert Haufrecht called "We've Come From the City," about New Yorkers and upstate farmers learning that they had a lot in common.

Wo-Chi-Ca also had a Winter Workshop Chorus, and I conducted it until 1947. We sang at union halls all over the city. Every Christmas we performed carols at the Schomburg Public Library in Harlem.

In 1945 the chorus of Camp Woodland joined us and we called ourselves the American Youth Chorus. We took part in a huge show at Madison Square Garden where we were the only youth group out of fifteen participating choruses. We sang Earl Robinson's "The House I Live In" and Bach's "Jesu Joy of Man's Desiring."

I remember how nervous I was leading the chorus onto that giant, star-shaped stage. But my kids, with their beautiful shining faces, reassured me: "Don't worry, we're going to be wonderful." And they were!

Our American Youth Chorus was invited to perform at a memorial for Franklin Delano Roosevelt in the Grand Ballroom of the Waldorf-Astoria. It was chaired by Walter Damrosch, music critic for the New York Times. We Wo-Chi-Cans wrote the entire narration! What a thrill to sing with Yarmilla Novatna and Carol Brice, two stars from the Metropolitan Opera.

During the winter I'd spend every spare moment in libraries and book shops looking for new songs. I learned many Chinese and Russian pieces from Liu Liang Mo, a visiting music teacher from China. I was a member of the American People's Chorus, and from there I brought to Camp songs of the European anti-fascist underground. I used to tell the chorus members "Music is a form of battle."

Such outstanding staff members at Camp! So many – Joe Wallace, Ada B. Jackson, Dick Crosscup, Butch Lasky, Grace Horowitz, Naomi Bassuk – played starring roles in the ongoing production that was Camp Wo-Chi-Ca. But behind the scenes, one woman, Eve Levine, served for ten years as stage manager.

A whirlwind of energy barely five feet tall, the Camp Secretary appeared to do ten things at once: type a letter at 120 words per minute, talk on the telephone, supervise a trio of teenage volunteers, and round up artists for a benefit concert.

Eve Levine was born to a poor immigrant family and grew up on the Lower East Side. When she was sixteen, her father died of tuberculosis and Eve had to leave school. She worked as a stenographer to support her mother and a younger sister and brother. Surrounded by poverty, stimulated by such writers as Jack London, Theodore Dreiser and Upton Sinclair, inspired by the revolutionary events of 1917, Eve became a radical early in her life.

Eve participated in rent strikes, went to union rallies, walked on picket lines. She married and had two children. She was militantly active in the schools, transforming her local PTA into a powerful force for quality education. At the public school her daughters attended, Eve convinced the authorities to install a library and an after-school arts program. Collecting money on street corners for Republican Spain, marching in May Day parades, Eve was proud to have her husband and both their daughters at her side.

Early in World War II, Eve worked for Amtorg, an organization that sent food and medical supplies to the besieged Soviet Union.

In 1943 Eve Levine became secretary/registrar for Camp Wo-Chi-Ca. In New York City she maintained a year-round office, the Wo-Chi-Ca nerve center. Here, single-handedly, Eve interviewed counselors, rented buses, and enrolled children in camp or placed them on the long waiting list. She sat on the Board of Trustees along with parents, union leaders, and Paul Robeson.

Arnie Weinstat looks back fifty-three years...

I had been a camper since 1939. Wo-Chi-Ca was in my blood, and even in winter I spent a lot of time at the office at 80 Fifth Avenue just to be around the 'feel' of Camp. Eve got me a job with the man who ran the mimeo machine on the sixteenth floor.

When it came time to register for the 1946 camp season, it seemed my parents missed the boat. When Eve told me that Camp was filled for the season, my only feeling was one of disbelief! I could not imagine myself without Camp, and I thought she might be pulling my leg. When I came to, I decided to make the best of it.

I told Eve she was stuck with me because if I could not go to Camp in New Jersey, then the next best thing was to be in 'Wo-Chi-Ca' in New York.

I was at the office almost every day after school, and when school was out I was there all day. Every two weeks when the buses took off for New

Jersey, I helped Eve schlep the files to Washington Square Park and back. One day she said to me "Arnie, I'm going to see that you go to Camp this summer even if I have to take the time away from my own daughter." And I think she would have done it too! But luckily, a cancellation came through and I was able to go for the last four weeks. It sure felt good to be that appreciated!

Another camper, Issar Smith, lived within walking distance of Eve's office. He too spent his spare time hanging around the 'Winter Wo-Chi-Ca:' "As a young person I used to love visiting Eve in the camp office near Union Square. In hindsight, I think I must have had a crush on her!"

After Camp Wo-Chi-Ca closed, Eve was secretary at a camp for children with heart disease. She refused several job offers from private camps; she could not bear to work for an institution run for profit.

Eve Levine suffered a stroke and died at the age of seventy-five. She left two daughters. Both had been Wo-Chi-Ca campers; one is co-author of this book. In their mother's papers, June and Pearl found an unsigned loving tribute:

Anyone who has ever had children and sent them to camp owes a debt of gratitude to Eve Levine. She has practically dedicated her life to children's camps. Most people are interested in their own children. What differentiates Eve is that she is interested in all children; she is a sort of universal mother.

If you were to judge her by her income, or the model of her car, the size of her television set, or the mink on her coat, she wouldn't have much of a rating. However, if you were to judge her by human values, then she would get the highest rating. She is the sort of person who cannot say 'no' to a request. Her basic philosophy is: "What can I do to help others?"

These days, when most people are concerned only with their immediate family and are indifferent to the rest of the world, people like Eve Levine are a rarity and should be treasured. Good human beings are the most valuable asset the world possesses. Eve is fortunate to be endowed with many human values: she is warm, sincere, unselfish, modest, steadfast and a true friend in the noblest sense of the word.

When I think of Eve, I am reminded of Emerson's quote: "A friend may well be reckoned the masterpiece of nature." Eve has hundreds of friends. I consider myself fortunate to have Eve Levine as my friend.

Eve Levine next to Paul Robeson, her daughter June by her side

Eve Levine died in 1975. In her will, she left five hundred dollars to her beloved Communist Party.

DEAR COMRADE-CAMPERS

Enthusiastic children, inspired artists, idealistic staff members – such a splendid combination attracted many eminent visitors to the utopian camp. Famous labor leader Ella Reeve Bloor came up often. The tiny woman with snowy white hair would tell stories of her life. But these were hardly tales of an old-fashioned grandmother knitting by the fire. Mother Bloor astounded the kids with her audacious adventures.

As a young girl I became friendly with an old man known as 'The Good Gray Poet.' On Mickle Street in Camden, New Jersey, I was one of the neighborhood children who loved Walt Whitman and gathered at the marble steps where he came to sit in the evening. Yes, we children sat and listened to his stories just as you are listening to mine now. Old Walt wore a gray plaid shawl around his shoulders and a big soft hat on his head.

He and I became fast friends, walking hand in hand around Camden and riding the ferry together to Philadelphia. Shall I read you some from my book?

Perhaps it was on those ferry boat rides that the course of my life was determined, and that Whitman somehow transferred to me, without words, his own great longing to establish everywhere on earth "the institution of the dear love of comrades."

In 1902 I joined the Socialist Party. I became a close friend of Eugene V. Debs. When he was arrested for opposing the war I led the nationwide campaign to release him from prison.

I worked with Upton Sinclair, exposing filthy conditions in the meat packing industry. I helped Sinclair with his book **The Jungle.** *That led to the creation of the Food and Drug Administration and the passage of the Pure Food and Drug Act of 1906.*

I believed fervently in women's rights, and I gave speeches all across Ohio on the Suffragist Platform. My suffrage speeches were always fiery class struggle speeches. I tried to make clear that the object of our campaign was not alone to win the vote, but to prepare women to use the power of the ballot to get decent pay and decent working conditions for women, and to strengthen the position of the whole working class.

"Walt Whitman, Gene Debs, Upton Sinclair, and the suffragettes too! You sure knew them all. But," the kids asked, "were things really so terrible for workers in those days?"

"Oh yes, and for the children of the workers too. That's just what you'll read in my book. Listen:"

Violence, even against children of striking workers, was rampant. In the 1913 winter, 15,000 copper miners in Calumet, Michigan were on strike against starvation wages. I was with the women's auxiliary of the Western Federation of Miners, and we organized a Christmas party for the children. In the top floor ballroom of the Italian Workers Hall, we put up a small Christmas tree and were serving cookies and punch.

Suddenly, from outside the building, a company provocateur yelled "FIRE!" Panic broke out. Before we could stop them, dozens of children charged out the door and down the stairs. But company thugs had sealed off the exit. Seventy-three little bodies lay suffocated to death.

"Oh, that's so awful!" the children exclaimed. "But tell us more, Mother Bloor."

"Well, the following spring I was in Ludlow, Colorado, and I saw another ugly labor massacre. We had set up a tent camp for striking miners because the bosses had kicked them out of the company-owned houses. Coal company guards and hired strikebreakers and even state militiamen raided the camp. They poured kerosene on the tents and set them ablaze. Then they opened fire with machine guns. As many as twenty were killed, including thirteen children and a pregnant woman.

Mother Bloor at Camp Wo-Chi-Ca

"I shall never forget the despair and agony on the parents' faces on the awful day of the funeral. The capitalist class, dear Wo-Chi-Cans, shoots down mothers and children. It stops at nothing, no matter how monstrous, to prevent the organization of the workers. I will read just a little bit more."

In 1919 I helped to found the American Communist Party and served on its Central Committee for sixteen years. I went to Moscow as a delegate to the 1921 World Congress of Trade Unions and made friends with Lenin and his wife Krupskaya.

Back in the States, I toured for three years trying to stop the frame-up of Sacco and Vanzetti – speaking at rallies, distributing the **Daily Worker** *at each stop. I was already sixty-three years old, but I hitchhiked from one end of the country to the other. After those poor Italian anarchists were executed, I delivered a eulogy for them to 100,000 people at Union Square in New York. During the Depression I traveled with my husband Andrew Olmholt throughout the Great Plains, organizing strikes and relief for farmers.*

"You must have been in every state in the whole United States!"

"Yes, I traveled across the country many times, raising money for striking textile workers, coal miners, family farmers. I was arrested thirty-six times! The last time, when I was seventy-three, I was thrown into a sweltering Nebraska jail for defending women chicken pluckers.

"But the state I've spent the most time in is Pennsylvania. I married very young, had five children, then divorced and went off to study at the University of Pennsylvania. In 1938, the same year that my book was published, *Women in the Soviet Union,* I ran for governor of the State of Pennsylvania.

"While I was a young mother alone with my children – why, one was just an infant, still nursing – I got a call to go to eastern Pennsylvania. Young children there were put to work in coal mines, in silk mills, and glass factories. The Socialist Party wanted to put an end to that.

"You know, the bosses swore that no one under sixteen worked in those factories. Well, you can see how small I am, just four feet tall. So I disguised myself as a twelve-year old and got hired in a glass-blowing department. And you know what I found in that furnace? Children just like you – exactly your age!

"We got child labor laws passed, we made our country safer for children. And when I see children like you, going to summer camp, black and white together, all nationalities and creeds, I feel so happy.

"How I wish my old poet friend could have lived to see Wo-Chi-Ca. This camp is Walt Whitman's dream come true."

An American labor organizer one day, a Chinese music teacher on another... A boyish-looking man with a crewcut and silver-rimmed glasses, Liu Liang Mo is author of *China Sings: Folk Songs and Fighting Songs of China*. In perfect English, he invites the campers to learn Chinese. "This freedom song, 'Chee Lai,' is a marching song of resistance against the Japanese. It has become popular around the world. Many of you have already heard it sung by my friend Paul Robeson; perhaps some have his recording at home.

"In China, I taught 'Chee Lai' to thousands of soldiers at one time. Each row learned a line and passed it back to the row behind, until all 10,000 were singing in unison."

Liu Liang Mo raises his arms, for today, using the same method, he will teach the Wo-Chi-Ca children – all two hundred of them.

> *Chee Lai, buon so nulee dee runmun...*

"You see, Chinese is easy. And when you know what it means in English you will never forget this song."

> **Arise, you who refuse to be bond slaves...**
> *Ba wo men dee sheero -*

"Yes, Chinese is easy when you learn to sing phonetically!"

> *- so shen wo men sin dee chun chung...*
> **Let's stand up and fight**
> **For liberty and true democracy!**

Arm in arm, two hundred boys and girls march out of the Barn:

> *Chee Lai, Chee Lai, Chee Lai!*

Liu Liang Mo lived in the States, busily raising funds for Chinese Relief and for the People's Army. But he made time to visit Camp every summer. He sent his son Kong to Wo-Chi-Ca. In the winter, Liu took groups of campers to the Chinese Opera where, in whispers, he interpreted the spectacle on stage.

"Wo-Chi-Ca children," he would say, "are like Chinese children. I guess I fell in love with Wo-Chi-Ca the first day I saw it."

From China, from India, from other far-flung lands, world-renowned men and women beat a path to the heaven on earth in New Jersey. Poets and playwrights, actors and singers, union leaders, political activists, musicians, painters, writers, dancers... – had all arrived at once, Camp Wo-Chi-Ca in the Schooleys Mountains could claim to contain the greatest aggregation of genius since Athens in the Golden Age of Greece.

"Othello" from Rockwell Kent's Illustrations for the Complete Works of William Shakespeare

One such genius was the artist Rockwell Kent. Indeed, art critics agree his work has the feel of ancient Greece. Kent, one of the most popular artists in the first half of the century, was born in Tarrytown Heights, New York. He was carpenter and lobsterman, sailor and architectural draftsman, printer and globe-trotting painter. And, most happily for Camp Wo-Chi-Ca, Rockwell Kent was also president of the fraternal organization that nurtured Wo-Chi-Ca, the International Workers Order. Kent visited Camp on July 22, 1947.

He shared with the campers the experience of one who had traveled in out-of-the-way places around the world, seeking beauty in the stark landscapes of Greenland, Tierra del Fuego, Monhegan Island off the coast of Maine. The artist brought to the children the passion of a man who painted somber moody landscapes and heroic, larger-than-life human figures. He inspired campers and staff with the talent of an artist who had illustrated Melville's *Moby Dick*, Chaucer's *Canturbury Tales*, and the complete works of William Shakespeare.

Kent had written extensively on art and children. "The child," he maintained, "is the perfect artist. The most that can be done for the child in art, beyond a little encouragement, and plenty of paper and chalk and pencils and watercolors and the like, is to make his life a pleasure. Give him some quiet hours away from boisterous play..." Kent's essay "Art and the Child" circulated among Wo-Chi-Ca staff as required reading.

A welcoming committee of campers and counselors showed IWO President Kent around the grounds. Resident art counselors Ernest Crichlow and Charles White demonstrated the camp's art program to the distinguished visitor. Kent lunched in the mess hall, surrounded by children. During Rest Hour, campers clustered around their tents to hear the artist tell folk tales from Greenland.

Shortly after his departure, camp directors received a note from Kent: "I have been bubbling over with enthusiasm about Wo-Chi-Ca and the grand spirit that prevails there. I would like to see a sort of 'Five Year Plan' undertaken, with its objectives clearly outlined and pictured. If my architectural training can be of any service to you, do let me know... Please give our best wishes and warmest greetings to all the kids."

In 1953, shortly before Camp was forced to close, Rockwell Kent was summoned to appear before the McCarthy Committee. This truly American artist was called a Communist and labeled "un-American."

As much as art, drama was vital to Wo-Chi-Ca. Each two-week camp period the children put on a skit, perhaps a play, even an operetta. For example, in 1941 alone, the campers dramatized John Brown's raid on Harper's Ferry, produced *Song of Victory, The People Yes, Plant in the Sun*, and with a cast and crew of seventy, presented *Haiti!*

What a thrill it was to have a visit from the Black actor who had played the lead role in the Broadway production of *Haiti!* Campers and staff lined up excitedly for the autograph of the famous Canada Lee.

Strikingly handsome, Canada Lee started out as a child prodigy in music. Forsaking his violin strings for horse reins, he worked at the Saratoga Racetrack, first as a stable boy, then a jockey, but returned later to music to lead a jazz band.

Next he turned his talents to boxing: in two hundred professional matches, he lost only twenty-five fights. Lee might have won the welterweight or middleweight championship, but suffered an eye injury and was forced to retire from the ring.

Thanks to the WPA, Canada Lee became an actor. In this arena too he fought to achieve dignity as a Black man. Lee chose to appear only in socially relevant dramas, acting, for example, in the anti-lynching play *Stevedore*. His portrayal of Bigger Thomas in *Native Son* evoked from the critics cheers of "magnetic!" and "overwhelming!" Lee was acclaimed "the best Negro actor of his time," and the *New York Times* said his was "the most vital piece of acting on the current stage."

Canada Lee took on Shakespeare, playing Caliban in Margaret Webster's production of *The Tempest*, and Banquo in Orson Welles' all-Black production of *Macbeth*. Canada Lee starred in *Othello* as well.

Lee also appeared in Hollywood movies such as *Body and Soul, Lifeboat,* and *Lost Boundaries*.

On the NBC radio network, master of ceremonies Canada Lee conducted the first radio program wholly dedicated to the condition and treatment of Blacks in America. He took a leading part in a huge Negro Freedom Rally in Madison Square Garden. Lee entered the U.S. Senate with a petition signed by 25,000 New Yorkers: it demanded that notorious racist Theodore Bilbo of Mississippi be banished from the Senate "for conduct unbecoming a member of Congress."

But as the Red Scare and Cold War heated up, Canada Lee was punished for his defiant stand against racism. As 'scoundrel time' took hold, frightened actors and directors caved in to the House Un-American Activities Committee. In "naming names," they named Canada Lee as a Communist. Called before the Committee, Lee himself repeatedly refused to name names. "They could not," the *Daily Worker* wrote, "make Canada Lee into a cold war stool pigeon."

New York and Hollywood studio heads placed Canada Lee on their blacklist. Forty radio and television shows banned him from the airwaves. Forced to leave the country to earn a living, Lee starred in a British film shot on location in South Africa – *Cry the Beloved Country*. His co-star Sidney Poitier called Canada Lee "one of the most courageous characters I have ever met." Though the movie was a hit in America, Canada Lee returned home to find that he was still blacklisted.

"I can't take it anymore," Lee wrote the president of the NAACP. "I am going to get a shoeshine box and sit outside the Astor Theatre. My picture, *Cry the Beloved Country,* is playing to capacity audiences and, my God, I can't get one day's work."

Canada Lee played his final scene on a stage in White Plains, New York, at a meeting to protest the tavern shooting of two Black men by an ex-policeman.

"Haply, for I am black and have not those soft parts of conversation," he began, quoting from *Othello.* Then, to the grieving audience, Canada Lee said "I am a black man, and black men have been killed. When I think that America, this great and tremendous country, has been built on the backs and sweat of my people; when I think that in every war my people have died for this country; and when I know that my people cannot walk the streets here in safety..."

Canada Lee

Canada Lee died of a heart attack on May 9, 1952. The ex-boxer was only forty-five years old. A major factor in his untimely death, his friends and family asserted, was stress due to McCarthyism.

Also a big hit with the campers was the music and dance team of Larry Adler and Paul Draper. Larry called himself a 'mouth organist' and was simply the best harmonica player ever. Musically precocious, at age ten he was already a cantor at an orthodox synagogue. Soon after winning the Maryland Harmonica Championship, Larry ran away to New York to play for silent movies and in vaudeville shows. He was only thirteen.

Larry Adler worked with Eddie Cantor, Jack Benny, Florence Ziegfeld, Paul Whiteman, George Gershwin, Duke Ellington, Fred Astaire... The harmonica became phenomenally popular; Larry Adler fan clubs sprang up everywhere.

Adler appeared in five films and composed scores for a number of others. For *Genevieve*, he received an Academy Award nomination for best musical score. Adler turned his attention to classical music as well, playing harmonica solos with symphony orchestras.

In 1940 Larry Adler joined forces with Paul Draper. Like Larry, Paul was unrivaled in his field, for he had created a unique dance style. He combined the popular appeal of tap dance with the glorious leaps and pirouettes of classical ballet. Together Adler and Draper were sensational, performing to a packed house at Carnegie Hall.

During World War II Adler and Draper worked with the USO, touring Africa, the Middle East and the United States. In the Forties, the Armed Forces were still segregated, but the Adler/Draper team refused to step on stage unless the audience of Negro and white soldiers sat side by side. In the Korean War, Adler and Draper again entertained troops, but their patriotism did not prevent McCarthyite cries of "Communism." Both artists were summoned before the House Un-American Activities Committee. Both were blacklisted.

On August 17, 1947, a muscular African-American man drove up the winding road to Camp Wo-Chi-Ca. He was Kenneth Spencer, a handsome actor and singer, master of a thundering bass-baritone voice. Spencer appeared on Broadway in *Showboat* and *Cabin in the Sky*. He played a leading part in the movie *Bataan*.

Born in Los Angeles in 1913, a graduate of the Eastman School of Music in Rochester, Spencer was the first Black American to sing with the Austin and Houston symphony orchestras. He was soloist with many major orchestras, including the New York Philharmonic, the London Symphony and the Vancouver Symphony. He performed with the St. Louis Opera Company.

Kenneth Spencer organized the first all-Negro USO unit, touring Caribbean and South Pacific bases. President Franklin D. Roosevelt invited him to sing at the White House. In New York, Spencer gave several concerts at Town Hall, all to rave reviews.

But his heart called him to Wo-Chi-Ca. The acoustics were terrible, children would overflow their hard wooden benches and spill onto the splintery floor, the microphone frequently failed. Still, no plush concert hall or Broadway theater could provide Kenneth the comradeship he felt at Camp Wo-Chi-Ca.

itle: Tales of Wo-Chi-Ca: Blacks,
Whites and Reds at Camp
ond: Good
ate: 2023-12-21 11:57:22 (UTC)
SKU: ZBM.1712D
SKU: ZBV 0971743509.G
nit_id: 13607231
ource: PAULA

ZBV 0971743509 G

delist unit# 13607231

Black and white children in a genuinely democratic camp moved Kenneth Spencer to declare:

It is wonderful to see here in Wo-Chi-Ca how the spirit of America is being carried out, the spirit that the men in the Revolutionary War fought for and that all true Americans wish for their children to have. That kind of America is here in Wo-Chi-Ca.

Spencer drove back to New York to raise funds for his beloved camp. His concert at Carnegie Hall helped to build the Paul Robeson Playhouse.

Kenneth SPENCER

The Great American Basso

A frequent visitor to Camp was the poet Aaron Kramer. He would often read aloud from his newest work. One day Kramer read a section from a long poem on the American Revolution. Portraying the celebrated crossing of the Delaware, he intoned "...the night was black for Washington's troops."

His listeners, though young, had super-sensitive antennae. Zealous senior campers thought they detected 'white chauvinism.' "Why always 'black' to denote the negative? Why 'black' for all things evil? Was this not unconsciously racist?"

The poet was somewhat taken aback. He used "black," he maintained, not in a derogatory sense, and not in relation to Negro people at all. He stood simply on the grounds that black night has always symbolized fear and danger. For hours, the poet and his teenage audience discussed word connotations and their effect on oppressed minorities.

Aaron Kramer agreed that the point of poetry is to choose precisely the proper word. He conceded that he might not be as sensitive as the interracial campers. Noting that nothing is all black or white, Kramer promised to cross the Delaware again, this time with a corrected compass!

Aaron Kramer at Wo-Chi-Ca

From the subcontinent of Asia, Kumar Goshal brought an international perspective to young Wo-Chi-Cans. Dressed in a Nehru jacket, the author of *People of India* as well as *20th Century India* spoke of the struggle against colonialism. "Like you Americans, we too must win our independence from England and make our own destiny."

During this period another scholar visited Camp. He seemed to be a mild unassuming man. But Albert E. Kahn hunted the most dangerous beasts: fascists, Nazis, and their counterparts in the House Un-American Activities Committee.

Kahn's best sellers – *The Great Conspiracy*, *The Plot Against the Peace*, *Sabotage! The Secret War Against America* – had exposed fifth column intrigue. *Conspiracy* was translated into fifteen languages. Kahn edited *The Hour*, a confidential newsletter that exposed German and Japanese wartime conspiracies in America. He was Executive Secretary of the American Council Against Nazi Propaganda.

Like Rockwell Kent, Albert Kahn was an officer of the International Workers Order. He served as president of an important branch, the Jewish People's Fraternal Order.

In the Fifties, the McCarthy blacklist would have silenced Albert Kahn had he not formed his own publishing company. He issued *False Witness*, in which Harvey Matusow confesses that he lied about hundreds of people he named as members of the Communist Party. "I was not a leader in the Communist Party. I was a communist flunky in a club on the Lower East Side of New York, and through a few lies I built myself up into an expert on communism."

Matuso's book was widely read. Harvey Matuso spent twenty-one days in jail for perjury, but the lives he shattered remained in ruins forever.

Albert Kahn, so active politically, had an exquisite artistic sensibility as well. He created an enchanting pictorial biography of Russian ballerina Galina Ulanova. Pablo Casals chose Kahn to assist him in writing his autobiography *Joys and Sorrows*. The quiet writer who turned out to be such a talented and courageous man was but one of the many extraordinary visitors to Camp Wo-Chi-Ca.

In the old structure called 'The Shacks,' where once the chickens roosted, and where now campers found spaces for clay work, arts and crafts, photography and journalism, the Gerald Feifer Library occupied a snug room. Its homemade pine shelves held an extensive selection of books by left-wing writers. Millicent Selsam's marvelous nature studies, Albert Kahn's alarming exposés, Jack London's *Iron Heel* and other class-conscious novels beckoned the young reader. In addition, the library contained at least one copy of every book by Howard Fast: *Freedom Road, Citizen Tom Paine, Conceived in Liberty, The*

Unvanquished, The Last Frontier....

Fast, on one of his many visits, came up to Wo-Chi-Ca early to help prepare the camp for opening day. He worked hours in the hot sun, hammering, hauling, scrubbing, and setting up tents with other volunteers. At sunset they all relaxed on the lawn, in a discussion of politics, history, and literature. Fast was deeply involved in all three.

In 1945 Howard Fast received a call from Dr. Edward K. Barsky inviting the well-known author to serve on the executive board of the Joint Anti-Fascist Refugee Committee. Spanish Republicans were still in exile in southern France, in desperate need of food and medical care. In America, people from all walks of life gave generously to 'The Joint' and provided sufficient funds to convert an abandoned convent in Toulouse into a hospital.

But only three months after Fast joined the Committee, its entire board was summoned before the House Un-American Activities Committee. Fascism was no longer the enemy. The adversary was now 'the Red under every bed.' Progressives and Communists who first warned of the fascist danger were now stigmatized as "premature anti-Fascists." The Joint Anti-Fascist Refugee Committee was ordered to turn over all records, including names of donors and "correspondence with persons in foreign countries."

Certain that harm, perhaps even death would come to Spanish refugees, Barsky and Fast and nine other board members refused to surrender the records. They were cited for contempt of Congress and sentenced to federal prison. The Supreme Court rejected all appeals; President Truman refused clemency. Outraged millions round the world protested.

Howard Fast was fined five hundred dollars and jailed for three months. Walking out the prison doors, he found himself in yet another prison: the blacklist. Libraries and schools removed Howard Fast books from their shelves. Not one major publisher would touch his work. Alfred A. Knopf returned a manuscript with a note declaring that he would not "dirty his hands" by opening an envelope sent to him by Howard Fast.

Fast, a close friend of Paul Robeson, had been one of his bodyguards at the shameful Peekskill incident; he described this event in *Peekskill, USA: A Personal Experience*. Though the book was printed by the Foreign Languages Publishing House in Moscow, in the USA only the Civil Rights Congress would publish it.

Determined to break through to a wider American audience, Fast turned to self-publication. He took subscriptions by mail to his new novel; the cover was to be illustrated by Wo-Chi-Ca artist Charles White. Howard Fast sold 50,000 copies of his self-published *Spartacus*. A few years later, the book became a triumphant

Hollywood movie.

In 1952 Howard Fast ran for Congress on the American Labor Party ticket. Two years later he was awarded the Stalin Peace Prize. Though in 1957 Fast left the Communist Party with a bitter denunciation, to this day the writer maintains his belief in the "inevitability of socialism."

Every day, it seemed, new visitors would come to Camp. Actor Will Lee, Marxist scholar Doxey Wilkerson, Africa specialist Max Yergan, *Daily Worker* artist Del who gave 'chalk talks' to demonstrate his cartooning style. The son of General Pershing dropped in, as did local celebrity James Boone, a descendant of Daniel Boone. Methodist minister Lynn Sprague, leader of a fight against police brutality near New York City, celebrated his thirtieth birthday at Wo-Chi-Ca. A Red Army officer, in the U.S. to raise money for Lend-Lease, brought greetings from Young Pioneers in the Soviet Union.

Crowds of visitors trooped around the 127 acres – groups of a dozen, even a hundred! A news article from a *Daily Wo-Chi-Can* of 1939 reads:

WO-CHI-CA WELCOMES I.W.O. DELEGATION!

One hundred members of the I.W.O. visited Wo-Chi-Ca on a bright Sunday afternoon and were thoroughly pleased with the progress the camp had made in its various activities.

A group from the Progressive Women's Council, which had raised over four thousand dollars for the building fund, came to see their money at work. Delegations from the Furriers Union, the Office Workers Union, the Mine, Mill and Smelters Union toured the buildings and explored the grounds. Were kids imagining it or were there as many visitors as there were campers?

In the summer of 1937, Dr. Edward Barsky had come to Wo-Chi-Ca. Children, counselors and cooks gathered on the grass to hear news of the Spanish Civil War. The renowned surgeon described how he set up operating rooms in trucks close to the front lines. Rapid treatment of wounded soldiers saved many lives.

With Dr. Barsky stood men and women from his medical team, as well as soldiers in red berets – members of the Abraham Lincoln Battalion. They spoke with passion of their determination to defeat the fascist armies.

The Wo-Chi-Cans hung on every word. Some of these International Brigade volunteers were their own sisters, brothers and cousins. In the group that day sat counselors Ralph Wardlaw and Wilfred "Mendy" Mendelsohn. These two came to a momentous decision: the best thing they could do to protect the young campers would be to go and fight in Spain. They would stop fascism before it came to America. When Camp closed for the season, Ralph and Mendy enlisted in the Lincoln Battalion.

The impression on the campers made by Liu Liang Mo, Rockwell Kent, Canada Lee, Larry Adler, Paul Draper, Kenneth Spencer, Aaron Kramer, Kumar Goshal, Albert Kahn, Howard Fast, Dr. Barsky and so many other illustrious visitors was incalculable and indelible. And these visitors themselves came away with profound affection for the camp and its children.

Mother Bloor, after one of her visits, summed up her feelings about Wo-Chi-Ca in a letter.

Dear Comrade-Campers,

All week I have been thinking of you all - wondering what you are doing. It is a wonderful place you live in, and I enjoyed every minute of my visit to you.

Keep on singing children; keep on cheering. Keep on working, and sometime we shall, all together, make it possible for all children to have such happy times and such beautiful places to live.

Let us get together all kinds of boys and girls - Jew and Gentile, Catholic and Protestant, black and white, all nationalities, all creeds. Let us get together quickly so that we can make this country of ours safe for little children.

Your proud loving,

Mother Bloor

PUREST KIND OF A GUY

So many lofty, imposing, splendid visitors to Wo-Chi-Ca! And yet one stood above all others – the tallest tree in the forest, Paul Robeson. The boy who would become Wo-Chi-Ca's great hero was a local lad: a grade school child in Princeton, a high school student in Somerville, a college man in New Brunswick – all in New Jersey, all only a short drive down the road from Camp Wo-Chi-Ca.

In the university town of Princeton – that "northernmost outpost of the Confederacy" – in a Negro neighborhood of neat frame homes, stood the Witherspoon Street Presbyterian Church. On April 9, 1898, in the church parsonage, Paul Leroy Robeson was born. The father of this youngest of five children was scholarly William Drew Robeson – formerly a slave in North Carolina, now pastor of the church. The child's mother, Maria Louisa Bustill, came from a long line of Northern free Negroes. Tragically, young Paul lost his mother before his sixth birthday when she died in a kitchen fire.

The entire Black community of Princeton helped raise the motherless child: "My early youth was spent hugged to the hearts and bosoms of my hard-working relatives. I remember the cornmeal, greens, yams, and the peanuts and other goodies..."

Paul's father, Reverend Robeson, outspoken in defense of Negro rights, was forced out of his position by the all-white church board. After twenty years he was reduced from parson to ashman, hauling cinders from furnaces and dumping them in his back yard. But soon Reverend Robeson decided on a change of religious denomination. He built a new church, St. Luke's A.M.E. Zion in Westfield, creating for himself a position as its pastor. For the first time his son Paul went to school with white children.

By and by, Paul and his father moved on to a larger parish in Somerville. Here Paul finished eighth grade in a segregated school, then entered Somerville High School; he was one of only ten Black students out of a total enrollment of two hundred. Paul had been a happy boy, a good scholar and athlete in elementary school. Now, in Somerville High School, he demonstrated the astonishing gifts of one destined for greatness.

Paul Robeson earned straight-A grades, was a dominant member of the debating team, and edited the sports page of the school magazine. As a member of the drama group he played Othello and Mark Antony. "In high school," Paul later recalled, "I had a very fine teacher whose passion was Shakespeare."

Paul Robeson, Rutgers football star

Paul sang in the bass section of the glee club; he was the star player on the football, baseball and basketball teams. Brilliant both in the classroom and on the sports field, the Black student was extremely popular: "It was a rich experience to have four years in school with as great a human being as Paul – to have him as a warm and loyal friend..."

White folks in Somerville were fond of Paul: "Everybody liked him a lot. He was entertained and dined at all our homes. Everybody's mother was crazy about him and was always holding him up as an example of what they would like us to be. We all felt Paul to be our superior, but we didn't resent it, he was such a great guy."

To cap off his fabulous high school career, Paul won a statewide competition for a four-year scholarship to Rutgers College. His tryout for the football team, for the right to wear the Rutgers scarlet, was a bloody beating which landed him in bed for ten days with a smashed nose, dislocated shoulder, and the nails ripped off all the fingers of his right hand. "They didn't want a Negro on their team; they just didn't want me on it!"

Paul's courage and talent did finally win him a place on the football squad – but not at the festive table: the banquets honoring the Scarlet Knights were only for whites. In an important game, Paul was removed from the lineup when Washington and Lee, a southern school, refused to compete against a team with a Negro player. Paul was not allowed to live with white students. As the only Black student on campus, he was made to live alone in an empty residence hall.

In spite of this initial bigotry, Paul became the legendary "Robeson of Rutgers" with "a name and a record equaled by none." "A football genius," Robeson was twice named to the All-American Team – the first Rutgers player in its fifty year gridiron history to win that honor. "Robey" was acclaimed "the best player in the country" and "the wonder of the age." Robeson also won letters in baseball, basketball, and track, playing on a total of fifteen varsity teams.

Just as impressive was Paul's academic record. He made the honor role consistently and took first prize annually in public speaking. At college Paul maintained his high school love of Shakespeare, naming *Hamlet* his favorite play. Paul's English professor, Charles W. Whitman, often took his star pupil to New York to see the Bard on Broadway.

In his junior year Robeson was selected for Phi Beta Kappa, the national honor society of scholars; in his senior year his classmates elected Paul to Cap and Skull, the fraternity composed of only four men, those who best exemplified the ideals of Rutgers.

At his graduation Paul gave the valedictory speech. The school magazine predicted that Paul Robeson would become governor of New Jersey. "He has dimmed the fame of Booker T. Washington," it prophesied, "and is the leader of the colored race of America." The comments concluded with an invocation: "May Rutgers never forget this noble son and may he always remember his Alma Mater."

For graduate studies Paul chose Columbia University Law School to be near the exciting neighborhood of Harlem where a cultural renaissance was underway. But Robeson was often absent from school and neighborhood – off to Akron or Milwaukee or Chicago. In order to earn tuition money, Paul cut classes on Friday, made tackles and caught passes with pro teams on Sunday, then hurried back to class for torts and writs on Monday.

In one rough game with the Akron Pros, Paul suffered a serious injury. Recovering from surgery in Harlem's Presbyterian Hospital, he met a pretty laboratory technician working there, Eslanda Cardozo Goode. Two years later, on August 17, 1921, Paul and Essie married.

After graduation from law school, Paul went to work for a legal firm on Wall Street, but only for a brief time. Among other indignities, a white secretary refused to take dictation from him and Robeson realized soon enough there was no future for him in law.

He took a part in a short play produced at the Harlem YWCA. Paul's role was that of Simon the Cyrenian, the Black man who helped Christ carry his cross to the Crucifixion. This performance started Robeson off on a long and distinguished theatrical career. Soon he was in England, acting with the legendary Mrs. Patrick Campbell.

Great Britain altered Paul Robeson's life. There he grew close to class-conscious laborers, absorbing their socialist ideals. By way of his many dockworker friends in London, Robeson discovered Africa, his ancestral continent. In Paul's tours around the countryside of England, Scotland and Wales, he was moved by the kindness and decency of ordinary working people – touched by their friendship and freedom from prejudice. Essie remarked that in London – unlike New York – she and Paul "could, as respectable human beings, dine at any public place."

Paul Robeson wearing Phi Beta Kappa key

In London, Paul made friends with Jomo Kenyatta, Kwame Nkrumah, and Jawaharlal Nehru. Robeson became a Man of the Left: anti-capitalist and anti-imperialist. Also in London Robeson met the American musician and folklorist Lawrence Brown. Larry would become Paul's collaborator and lifelong friend.

In 1925, at the height of the Harlem Renaissance, Paul – with Brown accompanying on piano – gave an historic song concert. To an overflow crowd at a Greenwich Village theater, Paul sang sixteen Negro spirituals.

This sensational concert – first ever of a Black soloist singing nothing but Negro spirituals – catapulted Paul to fame. The New York World spoke of "...a turning point, one of those thin points of time a star is born. Paul Robeson's voice is difficult to describe. It is a voice in which deep bells ring."

The singer had already attained celebrity as an actor: only a year earlier Paul had performed in three notable artistic productions. He starred in his first film, *Body and Soul,* working with African American director Oscar Micheaux.

At the Provincetown Playhouse in New York City, Paul appeared in Eugene O'Neill's *The Emperor Jones*. Theater critics called him "...as fine an actor as there is on the American stage today."

Bomb threats and talk of riots made for a tense opening of O'Neill's *All God's Chillun Got Wings*. Robeson was to play a young Black lawyer married to a white woman (the actress Mary Blair). With steelworker friends of the cast guarding the theater, no trouble occurred. Paul was praised in the press as "a genius," "a great actor," "a superb actor."

In 1928, Essie and Paul decided to move to England with their infant son Paul Jr. Appearing in the London production of *Showboat,* Paul stopped the show with his moving rendition of "Ol' Man River." This striking song by Jerome Kern and Oscar Hammerstein II became Paul Robeson's signature song, identified with him forever.

Invited to give command performances before the Prince of Wales and the King of Spain, Robeson toured the British provinces as well as Vienna, Prague and Budapest, giving concerts of Negro spirituals. On an American concert tour, Robeson twice appeared at Carnegie Hall.

Back home in London, Paul, long a lover of Shakespeare, took on the role of Othello. At one performance the audience called him back for twenty curtain calls. The English critics lauded him as "great," "remarkable" and "magnificent." The first of many biographies of Paul Robeson was published at this time: the author, Paul's wife Essie.

While at Rutgers and Columbia, Paul had tutored in Latin. In Europe he quickly learned French and German and began to study Russian as well as several African languages. He eventually would be proficient in thirty languages!

Paul accepted an invitation from film director Sergei Eisenstein to visit the Soviet Union. Robeson was tremendously impressed with the Socialist nation, especially the equality enjoyed by all races and peoples. He returned often, once staying an entire summer. "Here, for the first time in my life," Robeson exulted, "I walk in full human dignity." Paul and Essie enrolled Paul, Jr. in a Soviet school where the boy would not suffer the racism of America.

Returning to England by way of Germany, Paul condemned the Nazi oppression of Jews, and sang to raise money for refugees fleeing the Third Reich.

Robeson devoted an entire London concert season to benefit performances for the Republicans fighting the fascists in the Spanish Civil War. In spite of danger, Robeson visited the front lines in Spain and sang to the Loyalist troops. So enthralling was his voice that soldiers on both sides laid down their guns to hear him. After touring the battlefields, Robeson denounced the United States, France and England for refusing to aid the Republicans; he applauded the Soviet Union for its staunch support of the duly elected Spanish government.

Plunging further into political activity, Robeson joined with Africa scholar Max Yergan to found the Council on African Affairs, pledged to work for an independent Africa.

Paul's agent warned him that his outspoken politics would endanger his career. But Robeson persisted and remained enormously popular. At Albert Hall in London, Paul brought the audience to its feet when he changed the words of "Ol' Man River" from "I'm tired of livin' and scared of dyin'" to "I must keep fightin' until I'm dyin'." Everywhere he appeared he was greeted by adoring fans. A cheering crowd in Torquay lifted him on their shoulders and carried him into the concert hall. The British public ranked Paul Robeson among the top ten film and recording stars.

In the English film *Sanders of the River*, Paul starred as African chief Bosambo. Enormously excited, Robeson had hopes that the film would promote "understanding of Negro culture and customs." What a painful disappointment when the finished film portrayed Africans as childlike savages and the British as civilized gentlemen! In the end Robeson confessed "I hate the picture," regarding it as nothing more than a glorification of British imperialism.

Jericho, filmed in Egypt, Paul esteemed only a bit better. Two other British films in which Robeson starred – *Song of Freedom* and *King Solomon's Mines* – did treat Blacks with some dignity.

In *Big Fella,* Paul played what is perhaps his most endearing role in the movies, though he did portray the likable Joe in the lavish Hollywood version of *Showboat.* But of all the films Robeson made, unquestionably his favorite was *Proud Valley*, about a Black American miner in Wales.

In all his work, Robeson combined artistry with activism. His concerts in Oslo, Copenhagen and Stockholm spontaneously developed into anti-Nazi demonstrations. But by September 1939, the German army had invaded Poland and was poised for a blitzkrieg across all of Europe. It was time to go home. After twelve years, Paul Robeson, Essie and Paulie returned to America.

Immediately upon arrival in New York, Paul met with Benjamin Davis, Jr., a Black attorney and leader of the Communist Party. Paul offered to help register Negro voters in Birmingham. He also worked to free Angelo Herndon, a Black Communist sentenced to twenty years on a Georgia chain gang for leading an integrated demonstration of the Atlanta unemployed.

On the fifth of November 1939, Paul Robeson made radio history. At CBS in New York, he premiered a cantata written by John LaTouche and Earl Robinson. "Ballad for Americans" was a patriotic celebration of multiethnic and multiracial America. For fifteen minutes the studio audience stamped their feet and shouted "Bravo!" Phone lines were tied up for two hours, while for days letters streamed into the station. "Ballad for Americans" took the country by storm and Paul Robeson became a national hero.

CBS broadcast of "Ballad for Americans," November 5, 1939

This is the giant the Wo-Chi-Ca kids behold strolling up the dirt road on a summer's day of 1940 – the artist and activist who is coming to eat with them, play ball with them and sing for them. This is Paul Robeson on his very first visit to Camp Wo-Chi-Ca.

The day Paul arrived is ever in my memory. I danced on stage in front of my fellow work groupers; they were singing "Rise and Shine." I fell to the floor (deliberately) and hit my head (accidentally!). When Paul came on stage he stopped to ask me with great concern if I had seriously hurt myself. What happiness! My four beloved grandchildren and their parents have all grown up with my memories and stories of Wo-Chi-Ca and Paul Robeson. Is it otherwise with any of us?

RENA GLUCK

To this day, more than sixty years later, when Wo-Chi-Cans reminisce about Camp, their talks begin and end with the visits of Paul Robeson. He came up every summer at least once, and some years several times. Paul and Eslanda had enrolled their son Pauli at Camp, and the father would come to see how Junior was doing. Furthermore, Robeson arrived on camp business occasionally, as a member of the Board of Trustees. But every August without fail, he came up for...

PAUL ROBESON DAY AT WO-CHI-CA: The mess hall bell announces his arrival. A giant of a man emerges from the camp station wagon. Raising an enormous arm, he breaks into a big wide smile. If he is a giant, he is a gentle one.

I actually met Paul Robeson. He mesmerized me with his towering presence and booming voice. He had huge, gentle hands and a magnetic smile. When he sang for us, my love for opera was born. The camp paid tribute to him with the production of an original show. My group danced. Paul thanked us with hugs and warm praise for our endeavors. Many of us cried when he said goodbye.

SHEILA NEWMAN

Louder and faster clangs the bell. Campers and counselors stream down the hill flourishing painted banners: **PAUL ROBESON DAY. WELCOME PAUL!** Kitchen workers desert their pots and pans. Kids clamor and swarm over Robeson; he scoops them up in a warm embrace. Up the dirt road they throng, children perched on Paul's broad shoulders or clinging to his massive arms.

I remember Paul visiting when we performed "Ballad for Americans." At one point in the performance he let loose and sang along with us. (What a voice, I can still feel the vibrations!) Paul was always a name and a presence at camp, always loved...

SY ROSEN

In the mess hall a special lunch awaits. Lucky kids sitting at Paul's table heap his plate with fried chicken, his favorite dish. For dessert, they have hand-churned peach ice cream and the confection Robeson especially likes, peanut brittle.

Paul Robeson had just come back from Russia and I remember him talking about its monumental efforts at reconstruction. I recall clearly his voice and how familiar a presence he seemed to me, as though he had stepped out of his phonograph record that we had in our collection at home.

STEVE COGAN

On "Paul Robeson Day" even Rest Hour is suspended. Instead, everyone presses into the Barn. Paul sits on a hard wooden bench, surrounded by wide-eyed youngsters reaching out to touch him. The campers present four original skits on the life of their hero.

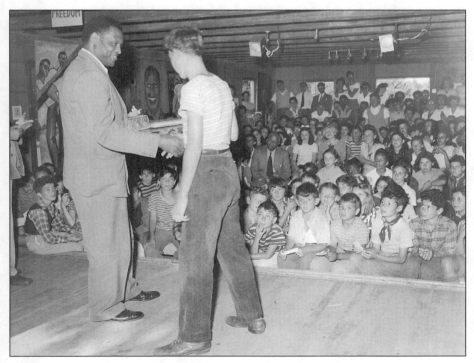

Paul and camper on stage in the Barn

Paul climbs the stage to thank the performers; the giant has tears in his eyes. He apologizes for not having time to sign all the autograph books. He has made arrangements with the journalism shack to mimeograph his signature so everyone can get a copy.

With Larry Brown at the old piano, Paul sings to wild cheers and applause: "Viva La Quince Brigada," "Joe Hill," "Shenandoah"... The campers sway to the music, arms around each other's shoulders. They join in the chorus of "John Brown's Body" and "Scandalize My Name." Still they call out "More, Paul, more!"

Then it's hurry on down to the ball field for a game between campers and staff.

Dear Dad,

Paul Robeson is here. I just took one picture of him but I'll take some more this afternoon. He is going to give a concert. We also have a program for him. I am proud to say that I can swim a few feet. All I need is a little more practice to become a good swimmer. Paul was wonderful. He sang a lot of songs. He certainly is a nice guy. Right now I have to run down to the ball field. Paul is playing catcher on the camper's team. I took eight pictures of him.

Love, Robert

'The Umpire' on
Wo-Chi-Ca's ball field

In shirtsleeves, baseball cap and catcher's mask, Robeson squats behind home plate. By the third inning the campers fall behind; Paul offers to act as umpire. Every call now favors the younger team. Serge Kanevsky reports for *The Daily Wo-Chi-Can*:

The game was a hilarious comedy from beginning to end. Paul Robeson did a fine job calling balls and strikes. One of the unusual features of this umpiring was the fact that Paul was able to call the pitch before the ball left the pitcher's hand.

Noticing that the old barn is far too small to accommodate the expanding camp, Paul offers to do a benefit concert to raise money for the building fund. He gives several performances in New York, all to full houses. Wo-Chi-Cans sell tickets in their neighborhoods, then usher at the theater. Paul and the campers earn enough money to build a new recreation hall.

On the 28th of July in 1948, Paul arrives at camp for the dedication of a shiny new Quonset hut, the Paul Robeson Playhouse. In the spacious new auditorium Paul sings "Freedom is My Land." He speaks of Jewish-Negro unity:

I have felt in my own struggles a very close bond with the people who gave to the Negro people in America their first ideas of courage, so that the folk songs of our people are the songs of Joshua, the songs of Moses, the songs of David... And I feel that there is no struggle closer than the struggle of the Negro people and the Jewish people.

Later that day, in the Whitey Melzer music room, Robeson listens to classical music with a group of campers. A young girl – moved by the day's events and the thrill of sharing a quiet moment with Paul – jots down a poem entitled "Dedication." Shyly she presents it to him.

It stands majestic, straight and tall.
On firm foundations it is built.
It symbolizes big-hearted Paul
Whose spirit will never wilt.

Like the courage of the Negro people
His great will shall never fall.
His spirit has been captured by
The Robeson Recreation Hall.

Laurel Field – age 12

In designing the stage of the new Playhouse, architect Irving Feirtag, a Wo-Chi-Ca parent, has remained true to the old Barn arrangement: in fine weather, the stage's back wall will fold away allowing performers to turn around and face an outdoor audience. Feirtag's plan, however, does away with the old practice of hauling wooden benches in and out of the theater. Instead, he envisions a sweeping stone amphitheater with broad semi-circular steps. It will seat the entire camp, in the sun or under the stars.

Counselors-in-Training proclaim their group the Robeson Youth Brigade and roll up their sleeves. Led by Paul Gipfel, classics professor at Brooklyn College, seventeen-year-old boys and girls swing pickaxes, shovel dirt, wrestle with wheelbarrows of cement. Laboring in the sun they sing.

> **Pick and Spade, Pick and Spade,**
> **We're the Robeson Youth Brigade.**
> **All speed the plan, shame the idle man.**
> **Pick and Spade, Pick and Spade...**

Tanned and muscular by the second summer, the young volunteers put the last stone in place just in time for Paul Robeson's annual visit. They lead the march into the new coliseum.

> **Off we go victorious,**
> **Confident, courageous,**
> **Children of the working class,**
> **Robeson Work Brigaders.**

On this Paul Robeson Day, Wo-Chi-Ca's foremost visitor arrives with his friend Mother Bloor. The entire Camp gathers in the amphitheater to hear Paul's emotional speech:

I thank you today for the play. I can't think of any greater gift or reward for anything I do than to see you playing parts of my life. Thank you.

I'm glad I got to know the International Workers Order and meet the children of Wo-Chi-Ca. I guess you know how I feel about Wo-Chi-Ca. I come to you not to tell you things, but to get strength from you. When I see you I know what I am fighting for and you can bet your life that I will be there to the very last moment. And I know Mother Bloor will live to see the kind of world we want because you are going to make it for us. We're going to help you but you're going to help us.

Paul Robeson
and Mother
Bloor
At Camp Wo-
Chi-Ca

I feel very deeply about what I saw in the Soviet Union where children of all kinds live on an equal level. I know what I have to do. It is important that I know the faith that you have in me. Mother says that we've got to drive others ahead. You drive me ahead. You make me rededicate myself to the struggle. I assure you and you know I mean it from my heart: I shall struggle against fascism with you. We will wipe it from the earth.

From the smallest of you, remember that we have a great, great responsibility to build the kind of world that we want to live in. I am proud to be here.

The campers too are proud – enormously pleased that Paul Robeson is their friend. Wherever Wo-Chi-Cans see Paul – singing at Carnegie Hall or playing Othello on Broadway – to call out "Wo-Chi-Ca!" is to utter the magic word that opens the dressing room door. A warm handshake and hearty hug is Paul's special greeting.

And so in winter and summer, in city or country, Paul Robeson and Wo-Chi-Ca stride arm in arm. Soon their fates will intertwine dramatically: the demise of Wo-Chi-Ca will be intimately related to the persecution of Paul Robeson. But that will be some years away. To the world, Paul Robeson was a famous actor, a concert artist, a star. But to Wo-Chi-Cans, he was the tallest tree in their forest, a sheltering sequoia, and a second father.

In 1941 we were part of a choral group, spending much of the summer rehearsing "Ballad for Americans." During the actual performance, a giant figure separated himself from the audience, mounted the stage and stretched out his arms in both directions, as if to embrace us all. It was he, Paul Robeson, and we sang with him. We sang the entire "Ballad for Americans" in the shelter of those arms. No one of us will ever forget the magic of that moment. We wanted it to last forever, to keep that feeling of absolute transcendence.

LUCIAN and GERRY KAMINSKY

Paul with campers on the field

New York City, a metropolis of over seven million, had its *Daily News*, its *Daily Mirror,* and its *Daily Worker*. With a population of three hundred, the little camp in New Jersey produced – every day through the summer – its own rag...

THE DAILY WO-CHI-CAN

No comic strip in these mimeographed sheets, but plenty of adolescent humor...

Question: Why do the girls always leave the campfire first?

Answer: Because the boys put the fire out peeing.

Did you hear about the male and female Hershey bars – with and without nuts?

MOSQUITOES WELCOME NEW ARRIVALS

The famous Wo-Chi-Ca mosquitoes licked their chops as new victims from the city were introduced to the old campers and workers last night at the Social Hall.

BAD POETRY

This is an example of unsuccessful poetry that was submitted to the paper by certain individuals who are connected with the kitchen:

Did you ever hear the story
Of the bad Wo-Chi-Ca boys?
They're always up to mischief
And a-making lots of noise.
At night they enter tents of girls
To have some fun inside.
And when the night patrol comes round,
Beneath the beds they hide.

ADVICE TO THE LOVELORN

Dear Lovelorn,

I have a terrific crush on one of the Spanish girls, but because of language difficulties I cannot express myself clearly. What shall I do?

A Worried Chum

Dear Chum,

Actions speak louder than words.

Bob Levine

More often the paper featured serious subjects.

JIM CROWISM IN BASEBALL

Among the baseball players on the Camp teams, DON IRISH and AL ANDERSON, two Negro boys, were standouts. In Professional Negro Baseball, Satchell Paige (quoted by JOE DIMAGGIO as "the greatest pitcher I ever faced") is a standout. All the local pro teams need pitching strength. By signing a Negro, they would solve a lot of their difficulties, but the unwritten law of barring Negroes from big league baseball has not yet been broken. Catch wise to yourselves, you big league magnates, and sign up these Negro lads who could show up some of the best stars you now employ! Wipe out Jim Crowism in the Major Leagues!

Wo-Chi-Ca campers ready to PLAY BALL!

"THEY SHALL NOT DIE"

LESTER CARTER, an important witness in the trial of the SCOTOSBORO BOYS, gave a few talks to the campers of WO-CHI-CA. He told us how these nine innocent boys were framed by "SOUTHERN INJUSTICE." Suggested by LESTER CARTER, the slogan "THEY SHALL NOT DIE" was adopted by every WO-CHI-CA camper. Five boys have since been freed but there are still four more. WO-CHI-CA will not rest until every boy has been pardoned in this atrocious frame-up.

WO-CHI-CA MARCHES WITH LABOR

One hundred campers of Camp Wo-Chi-Ca today took part in the Labor Parade held here in Washington, New Jersey. They were the largest and most impressive group in the parade. Several thousand people either watched or participated in the parade. The demonstration was the first in Washington's history.

Several bands led the parade and vied for the honor of being the best band of the day. Jack and Edmond, two Wo-Chi-Ca counselors, acted as judges.

The Wo-Chi-Cans traveled to Washington in the truck and in a big yellow bus, supplied by the Parade Committee. On reaching Washington they tooted horns, sang songs and in general made it obvious that they had arrived in the quiet little town.

Washington is a very conservative town. But people stared in wonder at the campers and remarked that "If they can do it, we too can do it." Hosiery workers of Washington, C.I.O. Cement Workers, A. F. L. Steel Workers, Masons, American Legion bands took part in the proceedings.

WO-CHI-CA GREETS WASHINGTON LABOR! Forward with American Labor! GIVE YOUR CHILD SECURITY; JOIN A UNION. Schools for Children, Unions for Workers. Marching with Labor, Marching with Progress. Labor is the source of all value (a quotation of Lincoln). WO-CHI-CA STANDS FOR LABOR, PEACE, and DEMOCRACY. These were some of the slogans carried by and sung by the campers of Wo-Chi-Ca.

UNION CARDS DISTRIBUTED

For the first time in Wo-Chi-Ca history, union cards have been distributed to all campers. Its purpose is to acquaint campers with the way in which unions are run. The campers will have their cards checked for every activity attended.

CAMP WORKERS FORM UNION

By Arty Bolton

The Maintenance staff has formed the first real labor union at Wo-Chi-Ca yesterday. The union includes Wo-Chi-Ca's basic industries: the dishwashers, vegetable peelers, pot washers, waitresses, firemen, chefs, docs and groundsmen. It aims to educate the camp workers, to protect the workers and to get further cooperation. Their first aim was to send a representative to the American Youth Congress in Philadelphia. He is Philip Furman. Their first organized drive is to get Vaino to join.

Vaino Hill, year-round caretaker

WHY OUR PARENTS
JOINED THE UNIONS

By Lefty Nichols and Sol Michtom

Our parents joined the Union because they felt that the solidarity of the working people was the basis of Democracy. By solidarity of the working people we mean organization of the workers into Trade Unions.

Our parents joined the union 'cause they felt and still feel that Unions fight for Higher Wages, shorter hours and better working conditions. Unions are real Democracies. Without the Union, our parents would never have been able to protest to the boss that hours were too long and the wages were too short. The boss would have fired our parents and hired somebody who was satisfied to work at scab wages. In Unity is Strength.

The Unions fight not only for better working conditions, but against discrimination of the Negro, Jewish and other minorities.

The newspapers said Unions were "Red controlled," "subversive," "against the interests of the people," "undemocratic," but our parents knew better, 'cause they voted for the officers, they knew that the unions really fought for the workers and that unions which had bad leadership were the exceptions to the good unions. And those bad ones were unions into which the bosses sent stooges and spies.

Our parents know that it was the common man, the union members, who really built America – the Engineer's Union, Union of Musicians, Street Cleaners Union, Ditch Digger's Union, Carpenters' Union, The Teacher's Union, Farmer's Union, Office and Professional Worker's Union, Truck Driver's Union – all of them. Not the Fords or the Morgans or the Rockefellers who claim all the glory of building this country when the common people built it!

Those are only a few of the reasons why our parents joined the union. There are many more – why don't you tell your friends about the Unions.

WCLC TO HAVE DISCUSSION

By Art Rosen

The Wo-Chi-Ca Central Labor Council is going to have a discussion on Negro discrimination. Recently a barbershop quartet won a contest but they didn't get the prize because they were Negroes. Wo-Chi-Cans resent this very much.

Like every good newspaper, The *Daily Wo-Chi-Can* reviewed movies and plays.

PLANT IN THE SUN

By Oscar Berland

Last night was one of our Gala Evenings. Ben Bengel's much talked about *Plant in the Sun* was presented by the Wo-Chi-Ca Theater Guild. The play – dedicated to Mike Quill, courageous leader of the TWU – shows how workers in a candy factory protest against threatened firings by their boss, and of workers who are trying to organize. The play ended with the entire cast leading the camp in the singing of "Solidarity Forever."

COUNSELORS TO PRESENT
WAITING FOR LEFTY

The counselors and staff production of Waiting For Lefty will be presented tonight as part of the Last Night activity. Waiting for Lefty is the play which proved such a success on Broadway. It was written by Clifford Odets who more recently has gained fame as a Hollywood script writer.

The play tells the story of the taxicab strike and the struggle of the workers against a corrupt union. The production was directed by Mr. Edward Kamarck.

SIGN UP NOW TO BE IN SCENES FROM GRAPES OF WRATH

CHORUS SINGS AT FURRIERS UNION CELEBRATION

CHICO STREET A HIT

This evening, the Senior Dramatic Group presented its production Chico Street at the Social Hall. The play concerned an East Side street where the boys had no nearby play street. One of their playfellows gets hit by a truck and so they ask the mayor of New York for a play street. He grants that a street be closed for them and has it named "Chico Street" after the boy who was injured.

Chico Street (also known as *Play Street*), written by a group of Puerto Rican senior campers, was so successful that Wo-Chi-Ca took it on the road.

TRIP TO NEW YORK

Wo-Chi-Ca's actors and dancers journeyed to New York to put on a gala show as part of the Children's Art Festival at the Central Park Mall.

The ride to New York was full of colorful events. The most surprising event occurred as the truck raced up Fifth Avenue. An open car came alongside as it stopped for a red light. It was the famous scientist ALBERT EINSTEIN. A rousing cheer was given for the great scholar.

A production of *Pinafore* met with great enthusiasm and was followed by another, more modern show.

OPERETTA WINS GREAT ACCLAIM!!

By Arthur Loon

Wo-Chi-Ca yesterday exhibited and cheered its marvelous vocal talents during the production of the operetta, *The Clock Shop*. The direction by Eddie Kamarck was excellent. The campers made their own costumes under the direction of Sally.

A NEW THRILL

By Cyril Tyson

Last night WO-CHI-CA had the greatest thrill since its opening. The first sound movie ever to be given in this camp was shown. It is very wonderful that we can have such things here.

The first sound picture was comedy. The next was named "Cumberland." It is the story of hard working folks who had to work very hard to be able to live. All they needed was to be united and the union did that. The picture shows that when the miners and farmers are united they are bound to win.

TALES OF MANHATTAN

By Phyllis

For the first few scenes, "Tales of Manhattan" is a passable picture. However, in the last scene sharecroppers in the south are depicted as ignorant, superstitious people, apart from the rest of America.

Paul Robeson's glorious voice and personality rescues it from the very worst kind of film, but apart from him, there is very little to recommend. Although it shows the Negro capable of managing his own community, there is not enough weight given to this in comparison to the complete negative picture of the Negro presented.

WE REVIEW NATIVE LAND

By Terry Chanzis

There aren't any stereotyped heroes or heroines from Hollywood in the film, "Native Land." It is not the story of one person, or a few people. It is the story of you, your neighbors, your family, and friends. It is the saga of a Kansas farmer raising wheat, of a factory worker, an office clerk, and their democratic struggle to organize and build unions in America. The enemies of America, the Ku Klux Klan and reactionary big business interests try their best to break up the progress of trade unionism, and abuse the Bill of Rights by violently attacking workers fighting for their union.

In a commentary at the end of the picture, Paul Robeson showed the relation of this struggle to the war today. Today also, defeatist elements not far removed from the Ku Klux Klan are trying to prevent the peoples' Victory in this war by blocking the demand for a second front. But, just as the trade unions grew in strength and organized against those who would destroy them, so right now we must strain every nerve to expose the appeasers.

THE BEST PICTURE OF 1937

By Hal Werner

To see "Emile Zola" is to experience a genuine thrill – to realize a glorious satisfaction upon watching unfold before you the life of a man who left comfort and calm to fight for reason and truth, because his restless, vital spirit, after having borne him through the struggles of early life to success and security, could not allow him rest in a world where there was so much more to struggle for. Emile Zola is a symbol. He represents unsung numbers of men and women who willingly chose and are choosing now, to open themselves to abuse, scorn, and bitter attack, by crusading with pen and tongue for certain ideals that must not be destroyed, and yet, would be unless defended. His life is a guiding star to all those who want truth, and are courageous enough to endure the dangers of seeking, finding, and teaching it.

One cannot discuss the acting in the film for the simple reason that there isn't any acting. The mere celluloid figures of light and shadow have been instilled with life – the cast lives its roles, as if they were fired by the inspiration and reality of their parts. PAUL MUNI is Zola, JOSEPH SCHILD-KRAUT Captain Dreyfus, GALE SONDERGARD is Madam Dreyfus – the many others in supporting roles all are worthy of the high plane and purpose of the picture. One feels like dashing to the library to read all of Zola's books, when with moist eyes and choked up throat, he or she hears the concluding words of the production as spoken by Monsieur Anatole France: "HE WAS A MOMENT IN THE CONSCIENCE OF MAN." Paul Muni as Emile Zola is unsurpassable!

Editorials in New York tabloids often dealt indignantly with political corruption. But when it came to righteous anger, these big city papers had nothing on the *Daily Wo-Chi-Can*.

EDITORIAL

By Faye Feinstein

It seems incredible that children from a Workers' Children's Camp should be accused of such pettiness as scribbling and defacing camp property. Nevertheless it is true. It was quite a shock to find that children whose parents sweat for a living and are workers themselves should not realize that those who built the camp were workers too. Camp Wo-Chi-Ca wasn't built on tin cans and buttons but on money that took quite a time to collect.

Campers' mothers and fathers tried hard to get their children into a camp which they knew would be different from any other camp; a place in which children would respect the rights of property because they themselves come from workers' families.

Found in the girls' washroom were enormous letterings of WHO LOVES WHO and various names of campers. The most astonishing fact, however, was that girls who have a keen sense of beauty should want to mar the walls of Wo-Chi-Ca. Those who have no regard for the sweat of the working class and a lust for destruction do not belong in a camp like Wo-Chi-Ca. THIS IS A WORKERS CHILDREN'S CAMP!

In a 1938 issue, we find columns of celebrated names. These were bunk designations, chosen by the campers, for it was a Wo-Chi-Ca custom to honor their heroes in this manner.

Jack London
Paul Bunyan
Anna Louise Strong
Elizabeth Gurley Flynn
Herndon-Browder
Dead End Kids
Tom Mooney
Organize the Workers

Susan B. Anthony
House of Democracy
Anti-Hearst
No Pasaran
Clara Zetkin
Hans Eisler
Progressive Girls of Bunk 13
Young Scottsboro Defenders

The articles and editorials, news items and movie reviews – advice columns too – written by a dedicated crew of campers, were printed on an ancient, leaky mimeograph machine. Just before lunch, the young journalists would put the paper to bed and run off to eat. Youngsters with dirty hands ordinarily would not be permitted to enter the mess hall. But when campers with ink-stained fingers joined the line, they were waved on through with an indulgent smile.

The range of subjects covered by these reporters is extraordinary, and the quality remarkable in light of the fact that the writers were between the ages of ten and fifteen. How many professional journalists today trace their careers back to those earnest beginnings on the old mimeo at Camp Wo-Chi-Ca?

WARTIME WO-CHI-CA

From 1942 to 1945, through all four summers of the grim World War, Wo-Chi-Ca continued to provide kids with country sunshine and fresh air. Wo-Chi-Ca would suffer hardships – from minor discomforts such as food and gas rationing to the major tragedy of lives lost in battle. Four difficult years through which the little left-wing camp in the Schooleys Mountains wholeheartedly supported the national war effort.

Wo-Chi-Ca's war ardor had not always been so strong. In fact, as late as 1940, most Wo-Chi-Cans objected to American entry in the European conflict. Campers and counselors – imitating their radical elders – opposed the deployment of American troops in an "imperialist war, a falling out among thieves." Irwin Silber, in the *Daily Wo-Chi-Can*, urged his campmates to oppose war preparations.

Contrary to the protests of 6 million of America's youth as voiced through the American Youth Council at its recent Wisconsin convention, the Wall Street controlled Congress prepares to once again make the world safe for American Imperialism.

The Congressional tools of Wall Street are all of a sudden interested in saving the democracy they are so much opposed to.

We in Wo-Chi-Ca can send letters and postcards to our Senators and Congressmen in protest of the draft bill.

How ardent and adamant was the fourteen-year-old writer for the *Daily Wo-Chi-Can!* Silber expands his views in an August 1940 article:

UNITED STATES, CANADA MAKE ARMS PACT

The United States and Canada will set up a joint board for North American "defense" it was announced today.

This pact is the longest step the administration of this country has taken in the direction of war. This pact lines us up directly with one of the belliger-

ents in Europe. Although the pact says the step was a defense measure, we can see how false this whole explanation is. If the British Government flees to Canada we will automatically be in the war.

The pact is another step by the war makers to get us into the Imperialist War raging in Europe.

We can demonstrate our opposition to this step – the so-called "defense pact" – by protest in the form of postcards and letters to our congressmen and to the president. Our slogan remains THE YANKS ARE NOT COMING!

In less than a year, this slogan turned to its exact opposite. By 1941, the Nazis had conquered most of Europe, and in June they turned eastward to attack the Soviet Union. Just six months later, the Japanese bombed Pearl Harbor. The U.S. declared war on Japan; Germany and Italy declared war on the U.S. Wo-Chi-Ca, like the rest of America, rallied to whole-hearted support of the war, for it was now a struggle against fascism.

DELEGATES BACK WITH REPORT

by George Paula

Leah Wellman, Ferman Philips, and Andy Hertz arrived late last night from Philadelphia's American Youth Congress. Attending were 1,200 delegates representing some 5,000,000 young people throughout the nation. Thursday night Paul Robeson delivered a speech. He said, "I took an active part in the Spanish struggle as to whether freedom would really come again to mankind or be stamped out by Fascism. I don't know how you feel but I am optimistic and happy tonight because Fascism has come to grips with one power that will give it no quarter."

OPEN UP THAT SECOND FRONT!

Feelings ran high against the enemy, yet Wo-Chi-Cans did not use racial slurs such as "Heinie," "Wop" or "Jap." The 'children of the workers' spoke respectfully of laboring people of all lands. The kids did, however, heap contempt on the hateful dictators. Campers square-danced to "Round, Round Hitler's Grave," while Albert Lannon and his pals sang a bawdy ditty:

Whistle while you work,
Hitler is a jerk;
Mussolini pulled his peenie
Now it doesn't work.

A more serious approach is reflected in an article from the *Daily Wo-Chi-Can* of July 19, 1941:

A MESSAGE FROM THE UNDERGROUND
MOVEMENT OF GERMANY

Bunk 13 has named itself 'Germany.' In so doing we wish to make clear whom we represent. We are not the Germany of Adolf Hitler. He only stands for a few rich men who have crushed the working people. He has done horrible, terrible things. For Germany, he has said the people haven't the right to live because they are Jewish or Negro or Catholic. He has killed millions of people because they spoke against him and for the workers.

We represent the Germany of Free men, the time when the working people shall run the land.

But such a Germany can come about only by the help of you – THE WORKERS OF ALL LANDS. We are struggling valiantly, underground to break the Fascist rule. But with the aid of his tremendous army he has kept us back and in addition has enslaved many other nations. He wants to make the world like Germany is today. Now he is fighting against the Red Army of the Soviet Union – the one great country which has built a Democracy like Camp Wo-Chi-Ca – where all are free and equal.

The people of the Soviet Union, together with the people of Great Britain and the United States, by stopping his Blitzkrieg Armies, are doing the only thing which will enable us to reestablish a people's Democracy.

WE MUST ALSO BUILD A MORE PERFECT DEMOCRACY HERE, IN THE UNITED STATES by guaranteeing the working of the democratic system of cooperation at Wo-Chi-Ca and fighting to build a more perfect Democracy throughout the country, no discrimination of races, jobs for all, this will demonstrate to the German people what they can gain from our victory... WE CALL UPON YOU, THE WORKERS OF ALL LANDS, TO SUPPORT THIS STRUGGLE, FOR OUR FREEDOM, FOR THE FREEDOM OF ALL COUNTRIES!

STOP HITLER - HALT FASCISM!

Wo-Chi-Cans were eager to do their part on the home front. To conserve paper, kids wrote their parents letters on the blank side of their *Daily Wo-Chi-Can*. The kitchen workers saved waste fats to return to the butcher: he paid them a penny a pound. As the young waitresses and pot wallopers scraped grease from frying pans they sang...

> **Stop! Don't throw those fats away.**
> **Stop! They'll make a bomb some day.**
> **Don't throw them down the drain,**
> **They can be TNT or cellophane.**
> **Stop! When you're through with your fry,**
> **Put those used fats by –**
> **Take them over to the butcher and get your change,**
> **Be a soldier of the kitchen range.**

Echoing chorus leader Naomi's motto, "Music is a form of battle," young camp singers gathered at Union Square in the city.

AMERICAN YOUTH CHORUS
FEEDS 3000 CHINESE CHILDREN

The American Youth Chorus sponsored by Camp Wo-Chi-Ca raised enough money to feed 3,000 Chinese children for one day. Singing at the corner of 14th Street and Broadway, the Chorus entertained passersby with "Chee-Lai," the marching song of China, songs of our armed forces, with solos by Ronnie Gilbert, "Freiheit" with solos by Albert Anderson and Ernie Lieberman, the "Song of the United Nations," and others that appropriately filled the program.

Henceforth, the Chorus will sing for other United Nations war relief, and hope to collect more and more money to help our fellow freedom-fighters, wherever they are fighting, all over the world.

From the most senior staff member to the youngest camper, the Second World War touched everyone at Wo-Chi-Ca. Many young children saw older brothers march off to the Army and Navy. With older male staff in short supply, sixteen-year-old former campers moved up to adult responsibility and became counselors. The senior boys made do with just night counselors; maintenance men from kitchen and garbage crews would sleep in their tents.

Wartime gas rationing meant fewer trips to town and a smaller number of visitors from the city. Then again, many parents of campers - mothers as well as fathers - worked long hours in defense plants. On Sundays they stayed home to rest rather than make the three-hour trip to Camp.

Before the war, a typical Wo-Chi-Ca meal might consist of chicken or beef, potatoes, two vegetables, bread and butter, plus a dessert. Large pitchers of milk and juice passed around the wooden tables and were constantly refilled. With the war, butter, sugar, meat and milk were rationed. Though no one went hungry, some felt deprived of favorite foods. A few children were heard to grumble.

The griping stopped dramatically one Sunday, and a *New York Times* reporter was present to write up the story for his paper's magazine section. Joy Glickman even today remembers it well: "Leaflets came down on campus telling us that the camp was invaded by the Germans. The senior campers, dressed as Nazis, routed us out of our bunks and marched us up to the ball field. To overcome the invasion we joined hands and sang 'Peat Bog Soldiers.'"

At mealtime a sign appeared on the door of the mess hall: "WE WILL EAT DINNER TONIGHT AS THEY DO IN OCCUPIED EUROPE." Tables were bare: no steaming casseroles, no butter, no milk. Each camper received only a small piece of dry stale bread, a few undercooked beans, and half a frankfurter. Pitchers on the table held only water. In shocked silence, the campers stared – the youngest with tears on their cheeks.

After a prolonged wait, the kitchen doors opened and out came waitresses carrying the real dinner: succulent fried chicken, corn on the cob, mashed potatoes, apple pie and ice cream. What aromas in the air, and what treats on their tables! Even with food rationing, Wo-Chi-Cans ate so much better than children under Nazi occupation. After such a day, no one at Wo-Chi-Ca ever again grumbled about food.

All were acutely aware of the war. When afternoon mail arrived, everyone rushed to read about bombings and battles, resistance fighters and refugees. Still, Wo-Chi-Ca summers were after all vacations, far from air-raid drills and scrap drives – a time to be just kids. Often, in the *Daily Wo-Chi-Can*, the war would share space with baseball games and bonfires.

THE RUSSIAN OFFENSIVE HAS BEGUN

DIMAGGIO HITS IN 55TH STRAIGHT GAME

THE GERMAN BLITZ HAS BEEN BLITZED...

TONIGHT'S MOVIE WILL BE CHARLIE CHAPLIN

HONOR JEWISH PEOPLE!

By Flash Kravitz

Keeping in line with the Wo-Chi-Ca policy of honoring all peoples and races, the camp tonight holds the third in a series of campfires. This evening's campfire is dedicated to the Jewish people. The two previous campfires honored the Negroes, Italians, and Indians.

Evening programs almost always reflected the War, whether in serious drama or in a comic vein.

SONG OF VICTORY

By Arty Bolton

Tonight's program is the long awaited play "Song of Victory" which the Drama Group is putting on. There will also be movies.

Boys and girls roared as Charlie Chaplin satirized Hitler in *The Great Dictator*. The campers applauded exuberantly at Soviet films, cheering when a smiling Joseph Stalin invariably appeared at the end. A favorite movie was Hollywood's *North Star*. Anne Baxter, Dana Andrews, Walter Huston, Farley Granger, and Walter Brennan portrayed Russian peasants in a village invaded by Germans. Two songs from the Aaron Copeland score – "Stranger On The Dusty Highway" and "If I Eat Too Much Jam" – became staples of the Wo-Chi-Ca Chorus.

DATE	NAME	PRODUCED
Sat. June 28	Vanka	USSR
	Bohemian Girl	USA
Sat. July 5	Teamwork	USA
	Chapayev	USSR
Sat. July 12	Indonesia Calling	AUSTRALIA
	La Marseillaise	FRANCE
Sat. July 19	The Year of Freedom	USSR
	Life at the Zoo	USSR
	Generals Without Buttons	FRANCE
Sat. July 26	The Floorwalker (Chaplin)	USA
	Road to Life	USSR
Sat. August 2	Tall Tales	USA
	La Maternelle	FRANCE
Sat. August 9	The Count (Chaplin)	USA
	Native Land	USA
Sat. August 16	Hymn to the Nations (Toscanini)	USA
	Youth of Maxim	USSR
Sat. August 23	The Fireman (Chaplin)	USA
	Return of Maxim	USSR
Sat. August 30	May Day, New York, 1946	USA
	Hello Moscow	USSR

But the screen war soon became all too real, touching the camp with tragedy. In July of 1943, Group Director Bea Melzer received a telegram: "We regret to inform you..."

While flying a bombing mission over Germany, Bea's son, popular counselor Whitey Melzer, was shot down and killed. The camp was stunned. What could campers say to Whitey's young sister Aurora and kid brother "Lucky?" Co-author June Levine was twelve at the time. She sat outside her tent with her best friend Nora Cogan, both weeping for hours.

More heartache followed. Counselor Sy Rosen entered the Army that same July. He was wounded, decorated for heroism, then sent back into action. Now came word that "Eggs," had been captured and was a prisoner of war in Germany.

Wo-Chi-Cans in uniform seized every chance to visit Camp, hitching rides on local farm trucks and hay wagons. Campers and counselors, soldiers and sailors all longed for an end to the war. But it dragged on two more years.

Late in 1944, more than 19,000 Americans were killed in France at the Battle of the Bulge. Another Wo-Chi-Can, Gerry Feifer, was among that number. His sister Pearl, in camp the following summer, still grieved over the death of her brother: at night her bunkmates heard Pearl weep into her pillow.

And yet, the supreme sacrifice of Gerry Feifer and thousands of his comrades may have saved the life of Pearl Feifer and many of her campmates. The pivotal Battle of the Bulge turned the tide against the Nazis. Allied soldiers forced the Germans into a crippling retreat, and Germany surrendered just three months later.

By the time Camp opened in the summer of 1945, Allied victory in the Pacific too was imminent. Everywhere, jubilant Americans raised hands in a "V for Victory" sign. Wo-Chi-Cans adopted the "V" to call for peace and quiet in the mess hall.

At Yalta in the Soviet Union, world leaders Roosevelt, Churchill and Stalin met to plan the postwar period. At Camp Wo-Chi-Ca in the United States, children gathered joyfully to learn the new "United Nations Hymn." To the music of Shostakovich and words of Harold Rome they sang...

> **As sure as the sun meets the morning**
> **And rivers run down to the sea,**
> **A new day for mankind is dawning.**
> **Our children shall live proud and free.**
>
> **United Nations on the march,**
> **With flags unfurled**

Together fight for victory,
A free new world.

What would it be like, this brave new world? Many Wo-Chi-Cans had visited the fabulous World's Fair of 1939, where the future was forecast with a display of gaudy consumer goods and technological marvels. But Wo-Chi-Cans had a different vision – a world free of hunger, prejudice and war. They put their hopes and dreams into an ardent Credo.

WORLD OF TOMORROW

This is our city - our city of tomorrow.
This is the city that we have fought and died for,
That has been built up on the struggles of the people.
This is a city built to plan.

Our houses are tall and straight.
Sunlight floods through the windows.
Everywhere there are parks with grass and trees.
Children play happily.
The mother wheels her child without fear.
Health is not bought with money.
Through the people's health plan
Medical knowledge has been brought
Within reach of the people.
Nowhere is there sign of want.

The people are well clothed and well fed.
Everywhere there is cleanliness and beauty.
Brown and white people go hand in hand
Sharing the fruits of the people's struggles.
The gangsters and the hoodlums are gone.
Vandalism is unheard.
A young girl can walk the streets at night without fear,
For people have learned to understand and trust each
**   other.**

Schools are free for all people
And everyone is taught to respect his fellow.
Education is a joyous experience.

The people learn to understand the beauty of living.
Song and dance fill the auditoriums.
The classroom radiates the meaning of Wo-Chi-Ca.

The girl who dreams of becoming a surgeon
Finds her dream come true.

Safe highways sweep to the outskirts of our city.
The factory units are clean.
The worker goes out in the morning.
At noon he chats and plays in the recreation centers.
He comes home at night without injury.
His job is secure.
There are no unemployed to haunt the gates.
All hands are busy at the tasks of satisfying the needs
That were not met in the past.

The highways speed to the countryside.
The tractors and the farm machines are not idle.
The farmer does not worry about debts.
He receives the fruits of his labor.
New forests continually arise
To replace the timber taken from the hills.

The valleys are no longer threatened with floods.
The river is harnessed.
It feeds water to the farmer's crops;
It lights his house;
It furnishes power for his tools.

Seawards from our city the ships sail.
Machinery for Africa, for China, for India.
There are no backward lands.
In each land the people is its own master.
Young people are able to travel to secure knowledge.
The geography book is lived.
The peoples exchange cultures.
The weed of fascism has been killed at the root.
There is no plot of earth that will ever nourish it again.

Freedom flourishes.
The German youth have been restored to a human world.
The Japanese people have thrown off their feudal state
And have taken their place among the democratic
    nations.
There is cooperation among all peoples.
There is no more reason for war!

This is our future.
This is the future for which we fight.
This is the future we will attain!

RED DIAPERS, RED BAITERS

I *was at camp in either 1947 and '48, or '48 and '49. My most vivid*
memory was of a girl in my bunk whose father owned a gas station,
and the torture she was put through by fellow campers because her
father was a 'capitalist.' Not a single adult came to her defense. She was
literally hounded from the grounds; her parents came to get her within
days of her arrival. Imagine what it must have been like in the Soviet
Union!

So reads a disturbing email received by the authors from a former camper.
Another Wo-Chi-Can sent a letter asserting that Camp was "an indoctrination
unit of a fringe party that was designed to develop a cadre of dedicated Party
adherents."

True, these were only two such messages among hundreds. And yet these two
raise disquieting questions. Was Wo-Chi-Ca indeed, as one historian character-
izes it, a "very hard-line camp?" Was the Workers' Children's Camp an indoctrination unit, "a summer camp for children of the Communist Party?"

It would seem so at first blush. Camp enrollment lists often included last names
that read like a roster of prominent U. S. Communists: Gerson, Gordon, Greene,
Jerome, Lannon, Mandel, Perlo, Starobin, Weinstock, Winter...

Kathy Perlo was the daughter of Marxist economist Victor Perlo, Bob Starobin
the son of *Daily Worker* foreign editor Joseph R. Starobin. Phyllis Mandel was
the daughter of Soviet expert William Mandel, "Rooster" Gordon the son of
Daily Worker columnist Eugene Gordon. Sue Weinstock's father Louis
Weinstock was a leader of the movement for unemployment insurance. Frances
Murray, the niece of Elizabeth Gurley Flynn, was also a camper.

Two close buddies at Camp were Fred Jerome and Billy Gerson. Their fathers
were V.J. Jerome and Sy Gerson, the former in charge of cultural affairs for the
Communist Party, the latter a top Party leader, arrested under the Smith Act.

Dan and Josie Green spent summers at Wo-Chi-Ca. Their father, a Party leader
who went 'underground,' eluded the FBI for five years. Their cousin Billie was
a camper as well.

I went to Camp in 1950 during a very difficult period in my life when my uncle, Gil Green, had been indicted as a Smith Act defendant during the McCarthy hysteria.

BILLIE GREEN ROTHMAN

Young camper Albert Vetere Lannon as an adult would write a biography of his father Al Lannon, maritime coordinator for the Communist Party. "Al Lannon," his son relates, "ran away from his Italian father who beat him, went to sea, visited the Soviet Union, and converted from lapsed Catholic altar boy to the reddest of the red." A graduate of the Lenin School in Moscow, the senior Lannon was a founding member of the National Maritime Union, a Smith Act prisoner, and a defender of the Soviet Union till his dying day.

A number of other campers were children of Smith Act prisoners, among them Michele Winter, daughter of Helen and Carl Winter.

I was a camper at Wo-Chi-Ca the summer of 1949, I think. Since I was only seven and Mother's not sure of this date, I'm guessing it was '49. That period of my life is remembered by BEFORE DAD WAS ARRESTED... DURING THE TRIAL... and WHEN HE WAS IN PRISON.

My dad was one of the twelve leaders of the Communist Party – along with Gus Hall and Henry Winston – arrested in 1949 under the Smith Act, tried and convicted in Foley Square, New York. Their 'crime' was that they thought that capitalism was bad for the people and that socialism would provide a better economic and social system providing jobs, education, health care, and equality... They spoke about it, wrote about it, and organized about it. The capitalists didn't like that, not one bit! The Communists were a 'threat' and something had to be done about it.

Dad and the others were sentenced. Dad served three years, eight months of a five-year sentence (time off for good behavior). After Dad was in jail, my mother herself was arrested, convicted and sentenced, although the Supreme Court overturned the Smith Act and she never served out her sentence.

After this period of time, Dad took on more public political work with the Daily Worker, eventually becoming editor. Mother, now ninety-two, continues to be active in peace activities, helping organize local People's Weekly World forums, giving leadership to the Midwest Labor Institute for Social Studies (which Dad founded) and the Communist Party where she is on the Michigan District Committee and the National Committee of the CPUSA.

Guess I'm proud of my folks. They were SECOND generation Communists; I'm a THIRD.

Camp was a unique time. It had the feeling of a safe, caring place where people were supportive and had anti-racist, pro-labor interests I was used to. What a wonderful time I had with singing, fun-loving children, and a staff sensitive to their needs.

Josie Green, Gil Green's daughter, had a cot across from me. She was from Chicago and I was from Detroit, a long way from home but at home with friends. I don't remember being afraid or homesick. I was among warm, supportive people who seemed to sing all the time. Even now, when life deals a tough hand, labor and liberation songs come to mind and help get me over.

I often tell people, when they ask how I got through the McCarthy period, that for an only child I had a very big family. A family of many people working for peace and civil rights: labor organizers and civil libertarians. Even as a young child I never felt alone. I knew there were good people everywhere. Wo-Chi-Ca was just such a place.

I have always been deeply grateful for the time at Camp. And the songs!

MICHELE WINTER ARTT

"Wo-Chi-Ca," we learn from historian Paul Mishler in his book *Raising Reds,* "was founded by people who had been active in the Young Pioneers, the IWO Juniors, and other sections of the radical children's movement in New York." The idea "came from people who had been involved in Camp Wingdale, a Communist adult camp."

I went to Wo-Chi-Ca in 1935 and '36 as a camper and worked there as a waitress in '37 and '38. My mother and father paid $22 per week and I went for two weeks. My father was a pushcart peddler in an open street market in Brownsville, so camp was quite a luxury for us.

The camp was quite a rustic affair. We slept in tents and in the morning we went outdoors to a long wooden cow-feeding trough to wash up with cold water. We then did vigorous exercises. Then the Red Flag with the hammer and sickle was raised: we raised our clenched fists in the air and sang the "Internationale."

MILI POLONSKY KLEIN

Mili speaks here of the camp's earliest years. But throughout its entire history Wo-Chi-Ca was home to a great many 'red diaper babies.'

I assume most of us were red diaper babies, and despite everything that has happened in the world, the values we grew up with and had reinforced at Wo-Chi-Ca have stood me in good stead... still do! I remember what the tents looked like, remember working on removing stones from a road, singing all sorts of songs including labor union songs, the wonderful sense of purpose, and freedom as well. And Paul Robeson visiting... Wasn't he our idol!
LENORE HALPERN MIGDAL-LLOYD, PhD

These red diaper babies were a significant presence, and those who were 'Smith Act Kids' enjoyed a certain distinction. On a recent TV talk show, the actor Marshall Brickman remarked that as a child he went to a left-wing summer camp. (Brickman attended Camp Wo-Chi-Ca in the early Fifties when it had changed its name to Wyandot.) Asked what he meant by a left-wing camp, Marshall replied that "it was where the most points go to children of Smith Act parents."

At that time no laughing matter! For progressives, the last years of Wo-Chi-Ca were dangerous and fearful. In September of 1949, at Peekskill, New York, a rock-throwing mob shouting racist, anti-Communist slogans ambushed audience members leaving a Paul Robeson concert. Many parents and friends of Wo-Chi-Ca campers were among those attacked. Children arriving at Camp the following summer came from an atmosphere heavy with apprehension. In the city the children undoubtedly felt endangered, but at their summer camp they found security.

Safety and comfort, as Riva Gurwitz Rosenfield makes clear, were of paramount importance to these Wo-Chi-Ca children:

To kids back home who were often isolated from peers – whose parents were in trade unions or had marched holding signs in May Day Parades – Wo-Chi-Ca was a place to feel safe. There was a special bond formed because we had similar backgrounds and this was the only place we could let it hang out without fear.

Close bonds formed in the summer often carried through the rest of the year.

At Camp in New Jersey we were close, living together, dreaming. Our clothes were jeans, cutoffs, T-shirts, or Army shirts hanging outside, with red bandannas hanging in our back pockets or tied around our necks.

But for me to survive, my Wo-Chi-Ca friendships in the City were essential. I lived for the weekends and parties and meetings and Marxist classes and folk song and folk dance rehearsals and performances. We were spread all over the boroughs.

My life is shaped by Wo-Chi-Ca. Wo-Chi-Ca lives on in my present, in my raised consciousness to those in need around me. As a pre-K teacher for twelve years I stressed freedom as my governing principle among the children in my classroom. I played freedom songs and lots of Seeger, Guthrie and Robeson records.

I believe that my husband was attracted to a spirit in me that was nurtured by the inspiring spirit of Wo-Chi-Ca. That time of kindness and unity, that single consciousness that we were the WORLD – a tight ship with a direction, sailing on a sea of danger. And if we did not let go, held onto each other, and each of us did a job, we would succeed, no matter how difficult it might be. Along the way, we would lift our spirits with our songs of sentiment, revolution, humor, and friendship. Each of us was capable of making up a rhyme and contributing it to the song. And thus the very hard job of living would proceed.

MARLENE ROSEN FINE

Bob Seborer also speaks of this Wo-Chi-Ca spirit:

Besides the great times that most campers experience, we at Wo-Chi-Ca got a connection to a larger movement, not a religious movement, not a nationalist movement, but an international revolution to end economic exploitation and racial persecution. We were given a glimpse of a very different kind of world. The message we were given was that all humans should be treated as equals. All of us, whites, Blacks, Latinos, Asians, people of all races were to be participants in the creation of this different kind of world. That's what many of the songs were about. It's as if a chip was added to our brain telling us that we were to try to make this a better world.

"And what if," some old campers now demand, "Wo-Chi-Ca *was* an 'indoctrina-tion unit?'" As John Vago bluntly puts it:

Many of us who remember the real Wo-Chi-Ca know what a valuable and wonderful institution it really was. If respect for the working class, opposition to racism, etc. are 'indoctrination' them I'm indoctrinated and proud of it.

Proud of the Communist character of Camp is John Vago – proud indeed are many others of their 'Red' Wo-Chi-Ca! But we must for the moment leave earnest endorsements of Camp and from serious stories turn to...

A COMIC TALE

Our story begins with historian Ronald Radosh, a gentleman who would never swell with pride at Wo-Chi-Ca's Communism. Writing recently in the journal *Heterodoxy*, Radosh considers his seven or eight years at Camp Woodland. It was, he explains, a "Popular Front" camp compared to...

...the overt Communist Party institutions, which included Camp Unity for adults, and two children's camps, Camp Kinderland (affiliated with the Yiddish Communist fraternal group, the International Worker's Order) and the very hard-line Camp Wo-Chi-Ca.

Perhaps the name was meant to confuse innocents, who might think that it was some kind of Indian name. But Wo-Chi-Ca stood for Worker's Children's Camp, to indicate its proletarian orientation, or to make it clear to Daily Worker subscribers that this is where their children should go. The camp named its social hall "The Paul Robeson Playhouse" and regularly engaged in open Party activities. During the great 1950's comic book scare... the camp's yearbook reported proudly that its campers were asked to all turn in their comics, which were then burnt in a huge evening public bonfire. In that manner, the Wo-Chi-Ca campers were purged of whatever racism and pro-Americanism might have been instilled in them by the dangerous cartoon strips. No Captain America for Wo-Chi-Ca campers!

When Wo-Chi-Cans today hear this tale of roaring flames they roar with laughter. A huge bonfire of burning books - just like the Nazis? Fanatic kids fervently tossing Captain America into the flames? What firebrands, what revolutionaries! And what rubbish. Is it not hilarious, Wo-Chi-Cans laugh, that Ronald Radosh was never a camper at Wo-Chi-Ca? He never set foot on the grounds! Where, then, does Radosh get this 'books in the bonfire' business?

That comic book pyre flares up in David Horowitz's autobiography, *Radical Son: A Generational Odyssey*. Davey Horowitz was indeed a Wo-Chi-Can: the young boy was sent to the Worker's Children's Camp by his parents, Phil and Blanche Horowitz, both New York teachers, both members of the Communist Party of the United States. Davey was at Camp during a dangerous time for American Communists, McCarthy time - "scoundrel time." Horowitz recalls this period in his memoir:

By this time, the Cold War was so close to being a hot one that it was as though we were behind enemy lines. The only time I felt politically safe was during the two weeks I spent at Wo-Chi-Ca, a summer camp for children of the Communist Party. My buddies there were Billy Gerson and Freddy Jerome, whose fathers were 'second string' leaders of the Party indicted under the Smith Act. Our camp life was flavored with progressive themes. Pete Seeger, Paul Robeson, and other Party artists made appearances, entertaining us with songs like "If I Had a Hammer" and "We Shall Overcome" which later became anthems of the Sixties protests.

Here, on page sixty-four of his book, Horowitz takes us straight to the bonfire:

Every summer there would be a campfire dedicated to the ritual burning of comic books that were 'imperialist' or had anti-Communist themes.

"Every summer!" Did Davey witness year after year this "burning of comic books?" How odd that no other camper saw these sensational bonfires. In fact, for the year 1949 at least, Davey's campmates categorically rule out a comic bonfire.

In 1949 there were complaints about comic books that were racist. However I don't recall any bonfires.

SERGE KANEVSKY

Arthur Komar states...

I was on the camp staff in 1949 and was present from before the start of the season, setting up, until after the close of that season, helping with the cleanup. Not only was there no comic book burning, but had there been any discussion or suggestion of doing so I would have been among the first to oppose it. The memories of Hiltlerism were too close to us at that time not to have missed the parallels.

And Mark Solomon says...

I was the not-so-magisterial 'political action director' for the staff in 1949 (a 17-year-old-near-know-it-all). I can say with absolute certainty that there was no comic book bonfire, no book burnings of any kind. The very idea of such a thing is so ludicrous that it's hardly worthy of serious consideration.

"I was a camper in '49," writes Sy Friedman, "and I have absolutely NO memory of any comic book burnings."

"Absolutely no memory of any comic book burnings!" Indeed, these campers deny such a thing. But comic book bonfires appear as a fact in Horowitz's autobiography! What's more, in a review of Horowitz's *Radical Son* from the *News & Observer* of September 7, 1998, Rob Christensen tells us that...

His [Horowitz's] parents were committed communists who sent him to Camp Wo-Chi-Ca, short for Workers Children's Camp, where the camp director would hold ritual bonfires to burn comic books considered imperialistic or anti-Communist.

The "camp director" too! This is no longer funny. It's quite serious, for now Wo-Chi-Ca's director is ordering the burning of books! Someone must get to the bottom of this and so your authors contacted the author of *Radical Son*.

Dear David Horowitz,

We should like to pinpoint the time of the comic book bonfire you speak of in your autobiography. In spite of Ronald Radosh's assertion, we can find no reference to book burnings in a Wo-Chi-Ca yearbook. Radosh refers to a 1950 yearbook, but to our knowledge there is no such publication. Yearbooks exist only for 1947, '48, and '49. Furthermore, many Wo-Chi-Cans explicitly deny that any such comic book bonfires took place. We would very much appreciate it if you would clarify this question.

Horowitz promptly replied.

Dear June and Gene,

I was at Wo-Chi-Ca three years (1949, 1950, 1951). I only attended two weeks a summer and I have no personal recollection of any comic book bonfire. I went on Radosh's word about this (he was particularly insistent that I include it). Radosh has a photographic memory, and I have never found him to be wrong. On the other hand, that doesn't mean he didn't make a mistake this time. If he did, I will correct it in future editions.

What? An ex-camper reports an incident he never saw, which was supplied to him by someone who was never there? A Comedy of Errors? A case of photographic memory with no film in the camera? More queer than comical! Your authors wrote to the historian.

Dear Ronald Radosh,

We are working on a history of Camp Wo-Chi-Ca. In the course of our research we came across claims that books ("imperialist" and "anticommunist" comics) were burned in bonfires at the camp. David Horowitz in his autobiography Radical Son, you in your article on Camp Woodland, and Christensen in his review of Radical Son all state this as a matter of fact. And yet we have been unable to locate one witness to these book burnings. On the contrary, quite a number of Wo-Chi-Cans explicitly deny such events took place.

We should like to inquire about your photographic memory. Were you in fact a camper at Wo-Chi-Ca and did you indeed witness the comic book bonfires in question?

Radosh responded to what he called "an obviously hostile nasty note from two people who are obviously writing a love letter to Camp Wochica."

...let me get some things straight. First, I never claimed to have ever attended Wochica. But I did see, at Woodland, a Wochica yearbook or publication that we looked at while preparing a Woodland book of similar nature. The Wochica book had a full page about the protest against comic books, including photos of campers throwing their comics in a bonfire. I do indeed have a photographic memory, and am not making this up. If anything, my response then was that unlike Woodland, Wochica was a true radical camp compared to a Popular Front camp that masked its true identity. The reason I remember this description and photo is because at the time, I was so impressed with it, wishing that Woodland would have acted in a similar fashion.

You can contest this all you wish; I know what I saw. You can attribute it to false memory, or you can look and see if the publication turns up, as I'm sure it will. But if you read what I wrote, it is more than clear that I never even implied that I went to the camp.

Corresponding rapidly by email now, the two parties write back and forth.

We do thank you, Mr. Radosh, for your prompt response. It is true we are writing a friendly account of Camp Wo-Chi-Ca. But also, we trust, an honest one! We ARE doing our research. We believe we have in our possession all the yearbooks Wo-Chi-Ca published; these are only three: 1947, '48, and '49. A discussion of comic books will be found in the 1949 Yearbook, BUT IN NONE OF THE THREE CAN BE FOUND "photos of campers throwing their comics in a bonfire." As to the other "publication" to which you allude, it has not turned up in our research, nor do the hundreds of Wo-Chi-Cans with whom we are in contact know of any such publication. These ex-campers are most distressed at this book-burning story. In fact, they feel their camp libeled.

The question they now ask is: How comes it that a respected historian passes off in his writing AS A MATTER OF FACT an event he did not himself witness, nor can substantiate with evidence? They feel you owe an apology, or a retraction of some sort.

It is truly a comic tale now, for here come the laughs:

Your reply does make me laugh. Frankly, there is so much about Wo-Chi-Ca that is deserving of it having a bad name that I hardly think my story is so profound that it alone "libels" the camp.

Indeed, a camp that was part of the Stalinist network and was part of a movement effort to create cadre for the international movement is far worse a crime than my remembrance of what I once read.

And so the quips pass back and forth...

Glad you got a good laugh out of our last message. This IS fun, in a nasty sort of way.

We got a big kick out of your attempt to charge US with finding evidence for your bonfire claim. That was really a riot! Does it not behoove YOU to produce that "publication?" Are we compelled to establish we did not burn books? Must we go about to prove a negative?

That's okay. We understand we are witches and witches must prove their innocence. Throw us into your bonfire with the comic books! We are "Stalinist" witches at that, and against such pariahs nothing is too outrageous, not even the smear that – like Nazis – we burned books.

We do not know if Radosh was having fun, but he certainly got all worked up.

The point about your beloved Wo-Chi-Ca is quite simple and was made by none other than the sympathetic pro-Communist historian Paul Mishler in his book on Communist summer camps. It is that Wo-Chi-Ca was part of the Communist apparatus, and was created in order to sustain that culture among young people - this in and of itself is as damning a point that can be made about that rotten camp.

But then comes a surprising admission:

Bonfires or not - and I readily admit that perhaps I was wrong about that - the camp did have a policy of asking their campers to turn in the offensive comics and to "combat the influence" of their pernicious ideas. No patriotic "Captain America" comic books for the little Reds in residence.

Well, the "little Reds in residence" are all grown up now. While a few are still Reds, many have migrated far and wide across the political spectrum. None quite so far, however, as little Davey Horowitz.

The aforementioned Rob Christensen informs us that "in conservative circles, Horowitz, a former editor of the left-wing *Ramparts* magazine, is revered for renouncing his former fellow travelers."

In a review of *Radical Son* for the magazine *Reason* (March 1997), Steven Hayward notes that Horowitz "...made a complete break with revolutionary socialism and embraced its opposite."

"Just like Whittaker Chambers," Hayward continues, "Horowitz is less a conservative than he is a 'man of the right' (as Chambers described himself) - i.e., against the left."

Steven Hayward further relates that...

Horowitz was a classic "red diaper baby," raised by communist parents in the hothouse atmosphere of New York City in the 1940s. His parents, he tells us, thought of themselves as secret agents and were in fact close to the chain of communications that delivered Stalin's orders to assassinate Trotsky.

Part of the plot to murder Trotsky! Extreme enough, one might think – indeed, murderously fanatic. But Hayward's next hilarious line shows us just how deep Horowitz sank:

Horowitz even attended Wo-Chi-Ca (short for "Workers Children's Camp"), a communist summer camp for kids.

EVEN! It was not radical enough that he had parents who assisted in the assassination of Trotsky, but young Davey even attended Wo-Chi-Ca. Now that's revolutionary! Nothing makes the Wo-Chi-Ca folks laugh louder than this four letter word "even" in the magazine *Reason*.

With such fun all around, Wo-Chi-Cans can take a tolerant view of things, and so are generous, even to David Horowitz. Witness Billy Gerson:

The summer of '51 was the best of all the summers that I spent at camp. One factor was that my bunkmates were an unusually bright, talented group of kids. My recollection is that we always came up with the best skits, won the treasure hunts, beat every-one in softball... We were the nucleus of the Group C softball team that beat the older group in an inter-group game - the only time I can remember that occurring while I was at Camp.

1951 was pretty much the height of the anti-Communist hysteria. I came to camp just two weeks after the arrest of my father Si Gerson, an official of the New York State Communist Party. Although I was not really very aware of it at the time, this probably gave me a little extra status with my campmates. I remember one boy telling me – a little bit hopefully (!) – "I think my father's going to get arrested soon too.

"That summer at camp recently got me a cameo appearance in the book Radical Son, an autobiographical work by David Horowitz, one of my former bunkmates.

Horowitz is a Red Diaper Baby gone wrong. He's now an ultra-conservative who is anathema to many of his former acquaintances. But so powerful was the effect of that glorious summer at camp that I can't get too angry at Horowitz. Rather than thinking of him as the jerk he's become, I remember him as the pitcher on the bunk ball team when I was the shortstop, or as Ivan Skavinsky Skavar opposite my Abdul Abulbul Amir in our campfire skit.

It was one hell of a great summer.

Group C, Bunk 11, 1951,
Front: Bobby Epstein, Billy
Gerson, Davey Horowitz, Larry
Liebman Back: Willie Ford,
Fred Jerome, Alan Fink, Dave
Slapershnik, Bobby Pilgrim,
Steve Rosenfeld

So what did happen to the kids' comic books if they were not burned or banned? Were they simply ignored? Let us look at the 1949 Wo-Chi-Ca Yearbook that features a two-page spread on the subject:

Our progressive parents are doing their utmost to make this one democratic world. We, as their children, should help them as much as possible. We, the children of Wo-Chi-Ca, no different from other children, enjoy reading comics. Because this is so, we have had several discussions on this topic. We have found both good and bad points in them, but I might add, mostly bad.

From the 1949 Wo-Chi-Ca Yearbook

Comic books draw your attention because of their bright colors and attractive pictures. Their ridiculous, unreal situations make them utterly fantastic and they are, in one way, a bad escape from reality. We have also found that reading comics dulls your taste and interest for good books. There are many children's books which would be of a much greater interest and enjoyment if you would just take the time away from comics to read them. Comic books also take your time away from sports. Children of our age should get more air and play more active games. It is so much healthier than just sitting and reading a joke book.

Comics, besides taking up good time are a bad influence on the growing mind. Have you ever noticed, when reading a comic, how handsome a hero is made to look? Does this mean that only handsome men can be heroes, or that "ugly" people are thieves, murderers, robbers, etc.? Have you ever noticed the foreign, minority-group names given to the bad, and that the good receive only the plain, simple, Anglo-Saxon names? Most comics, instead of helping us to respect people of different backgrounds, prejudice us against them.

If we care at all about what our parents are doing we should try not to encourage for ourselves and our friends the prejudiced and undemocratic things that joke books would teach us. The children of the future should not grow up in the fantastic world of comics.

BY AMIE BLUM

Dave Sear, a counselor in 1951, found a creative way to do away with a quite a few comic books:

My solution to the problem was to turn my group B boys loose with their comic books, swatting flies at rest period after lunch. This destroyed the comic books and got rid of the flies.

Comic books were not the only undesirable items to turn up at Camp. In 1949, a camper received a gift from his parents – a target game in which children were to throw darts at "Black Sambo," a hideous racial caricature.

Educational Director Morris Salz (in winter he taught school in a largely black school in Brooklyn) drafted a letter to the game manufacturer which was sent along with a petition signed by the campers. His letter and the company's reply were published in the 1949 Yearbook along with the picture of the offensive game. Twelve-year-old Crystal Field (nicknamed "Crisco") summed it up:

I think that this year Wo-Chi-Ca has brought us a very important lesson in how to live together.

During the last two weeks, a target game was brought to camp. On the target was a caricature of a Negro child. We were surprised, shocked, and bitter that such things were being sold to kids.

After many discussions on the game we decided to send a letter to the manufacturers of the game...criticizing them and asking them to take the game out of circulation.

Our answer came in the form of two attractive target games, one of a clown, and another of some monkeys climbing a tree. We were a little confused, as no letter had come with the targets.

We sent a letter to the company, thanking them for the games, but repeating what we had said in our last letter.

Finally a reply arrived stating surprise that this target game was still on the market. After protests by the National Association for the Advancement of Colored People the game had been discontinued.

In discussing this we came to the conclusion that the only way to remove games that caricatured a minority group would be to see that laws are passed making such games illegal.

If only we could make illegal the immoral games of our 'Captain America Radosh' and his sidekick 'Bucky Barnes Horowitz.' In their battle for truth, justice and the American way, these super heroes defame Wo-Chi-Ca, charging it with a practice so vile it borders on the fascist. Any honest investigator will discover only earnest kids and counselors advocating education, demonstration and legislation as the means to combat racism. No comic books heaped upon bonfires, no tossing of games into flames. Libel is no laughing matter, but so ends our comic tale.

How **do** Wo-Chi-Ca alumni, sixty years later, remember the politics of Camp?

Wo-Chi-Ca was a phenomenon not only because of its leftist origins and persuasion. Its significance as one of the few interracial experiences for white and black kids should not be understated. Yes, there were labor songs, and in the earliest years there were red bandannas. But it was more than a red diaper camp. Wo-Chi-Ca was an idealistic foreshadowing of the kind of integrated loving world we all hoped would follow World War II.

JACK BROITMAN

Many do not feel that a political atmosphere pervaded the camp, and they dispute "indoctrination."

My experiences at Camp Wo-Chi Ca from 1942-1947 (ages 8-13) were very positive ones. I met campers and counselors of diverse races and religions from different parts of the country, and realized that not everyone was Jewish or Italian like in the Bensonhurst section of Brooklyn where I was growing up. We sang songs of brotherhood and learned about tolerance and caring for each other. It didn't make any sense to me that we were considered to be 'subversive' a few years later. We were anything but subversive. The values emphasized at Wo-Chi-Ca were Peace, Love and Tolerance.

I may have been a naive little pisher from Brooklyn, but I don't remember any Communist indoctrination at Wo-Chi-Ca, unless you call singing songs like "Freiheit" and "Peat Bog Soldiers" indoctrination.

I have a lot of trouble thinking of Wo-Chi-Ca as a 'Communist camp.' It surely was not that to me. It was a place in the country where I had fun and enriching experiences – doing arts and crafts, playing ball, swimming, hiking, roasting marshmallows at bonfires, learning how to folk dance, singing songs in different languages about Peace, Brotherhood, Freedom, Labor Unions, and the Spanish Civil War.

ROY DOMBRO

I went to Wo-Chi-Ca in 1947, '48, and '49. I don't recall Communist Party activities in the Paul Robeson Playhouse although we sang a few songs like "Avanti Populo" and "Freiheit." I did not consider Wo-Chi-Ca a hard line camp. In fact, none of the kids, including myself, read the **Daily Worker.** *My counselors did not push any political ideas and nobody raved about the* **USSR.** *I thought we were progressives and I preferred to leave it at that.*

SERGE KANEVSKY

Progressive indeed, and certainly an outdoor space with a whiff of Marxism in the air. With so many left-wingers among visitors and staff, Wo-Chi-Ca kids might hear Marxist talk at Camp much as they did back in New York when their parents had friends over for an evening. But just as at home, such talk was taken for granted by the young campers, to the point that it was often ignored.

Camp was a place for fun in the sun – hiking and swimming – hardly a school where revolution was taught along with arts and crafts! No formal classes in Marxist theory were conducted at Camp Wo-Chi-Ca. The Marxism the kids experienced was in the fee structure that subsidized the poorest children, in the co-op where wealth sharing was applied to daily distribution of candy bars. Marxism was in the internationalism the kids were taught, in the songs they sang, in unionism, and foremost in black-white unity.

Did the Communist Party control the camp? A surprising assessment comes from camper Dick Flacks. His mother and father were New York public school teachers as well as members of the Communist Party. Dick, today a sociology professor at the University of California at Santa Barbara, recalls that...

...Wo-Chi-Ca was run as a model of participatory democracy. Each bunk had meetings. A camper council of bunk representatives was convened. A weekly town meeting run by campers was held. These helped instill in me a life-long passion for participatory democratic process. (Even if in reality the campers didn't have 'power,' there was a strong democratic message being communicated.) The revelations about the USSR and the CP had a powerful impact on me because I was so imbued with democratic perspectives. I could see quite quickly how one had to reject Stalinism and the Party in order to defend a genuine democratic movement. I was 'indoctrinated' with ideas, if you will, that helped subvert the authority of the CP rather than enhance it. And I am willing to bet that quite a few others had the same experience.

Another feature of the years I was in Camp was the rise of repression, exemplified by the Smith Act children in Camp. Many intense discussions of civil liberties were crucial in developing my political awareness. The camp was not regimented. It fostered individual self-expression and created a space in which adult authority could be questioned (and was!). None of this helped the aim of Party indoctrination, if there was such an aim.

Participatory democracy meant respect for other opinions and beliefs. Churchgoing children attended Camp and were taken to Sunday services. At least one loyal Republican is remembered with affection. Many campers looked forward to careers in the professions and a middle-class life. Franklin Roosevelt's 'New Deal' and 'town hall democracy' inspired kids as much as did Stalin and the Soviet Union.

This is all quite different from our initial impression. Even the charge of discrimination against 'bourgeois children' is here refuted:

I was the son of a capitalist and as a camper the issue never came up, though I am sure that many of the staff knew it. When I was a counselor, the last year in New Jersey, that fact was well known by any who cared to know. At no time was there any negative reaction.

BOB STACK

No, Wo-Chi-Ca was not exclusively "a summer camp for children of the Communist Party." At least six hundred kids attended each summer, and the number of red diaper babies was a modest portion of that total. A great number of children came from ordinary working-class families - Italian, Jewish, Irish, Slavic, Latino, African American, and Asian. Liberal they surely were, progressive yes, radical often. And if they were sympathetic to the Communist Party they were hardly alone. The Party during the Depression and War Years enjoyed widespread prestige. In 1943 it counted in its ranks 100,000 members - 15,000 serving in the Armed Forces of the United States.

No, Camp Wo-Chi-Ca was not an "indoctrination unit of a fringe party that was designed to develop a cadre of dedicated Party adherents." It was, however, a place that tried to turn out children who would make this a better world. Many Wo-Chi-Cans entered the helping professions. An eminent Harvard psychiatrist, recalling the camp's influence, tells of...

...a place very dear to my heart, Camp Wo-Chi-Ca. It had an enormous impact on me during the time I attended there and has greatly influenced my entire life, including my values, politics and commitments. When I first went to Camp, I was about ten years old and from East Harlem. I

lived in a very narrow world – a community that was often cruel with a great deal of fighting, teasing and provocation. In fact, the environment often seemed downright depressing, although I had many friends in the neighborhood.

When I entered Camp Wo-Chi-Ca, an entirely new world opened up to me in every way. It was my first opportunity to have real social experiences and interactions with kids - particularly white kids - from a variety of backgrounds. I was also greatly impressed by the respect that the staff showed children, as well as the camaraderie and spirit that enveloped the Camp. It was a very kind and caring atmosphere.

At Camp, we all felt that we had a sense of mission in fighting discrimination and fighting for oppressed people around the world. It was eye opening to me politically and stirred up all of my brain cells to a new intellectual fervor. Because of my Wo-Chi-Ca experience, I became much more interested in school and in expanding my mind. Because of this social and intellectual stimulation, I blossomed in the junior high school in my neighborhood and then later went on to Stuyvesant High School. I was perhaps one of the few kids from our neighborhood who attended Stuyvesant. If I hadn't had the experience of Wo-Chi-Ca, I would never have gone in an academic direction and achieved what I achieved.

Because Camp left me with a strong interest in people, I was always involved in civil rights, and eventually joined the civil rights movement after becoming a psychiatrist, and went to Mississippi from 1965 to 1967 to assist civil rights workers. I believe that choosing the field of psychiatry was influenced by my humane commitments that had their beginnings in my summer experiences in New Jersey. Even today, I often yearn for the spirit and closeness that I felt with the many campers and counselors at Camp Wo-Chi-Ca.

The Wo-Chi-Ca spirit remains an ideal that I continue to encourage as being fundamental to a sound democracy. It is appreciating and respecting the differences in people, honoring their rights, and striving for a strong sense of community where people truly care about one another.

I still recall many incidents from Camp and I still remember many of the lyrics of the songs and dances learned there. Wo-Chi-Ca has unquestionably enhanced and impacted my life in a very positive way.

ALVIN F. POUSSAINT, MD

Another Wo-Chi-Can at Harvard declares...

I attended Wo-Chi-Ca for two weeks in 1948 and three weeks in 1949. These were some of the best experiences of my youth and I wish I could have stayed longer.

I am now a Professor of Psychiatry at Harvard Medical School. Interestingly, Dr. Alvin Pouissant, my fellow Professor of Psychiatry at Harvard also attended Wo-Chi-Ca in 1949. Another Professor of Psychiatry (at Columbia), Dr. Fred Quitkin, was also at Camp in 1949. I'm not sure what this says about Wo-Chi-Ca and psychiatry but I know the three of us share a commitment to caring for those less fortunate than ourselves.

Among the great Wo-Chi-Ca experiences was learning to understand the racial and ethnic differences among campers and to appreciate differences in financial resources as well. Some of us had more than others. But we all shared, and in doing so, developed an incredible sense of camaraderie. I had never been away from home, never lived with others who were different from me, and never shared what I had with others who had less. I remember Canteen at night, sharing candy, and listening to discussions of prejudice, bigotry, and the importance of fairness.

CARL SALZMAN

A social worker reflects that...

...Wo-Chi-Ca was unique; it was ahead of the times. We lived integration... and with equality among females and males. Above all, we were taught to appreciate other cultures, to understand the plight of people and to strive to create a change in the ills of the world by bettering the lives of all people.

This may sound silly, but at camp we were curious about the hair texture of Black youngsters. A smart counselor had us play Blind Man's Bluff so as not to offend anybody and still be able to satisfy our curiosity. I later used this experience when I had a blind child in a sighted group.

JOY GLICKMAN

A retired social worker:

Wo-Chi-Ca was the defining experience of my youth. Although I came from a radical, Socialist-Bolshevik background, and even lived in a racially mixed neighborhood and had Black playmates, it was at Wo-Chi-Ca that my basic value system was formed and reinforced.

Wo-Chi-Ca taught me the importance of community, respect for individual worth, and the principle of the brotherhood of man based on human dignity regardless of race or religion.

My participation in various work projects – building a stone and wood cabin, laying out a soccer field, taught me about the dignity of work and the pride in collective effort.

I remember once when a group of boys, myself among them, pulled a 'raid' on another bunk, which included some damage to beds and people's clothes. The head counselor spoke quietly, and asked for the guilty parties to come forward. We all did so, expecting some horrible punishment. Instead, we were treated with such dignity and respect that we never misbehaved like that again.

In my later life, I always felt a sense of responsibility, as if my actions as an individual mattered.

I went on to be one of Paul Robeson's bodyguards at Peekskill, and when I was a student at CCNY, to be one of the leaders against discrimination toward Black students and Jewish teachers.

I became a social worker, working in community centers and settlement houses. I eventually emigrated to California to teach Social Work at Cal State University in Sacramento.

I don't know how my life would have developed without Camp Wo-Chi-Ca, but I do know that the Wo-Chi-Ca experience shaped the adult I became.

SOL SPECTOR

And still another social worker...

My sister and I (fraternal twins) were at Wo-Chi-Ca in 1946 and 1948, when we were ten and twelve years old, and it was a truly wonderful experience for me! I loved the atmosphere, the feeling of camaraderie, of working together for an ideal...

I've certainly told my daughter about my experience in Camp, and also have told my husband and my close friends. I am a product of that whole environment and proud of it.

LENORE MIGDAL-LLOYD

Many Wo-Chi-Cans went into teaching – Sheila Newman, for example:

I lived in a Jewish middle class neighborhood in Brooklyn and my parents, who were leftists, wanted me to have the opportunity to meet people from other backgrounds.

The moment I arrived in Wo-Chi-Ca, I realized I had found 'my own kind.' At last I belonged. From age nine through fifteen I attended Wo-Chi-Ca. From my first summer to my last, I couldn't wait for the other ten months to pass!

I hated coming home to Sheepshead Bay in Brooklyn when Camp ended. There, the only Blacks you saw were domestic servants. I was the only child on my block who was not Kosher and didn't attend synagogue. I perceived my neighbors, even children my age, as capitalists who only cared about material things. Being religious made them hypocrites.

Wo-Chi-Ca was my ideal world. It was there, at ten years of age, that I found the first of my boyfriends and true comrades. How fortunate I felt in later years not to be involved in 'bourgeois' dating!

In Camp, we were taught to be aware of 'male supremacists' and 'white chauvinists.' We performed in plays dealing with Black slavery and the Jewish Holocaust. I became aware of the analogous histories of Blacks and Jews.

In Wo-Chi-Ca, I met many interesting leftists. The most exciting was Paul Robeson. It was a great thrill to perform a dance choreographed to a Langston Hughes poem in his honor.

Shortly after marriage, I was appointed to teach in a Harlem elementary school. I was very pleased at the opportunity to work with Black children. Throughout the years, I have used my Camp songs such as "Take this Hammer" and "Midnight Special" to enhance my teaching.

Today, at fifty-seven, I'm still married and still teaching in a predominantly Black school in Brooklyn. I feel grateful to have had a leftist background. It has made me a more compassionate, caring and productive human being.

Today's alumni, now in their sixties, seventies, even eighties, still fiercely defend their childhood Wo-Chi-Ca, still cherish their Workers Children Camp.

I am pained that there is any questioning of the sincerity, decency, courage and dedication of the martyrs for a better world, however naïve or misguided history may have proven them to be. It is their humanitarian values that most of us have learned and absorbed at Wo-Chi-Ca for which I, for one, am very grateful and respectful.

ARTHUR KOMAR

A hard-line camp? Hardly! Most of those running the camp were softies, and with few exceptions people recall Wo-Chi-Ca as an oasis of kindness where idealism bloomed, equality thrived and free thought flourished. Red diaper babies? Counselors assigned to care for bedwetters would have settled for diapers of any color! Proletarian? Assuredly. Wo-Chi-Cans in these pages reflect that perspective proudly. And half a century later, the Wo-Chi-Ca sun still warms the autumn of their lives.

We, Lucian and Gerry Kaminsky, were, are, and always will be Wo-Chi-Cans. Gerry Kaminsky (nee Gottlieb) started at Wo-Chi-Ca in 1937; Lucian started in 1940. There's a love story here, actually two – one between us, and one from us to Wo-Chi-Ca. We met at Wo-Chi-Ca in 1940, as senior campers. Excluding World War II, we have been together ever since.

We came from Eastern European families with progressive leanings. I, Lucian, was from Manhattan, and a red diaper baby. Gerry came from Kearny, a small town in New Jersey.

At Wo-Chi-Ca we lived, sang, played, occasionally protested, all with the leitmotif of domestic and world politics, in an atmosphere which got us to think, and to feel. Kids from almost every nuance of political background sat and discussed things like the Nazi-Soviet Non-Aggression Pact and what it meant (and how it hurt). We discussed the stalemated Western front.

In the summer of 1941, we hosted people the likes of Max Yergan, Canada Lee, Mother Ella Reeve Bloor, and other well-known Americans. Where else could such a gathering exist?

This was the time when the Nazis invaded the Soviet Union and the war was even more on our minds, and for some, a specter looming over their futures. We all knew that we would be involved, sooner or later.

Pearl Harbor intervened and the guys went their separate ways all over the world (some, like Whitey Melzer, never to return), while the girls involved themselves in the war effort. In our case, Lucian became a Naval Officer serving in the Pacific, while Gerry served as a Cadet Nurse in the U.S. Public Health Service. The cap to our personal story is that we were married in April of 1945.

Our Wo-Chi-Ca is the story of our lives together. It began there, we grew there, we fell in love there, and every so often in our later life we drive there to try to get that Wo-Chi-Ca feeling.

As our kids grew up, we searched for another Wo-Chi-Ca for them. We never found it. We never found that indefinable something that made Wo-Chi-Ca so special. Maybe it was the time, the world as it was, or simply us.

We live now in South Florida, and Wo-Chi-Ca is in our hearts and minds. Together in a single frame on our wall are two mementos that will pass down to our children and to their children. They are a simple Wo-Chi-Ca yellow-and-blue felt patch, and a little Russian dancing doll, band-sawed out in 1940 by Lucian and painted by Gerry.

As long as there are Kaminskys, Wo-Chi-Ca will have special meaning for them.

LOVE AND LAUGHTER

Red diapers aside, Wo-Chi-Ca was, at bottom, a summer camp, a place for
fun. Children off on holiday customarily engage in pranks, tricks and
games – even indulge in mischief. Wo-Chi-Ca kids were no different.

*I remember some glorious after-lights-out pillow fights. In '48 I was in
one of the platform tents. Someone threw a pillow, which caught on a
protruding nail high up in the center post. Someone else then grabbed it
and threw it – hard! There was a blizzard of feathers.*

JOHN VAGO

*Danny Green told me he was immune to poison ivy. I didn't know what
poison ivy was but could not let him be one up on me, so I said I was
immune also. We found a patch of poison ivy and rubbed each other
down with it. Had to take sleeping pills at night, and photos of our
calamine lotion carcasses made the Yearbook.*

ALBERT V. LANNON

These are standard antics of kids at summer camp. But the two in the poison ivy
prank were children of conspicuous political parents: Gil Green and Al Lannon
were both prominent Communists.

Let us follow more 'Communist kids' off on a lark:

*Billy Gerson, Eppie, Davey Horowitz, and I decided to run off to visit the
town, contrary to regulations. Rebels that we were, we made it outside
the campgrounds and on our way to town. Then we saw the camp car
coming down the road. We dove into the bushes on the side of the road,
figuring we'd hide. Bad judgment on two counts: first, the counselors in
the car had already spotted us. Second, the bushes were poison ivy.*

*Of course, Billy and I got a special dressing down from someone whose
name doesn't matter because his type is so familiar. He told us that we
of all people should know better than to violate Camp rules – our fathers
would be ashamed of us if they ever found out. But not to worry because
no one would tell them and we should just suffer our punishment,
probably three days without softball or some such thing. I don't really*

remember the punishment, but the pompous punisher remains vivid in my mind. Also the itching from the poison ivy!

FRED JEROME

Some wore coats of calamine. Others cast off shirts, pants – all clothes whatever. They bared everything!

The camp had a small swimming area and we did a revolutionary thing – nude swimming! This was done at night by moonlight, but car headlights shone on us for safety. We did not escape notice. When the townspeople and some of the parents got wind of this, there was quite a controversy and the nude swimming stopped. But this has been a lifetime asset for me because the emphasis was in not being ashamed of the natural beauty of our bodies.

And so I learned – even though at times I did not enjoy my physical appearance – that nudity was okay and to be enjoyed. I have always been comfortable with swimming, hot-tubbing, group massage, etc. in the nude, which in the Seventies was very 'in.' My back yard in California was a delightful nudist colony.

MILI KLEIN

Wo-Chi-Cans in the nude! Other versions of this caper, however, have long been in circulation. Some remember that counselor Ralph Wardlaw (later killed in the Spanish Civil War) wanted to discourage the necking and petting prevalent among older campers. He organized a nude swimming party. After the swim, all snuggled into warm blankets while Ralph gave a lecture on human biology. In no time, everyone fell asleep. On top of that, it began to rain really hard. It drove everyone indoors in the middle of the night. All this taken together put a damper on the youthful enthusiasm for sex.

Falling asleep! So much for the mystique of the opposite sex! Friendship, comradeship, a vast array of diversions and distractions kept sexual activity at a minimum. This was, after all, a more innocent era. If there was a small amount of coed nudity and 'snuggling in blankets,' it did not lead to big problems. Wo-Chi-Ca was, as Irwin Silber points out, a progressive but hardly a free-love camp.

Wo-Chi-Ca was on the cutting edge... establishing approaches to the development of young people – both campers and counselors – which were way ahead of their time. Wo-Chi-Ca was a thoroughly coed camp. Most children's camps at that time were single sex. And those that were nominally coed, with a few noteworthy exceptions, kept boys and girls strictly separated and closely supervised. At Wo-Chi-Ca, by contrast, virtually all activity except for bunk arrangements was integrated across gender lines.

And despite the ideological limits of the time, I think the young women coming through the Wo-Chi-Ca experience had a keener sense of self-worth than most of their contemporaries, while the young men for the most part were at least a notch or two more sensitive to the practices of sexism.

There was undoubtedly a considerable amount of sexual experimentation if not consummation that went on. But I doubt whether more than a small handful left their virginity behind after a summer at Wo-Chi-Ca.

Staff members, often still teenagers themselves, sometimes unintentionally provided their young charges with examples of responsible adult behavior.

One day when my bunkmates and I were straightening our shelves, and our counselor Hi was off somewhere, one of us found a wrapped condom on the floor in front of Hi's shelf. It's probably impossible for anyone who wasn't around then to know how much importance in 1944 was attached to a condom.

A staple theme of risqué humor was the embarrassment associated with buying condoms. There used to be guys who would come up the freight elevators of New York City factory buildings and peddle condoms as if they were hard drugs.

And Wo-Chi-Ca – always sensitive to the danger of scandal that might be used by enemies – was quite puritanical. So, finding a condom was a big deal. We speculated about what we might be able to extort from Hi with our forbidden knowledge, but finally decided just to hand it to him and see his reaction.

Spotting Hi returning to our bunk across the Lower Campus, we ran out to him and presented our find. He was pretty cool about it, and thanked us ironically for returning it. Then he turned to me and said that he trusted I would not mention the incident to my parents, who were counselors at Camp. I assured him that I would not. I was hurt that he would even think I might consider betraying him – I loved him dearly as did all my bunkmates – and I was astonished that he could imagine me discussing condoms with my parents!

DAVE GREENWOOD

Sexual curiosity, erotic awakening, crushes, disappointments, adolescent yearning and anguish. Passion and politics intertwined...

I had the misfortune of being the child of an employee of the Daily News. (The fact that my father was known as 'The Red' within the corrupt Newspaper and Mail Deliverers Union and had his head beaten after he declined to say how he had voted at their election of officers availed me naught.) Also, I was plagued by allergies which gave me an unattractive and snotty nose in the pollen-laden August air. So I was considered lucky to find a guy who didn't hold all that against me in my Wo-Chi-Ca summer.

Although we were not ideally suited, I was happy enough. But he wanted either more or less (I can't remember which) than I was willing to offer during a two-week stint at summer camp. Rather than do the confrontational and correct thing to blow me off, he created a devious and humiliating method of saying it was over. He installed in the rear pocket of his jeans an enormous sprig of ragweed for my bunkmates and all the world to see. The message was clear to my eyes and nose. We never spoke again.

ROKKI KNEE CARR

When it came to romance, Mili Klein – revolutionary though she was – remembers not the politics, only the passion.

When I was a waitress at Camp I had my first important love tryst with George. I never forgot him. Ah, he was so handsome – my body still shivers with delight when I think back to those first warm embraces. He looked so wise smoking a pipe, as later did my husband of thirty-eight years.

Mili did not marry her camp sweetheart. But many a Wo-Chi-Can flirtation did lead to marriage. Fifty years later, many of those couples are still together.

Sy Rosen – a camper in 1938, '39, and '40, – had his summer as a counselor in 1943 interrupted by the draft. He was wounded, captured, then confined in a German prisoner of war camp. Sy returned home in June 1945 wearing a Purple Heart, a Bronze Star for Bravery, and a Silver Star for Gallantry in Action. How did he choose to spend his sixty-seven-day army furlough? As a counselor at Wo-Chi-Ca!

On my first night in Camp, I went out on the truck to bring food to seniors on an overnight hike. As I was getting off the truck I noticed a woman wrestling with a senior boy. Eleven months later I married that woman. She was Bunny Malkind, the swimming counselor.

Bunny Malkind Rosen reminds her husband that she was known as the 'no-swimming counselor' that rainy summer, and that their engagement was "a bit longer" than Sy remembers.

I met my future husband at Camp. After three days we decided to get married, but fortunately, we had the sense to wait a year before we did. We are still together after fifty-three years – two wonderful children and two grandkids later.

Lucian and Gerry Kaminsky, Sy and Bunny Rosen: just two examples among dozens of couples who met at Wo-Chi-Ca, got married, and still – all through the years – cherish the summer camp where their love blossomed.

A rarer bud, a beautiful bloom of black and white, also thrived in the garden that was Wo-Chi-Ca. Here, no wall stood between the races to keep campers from falling in love. Dave Tyson, a talented Black athlete, and Blanche Gross, a Jewish girl, found each other at Camp. Al Kisseloff, a Jewish boy, married Peggy Mair, the gifted Black girl who sang the lead in the camp's production of a Mozart opera.

Yes, Blacks and Jews grew very close at Camp. Some married; all formed fast friendships.

Weren't we a truly privileged bunch of kids to have gone to camp together at a time when Blacks and Jews found common cause, and to have been exposed to so much creative talent and intellect?

What a privilege it was to have the painter Jacob Lawrence as my arts and crafts counselor, the modern dancer Pearl Primus as my dance counselor, the painter Charles White as another arts and crafts counselor, and to be in the presence of that giant of a man Paul Robeson.

I am filled with sadness as I compare the current state of race relations in America with what we lived at Wo-Chi-Ca. But even back then we were labeled 'Reds' for being part of a truly caring community. Wo-Chi-Cans cared about the Spanish Civil War, a fair deal for laborers, world peace, and so much more.

RICK HAYNES

"When Blacks and Jews found common cause...." Rick Haynes puts his finger on the basic pulse of Wo-Chi-Ca: a Black/Jewish synthesis – certainly political, but also cultural. This unity expressed itself not only in romance – in love and marriage – but often in a familiarity born of shared living.

Each day, rain or shine, I would awake an hour before the other kids. I would hunt for flora and fauna to bring to the nature shack. I usually found salamanders and insects and occasionally a garter snake. But one morning I was not the first one up. I saw Mamie hurriedly dressing. As she slipped out the bunk door, I rushed after her, carrying my sandals.

"Hey! Are you following me girl?" she asked. She was definitely not glad to see me. "What you doing up so early?" she grumbled. "Oh, you know, I catch things," I replied.

Mamie was 'ten going on thirty.' She had a short compact body with dark chocolate skin. Her straight shiny black hair was pulled back in a ponytail. She had scowling brown slanted eyes, a prominent nose and thin lips, high cheekbones and underslung jaw. I knew she liked me since I was the only one to whom she told her whole name: Mamie Vestal Maria Agnes White.

Just then Deedee and Brenda emerged from the adjoining bunk carrying laundry bags filled with heavy items. They said "Hi" but their expressions made it clear I was not welcome. The three Harlem girls huddled together. Both Brenda and Deedee were tall and slender. They were light-complexioned and wore their brown hair in multiple braids. I heard Brenda yell, "But this is private!"

Then I heard Mamie tell them that I had caught a big snake. They finally agreed to take me along. Mamie linked her arm with mine as she led us into the woods. I knew we were off limits but didn't dare mention it. They made me promise not to tell a living soul.

The path led to a cluster of thick pine trees. We sat on some rocks, and the girls emptied out the contents of their bags: two cans of Sterno, two curling irons, two jars of Georgia Peach Hair Pomade, brushes and combs. Mamie took out a book of matches from her back pocket. When she ignited the Sterno, I shuddered to think of the consequences if we were caught. But I was fascinated watching the girls unbraid their thick hair, one section at a time. After brushing and combing each part, they liberally applied the pomade as Mamie heated the irons. She assisted her friends as they straightened their hair with the sizzling instruments. When the operation was completed, they used rubber bands to make two pigtails.

That morning, I discovered that not all girls curl their hair. After hearing Mamie's rendition of blues lyrics, I also learned why men fall in love.

> I met a bow-legged woman last night,
> I met a bow-legged woman last night,
> I fell in love with her right from the start
> Because her big fat legs were so far apart.

Mamie and I became close buddies for the remainder of her two-week stay. When she went home, I missed her a lot.

SHEILA NEWMAN

Nude swimming and heartthrobs, poison ivy and heartaches, bridges across the cultural divide. As many tales of Wo-Chi-Ca as campers and counselors... Dick Willing, (*Daily Wo-Chi-Can* reporter and 'mimeo inkslinger,') even offers a story of Camp with an altered name!

The Wo-Chi-Ho-De I Knew

The great mystery of my childhood was how my parents managed – even with IWO support – to send me to Camp as much as four to six weeks (every year but one) from 1938 to 1945. From the first moment I sensed that my time there would be important, almost magical. My parents surely foresaw the enriching and durable fruit their sacrifice would bear.

But why "Wo-Chi-Ho-De?" It stood for Workers' Children's Hotel Deluxe, a good-natured reference to sleeping in patched army tents and taking cold showers; to hand-cranking ice cream on Sunday; to not swimming unless we brought two stones to line the muddy pool bottom – hence the name "Two-Stone Pool."

The walk in the cool damp morning to the mess hall where inside enthusiastic chatter rises to deafening cacophony...

**Pass the moo-juice; slide the grease –
We would like some quiet please!**

The archy-craft shacks: papier-mâché, reed & raffia, woodworking, journalism, painting... Combining all these for a gala production in the 'Wreck Hall.'

**...I joined the drama group, acting every day –
Always in rehearsal but never in the play!**

**...I joined the chorus, sing and never tire –
Always in the bathtub but never in the choir!**

Baseball: "Pitcha's gotta bellyache!" Soccer, volleyball, Olympics, color wars (happily, only blue versus red, for "Black and white, we are united..." is part of our camp anthem).

Special treats: visits from great artists, writers or leaders like Liu Liang Mo, Canada Lee, Kumar Goshal, Mother Bloor and, of course, the incomparable Paul.

Overnight hikes: "We bin walkin' foreva from Morristown – how much foida 'til we get back to Camp? Is da truck comin' for us? Anyone got any watta left?"

'Archy-Craft' shacks

'Woody' the Camp Sta[
Wagon

Rest Hour: Dvorak, Bach and Beethoven over the loud-speaker. Readings from **The People, Yes!**

My children and grandchildren have been to camps, but nothing like Wo-Chi-Ca. Yet for all the mystique of the old site, it was first and foremost the people. Not just Matt, Butch and the other founders, not just Vaino Hill and Joe Wallace, but every parent, camper, counselor – every maintenance worker – contributing to that special moment in time that was Wo-Chi-Ho-De.

TRIPLE CROWN

"**N**othing like Wo-Chi-Ca...." Is it possible? Could no other summer camp compare to the Workers' Children's Camp?

My own children never attended Wo-Chi-Ca but they did go to Calumet, Webatuck and Kinderland. My grandchildren go to Kinderland. All of them have benefited from going to progressive camps. But in my own heart there was only one camp for me and that was Wo-Chi-Ca.

ED SMITH

If Wo-Chi-Ca was unique, that distinction lay first and foremost in its integration. The extensive ethnic mix and especially the large African American enrollment placed Wo-Chi-Ca in a class by itself.

Although Wo-Chi-Ca was never the fully interracial camp it aspired to be, it was still miles ahead of even the most progressive camps. Wo-Chi-Ca reached out to minority communities in practical ways that helped bring more Black and Latino children to camp. And it certainly inculcated a set of anti-racist values that Wo-Chi-Cans carried with them through their personal and public lives. Paul Robeson's close association with Wo-Chi-Ca over the years enabled all of us – black and white – to adopt him as a role model.

IRWIN SILBER

Black and white kids sleeping in the same bunkhouse, eating at one table, playing as teammates, singing in concert, putting on plays, sharing their culture....

"I will never forget my bunkmates from Harlem who taught me about African American culture and life. They turned me onto bebop – Charlie Parker, Dizzy, etc."

ISSAR SMITH (SMITTY)

"Butch" Stoller too was very close to Black kids at Camp. Today, Mike Stoller is famous as the composer of rock 'n' roll classics "Charlie Brown," "Yakety Yak," "Kansas City," "Hound Dog," "Jailhouse Rock," "Stand By Me" and others. "Poison Ivy," a golden million hit Mike wrote for the Coasters, seems especially to hearken back to those itchy New Jersey summers.

It was in 1941, when I was eight. I heard some very seductive music coming out of the barn. I wandered in and watched and listened intently as a black teenager played boogie woogie on the old upright piano. I don't think the musician was aware of my presence. When he abandoned his practicing and left the barn, I went to the piano to try to make my fingers do what I'd seen his fingers doing, so that I could make this wonderful music too. I feel that this moment was a major influence on me and my life.

MIKE STOLLER

Also, from Margie Schrier Katz:

At Camp, we sang "Lift Every Voice" and it has stood me in good stead ever since. We sing it at Black History Month programs in the multiracial senior building where I now live. I am always pleased to be seen with my head high instead of buried reading the words.

To this day I am the envy of friends who did not have the opportunity to experience what camps like Wo-Chi-Ca and Kinderland had to offer.

And from Sheila Newman:

The song "No More Auction Block for Me" gave me insight into the horrors of slavery. I learned that African-Americans were still not free in parts of the South. We sang "Lincoln Set the Negro free, Why Is He Still in Slavery? Jim Crow!"

CAMPERS

Prudence Hoy – Age 9 1/2

"I like Wo-Chi-Ca because it is
for all races and all religions.
It's not just for one race and
one religion. And you work and
play together. It is fun.

I love to play baseball. And
lots of other games. I have
learned not to be selfish and
not to boss people around. I
love Wo-Chi-Ca."

Alan Natapoff – Age 11

"I came to Wo-Chi-Ca on August
eight.
I will always remember that date.
About Wo-Chi-Ca I didn't know
Who was there or where to go.
All my bunk mates were introduced
to me
And I was completely surprised
to see
Negroes in the same bunk with me.

I don't hate Negroes; I like them
well.
They are intelligent; in sports
they excel.
Their fathers are workers like
mine and yours.
They are lynched. Why? What for?
The principles of freedom are
clear to me.
Why not live in harmony
and over Jim Crow score a victory?"

from a parent:

Dear Morris and Lally,

When Robert came home from camp, he made for his room and cried his heart out. Later he told me why. There are no tents here, he said, and no bunk mates, and no Dick Loring, and no wonderful activities such as he had enjoyed at camp. Why hadn't we arranged to have him stay longer? This world was not the same as the world he had just left. The other was so beautiful.

Robert and I were together for the next twenty-four hours. During this time he didn't stop regaling me with songs and accounts of happy experiences and raptures about the camp, its counselors, its activities. I couldn't get a word in, he was so talkative, so happy we had sent him to Wo-Chi-Ca.

I guess I don't have to tell you that it was by far the finest experience he has ever had. I understand that most kids bawl when they enter the busses to leave camp for home. And that isn't because the kids are mistreated at home, you may be sure.

I am very glad that I visited the camp during the two week-ends. What I witnessed enables me to understand Robert's love for it. He tells me that he helped a little in the building of the Robeson Social Hall. This seems to have been a most enjoyable activity. During my first visit to camp I asked him, "Have you anything to show something you've accomplished, besides catching twenty-one frogs which you let go?" He had no drawings or paintings or clay work at that time so I felt a little disappointed. Then he pointed to beautiful Robeson Hall and said, "There's something I helped build." Even if he only swept away a few pebbles or brought a couple of nails to the builders, he is very proud and happy.

I doubt very much that there is a happier bunch of children anywhere than I saw at Wo-Chi-Ca. Robert has already visited on his bike a Negro bunk mate as well as a white. This is one of the many evidences I have that he lived in a democratic community for one month, one very short month at the end of which he cried longingly for more of it.

The letter which I am enclosing is the last one Robert sent me from camp. It will explain itself. Incidentally, my boy wrote to me very regularly which is probably unusual as I have known parents to worry because they didn't hear from their kids; every letter I sent to my boy enclosed a self-addressed and stamped envelope or post card. I think this did the trick.

Fraternally,

NOAH

The Log Cabin

This page and the preceding from the Wo-Chi-Ca Yearbooks

Bob Friedman also picked up a life-long precept at Wo-Chi-Ca: "What did Camp teach me? Very simply, we are all equal and can all live as brothers."

Florrie Schenkler Forrest came to Camp from a lily-white town in Long Island. "I discovered that there was a whole world of kids and grownups out there from different walks of life, different colors, different religious backgrounds, and we could live together. Wo-Chi-Ca changed my life."

Kids from Harlem also found Wo-Chi-Ca a life-changing experience.

I was a sixteen-year-old wandering through the confused world of the upwardly mobile West Indian segment of the "Sugar Hill" New York Harlem community. Life was characterized by the family dictum to "improve yourself" – become a doctor, lawyer, or at least a minister. My father worked as a short order cook and went to night school to get a high school degree. He finally managed to get a civil service job as a hotel clerk. My mother waitressed and improved her clerical skills, eventually ending up as an entry level secretary. My three older sisters 'ran the house' while my parents worked to support us.

The Wo-Chi-Ca counselor job I got was a step up from expected summer work as a busboy or dishwasher. That summer of 1945 was confusing, scary and exciting. I was propelled into a world of people with a totally different, and for me, an intriguingly new way of thinking and living.

At Wo-Chi-Ca, girls and women were viewed as companions and peers, not merely as sex objects. Racial and ethnic differences were celebrated rather than feared, and working class people were respected and dignified. I made friends with women, learned to trust whites not to do me in because I was Black, and found pride in my working class roots.

Those ten weeks changed everything for me. I was swept up in multicultural music, dance and drama. Most importantly, I found peers and mentors in the quest for knowledge as well as the satisfaction that derived from helping others. Getting into New York City College became a definite priority for me. My goal became to enter Columbia University School of Social Work. I wound up as a university professor and licensed psychologist. My path was set that first summer at Camp Wo-Chi-Ca.

FRED MOORE

Maintenance worker Fred Wilson states that...

Wo-Chi-Ca had a profound effect on my life. It was the first time I came in contact with organizations that were not just giving lip service to the struggle to end racial segregation, but actually had programs to eliminate it and were putting their bodies on the line.

I moved to New York and worked with progressive organizations, walked picket lines, went to Washington on protests, and learned a tremendous amount about Socialist and Communist philosophy. It was at Wo-Chi-Ca that I first experienced an organized community in the U.S. where race didn't matter.

Yes, when Wo-Chi-Cans sang the camp anthem they meant every word of it.

> **You are the best, I love you best,**
> **Your fame is known from East to West.**
> **Oh camp so fine, Wo-Chi-Ca mine,**
> **There's not another camp like mine!**

The Wo-Chi-Ca spirit, then – if one could put a finger on it – could be found in the practice of racial equality. It is this feature of Camp that most alumni recall, the youthful ideal that remains with them all their lives.

The second pillar in the camp's foundation was music. "I Hear Wo-Chi-Ca Singing," Walt Whitman might have proclaimed had he strolled through the camp gates. Children sang constantly – arm in arm down the winding dirt road to the swimming hole, on the 'Appalachian Trail' to the mess hall, tooling leather in the craft shacks. Banjos and guitars twanged and thrummed everywhere. The old piano in the Main House jumped with the rhythms of Count Basie and Duke Ellington; during Rest Hour loudspeakers broadcast Bach and Beethoven. Evening programs always began with music, and "Irene, Good Night" was always the last song of the night. At the end of each two-week session, as weeping children climbed aboard homebound buses, they were sent off with choruses of "So Long, It's Been Good To Know You." Wo-Chi-Ca's soul was expressed in song.

Singing was an integral part of everything in Camp. We sang everywhere: walking from one activity to another, at meals, campfires, informal gatherings, formal chorus programs. You could do a whole "Ballad for Americans" or other cantata while cleaning the bunk.

I learned "Freiheit" that summer by sitting with the album **Six Songs for Democracy**. *It was a hit and my career was launched. I became a sensation at Camp and got laryngitis – as did others. It was de rigeur to walk around sucking lemons for your sore throat.*

We learned other songs of the Spanish Civil War, partisan songs from Europe and China, Russian and American folk songs of all kinds. We even did a Mozart opera. I wrote (with Hal Colter) a song, "To the British People," which was given to Paul Robeson when he visited Camp.

Everybody got tired of waiting for summer, so Wo-Chi-Ca started a winter program. It included a chorus which made every Saturday in the city like a day at Camp. We sang the same songs, but now for a wider audience. Being interracial and non-denominational we were accepted everywhere: The New York Fresh Air Fund, churches in Harlem, Russian War Relief...

I grew up in a unique set of circumstances provided by the Communist-led Left in that historical moment that paralleled my growing up on the streets and in the schools of Brooklyn. The Left provided me with caring adults, friends, a culture, an ideology, and a community. It gave me peers to learn from, taught me a vocation, and gave me the opportunity to practice it.

ERNIE LIEBERMAN

Another professional musician also credits his career to his years at Camp.

It was in the cool, quiet confines of the Whitey Melzer Music Room, my first summer at Wo-Chi-Ca, that I heard for the first time the recorded voices and instruments of the people who would determine the future course of my life.

First and foremost there was Woody Guthrie, then Pete Seeger on the five-string banjo. The Almanac Singers (Woody, Pete, Lee Hays, Millard Lampell) stopped me dead in my tracks. Josh White – how he made his guitar sing! I found Paul Robeson records also in the Music Room, and in that summer of 1945, I saw him there IN PERSON!

On my return home I asked my father to buy me a guitar. Next summer I was back in camp, guitar in hand. Fred "Doc" Gerlach, fresh out of the army, used to spend hours – when he was not working in the kitchen – pounding out boogie-woogie at the battered upright piano in the Barn. I tried to get the feel of it on my guitar. Joe Jaffe, a couple of years my senior, was a smoothie on the guitar and the five-stringer. Joe was learning banjo licks from Pete Seeger, also just mustered out of the army.

By the summer of 1947 when I was hired as a counselor (imagine, actually being paid to spend a summer at Wo-Chi-Ca!) I was ready to change the world with my guitar. That same year I joined Dave Sear on WNYC. That radio station's "Folk Song Festival" was hosted by Oscar Brand.

The cafeteria at City College was a hotbed of Wo-Chi-Ca-driven folk music. Every Thursday from noon to two, classes were suspended for student activities. Our folk music featured Wo-Chi-Cans Dick Willing, Moe Hirsch and Joe Jaffe along with non-Wo-Chi-Cans like Tom Paley (later with the New Lost City Ramblers). The spring semester of '48 witnessed the great student strike and sit-in, protesting the anti-

Semitic and Jim Crow practices of two faculty members. We were right there with our guitars, banjos and protest songs.

Sing Out began publication in 1950. Its first issue listed among its contributors Ernie Lieberman, Paul Robeson, Howard Fast, Aaron Kramer, Earl Robinson, Irwin Silber and Pete Seeger – just to mention those associated with Wo-Chi-Ca. In August 1951, I joined the magazine's music staff, eventually becoming music editor, a position I held until 1964.

So, thank you Wo-Chi-Ca for keeping the music going. I couldn't have done it without you.

JERRY SILVERMAN

Dave Sear, half a century after he plucked his banjo at Wo-Chi-Ca, is fondly recalled by Harvard professor Carl Salzman:

I remember the singing at Wo-Chi-Ca, which seemed to go on non-stop. In 1949 my counselor Dave Sear practiced the banjo incessantly. Dave was already playing with Oscar Brand on WNYC and on folk music records that I listened to as a teenager.

I remember sitting on the floor of the bunk watching his metallic finger picks flash, and listening to the 'hammering on.' I watched, fascinated, and I also wanted to play the banjo.

Because of Dave, I began to play the guitar, then bought my first banjo at age seventeen and learned the Pete Seeger style of plucking and frailing. I developed a permanent love for folk music as well as work and protest songs. At college, I drove my roommates crazy practicing banjo and guitar continually.

By the time I reached psychiatric residency, I had a fair proficiency, and played with classmates and friends. I met my wife singing labor songs, and at my recent 60th birthday, a group of us gathered, with guitars, banjos, harmonicas, etc., and sang the night away in good Wo-Chi-Ca style.

Now, in my early sixties, with graying hair and a beard, I still sing and play and listen to the old songs. My collection of union and labor records is well worn, and I remember the words of the old songs better than anything I learned yesterday. Fifty years later, I would rather sing these songs than any others.

Dave still remains in my mind as a model. I continue to play banjo and guitar and sing the songs of union, labor, and struggle. I feel the Wo-Chi-Ca heritage fifty years later.

Thank you Wo-Chi-Ca for the central role of union/work/labor songs that have carried through my entire life. Thanks for helping to develop another citizen with a reasonable social conscience and 'helping career.' And especially, thanks to Dave Sear!

THE SONGS OF WO-CHI-CA

A Sampler

"A Singing Camp"

WO-CHI-CA WE WILL SING TO YOU

Wo-Chi-Ca we will sing to you
In one accord,
And may your fame be spread
For miles and miles abroad.
We will join our hands
In all our strife,
And we'll always try to do
The thing that's right.

Our motto is to build
For character not for fame,
Wo-Chi-Ca will forever reign,
May we forever as comrades be,
Wo-Chi-Ca, we sing to thee.

WO-CHI-CA CAMPFIRE SONG

Round about
The blazing firelight
We have met
In comradeship tonight.
High above, the whispering trees
Guard our golden memories.
So now before
We close our eyes in sleep
Let us pledge each other
That we'll keep
Wo-Chi-Ca memories
Strong and deep
Till we meet again.

Ernie Lieberman

WORLD YOUTH SONG

Everywhere the youth
Are singing Freedom's song,
Freedom's song,
Freedom's song.
We rejoice to show the world
That we are strong,
We are strong, We are strong.
We are the youth,
And the world acclaims
Our song of truth,
Everywhere the youth
Are singing Freedom's song,
Freedom's song,
Freedom's song.

FREIHEIT

Spanish heavens spread
Their brilliant starlight,
Far above our trenches
In the plain,
From a distance
Morning comes to greet us
Calling us
To battle once again.

Far off is our land,
Yet ready we stand.
We're fighting
And winning for you...
Freiheit!

Jerry
Silverman

BELOVED COMRADE

To you, beloved comrade, we make this solemn vow,
The fight will go on, the fight will still go on.
Like you, beloved comrade, we pledge our bodies now,
The fight will go on, the fight will still go on.

SAME MERRY-GO-ROUND

It's the same, same
Merry-go-round,
Which one will
You ride this year?
The donkey and elephant
Bob up and down
On the same merry-go-round.

TUMBALALAIKA

Tumbala, tumbala, tumbalalaika
Tumbala, tumbala, Tumbalalaika
Tumbalalaika,
Shpiel balalaika
Tumbalalaika,
Fraylach zol zain.

NEW WORLD A-COMING

There's a new world a-coming, come on,
There's a new world a-coming, come on,
Come on from every country on this earth,
Fight for the rights you had from birth.
We've beaten Jim Crow and we'll keep him down,
White supremacy has no crown.
With hand holding hand against the foe,
We'll rise in a brighter world we know.

UNITED NATIONS HYMN

The sun and the stars all are ringing
With song rising strong from the earth,
The hope of humanity singing
A hymn to a new world in birth.

United Nations on the march
With flags unfurled,
 Together fight for victory
 A free new world.

As sure as the sun meets the morning
And rivers go down to the sea,
A new day for mankind is dawning,
Our children shall live proud and free.

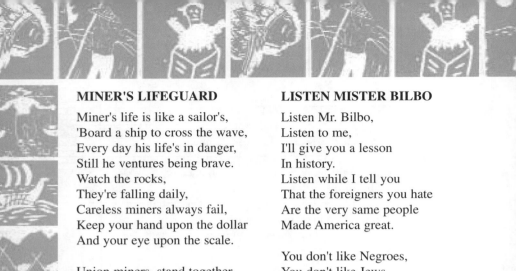

MINER'S LIFEGUARD

Miner's life is like a sailor's,
'Board a ship to cross the wave,
Every day his life's in danger,
Still he ventures being brave.
Watch the rocks,
They're falling daily,
Careless miners always fail,
Keep your hand upon the dollar
And your eye upon the scale.

Union miners, stand together,
Heed no operator's tale,
Keep your hand upon the dollar
And your eye upon the scale.

LISTEN MISTER BILBO

Listen Mr. Bilbo,
Listen to me,
I'll give you a lesson
In history.
Listen while I tell you
That the foreigners you hate
Are the very same people
Made America great.

You don't like Negroes,
You don't like Jews,
If there's anyone you do like
It sure is news,
You don't like Poles, Italians,
Catholics too;
Well, dead or alive, bud,
We don't like you.

SONG OF THE RESISTANCE ARMY OF EUROPE

We march in the ranks behind our tanks
And in the guerrilla band,
Freedom is our language
And the world is our native land.
And every woman and every man
Who will not be a slave
Is building a tomb for a fascist
And digging a fascist grave.

When the last enemy plane is shot from the skies
And the last gun rings from the hill,
There'll be land for brothers to plow,
There'll be factories for brothers to run,
And we'll live free 'neath the friendly sun
In the homes that brothers build.

Close ranks and forward march,
You armies of free men;
We'll free the lands from the dead man's hands
And give them to living men.
Yes free the land from tyrants hands
And give them to living men.

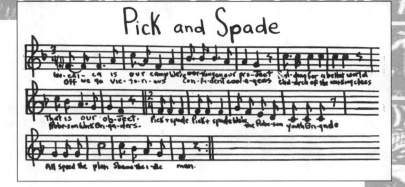

FREEDOM IS MY LAND

Wherever men love Freedom, I clasp them by the hand,
I call them all my brothers, for Freedom is my land.
I hear a million voices, with them I take my stand,
The people are my brothers, and Freedom is my land.

For liberty has one design for everyone to share,
It's like the sun that has to shine on people everywhere.
I hear the millions marching, with them I take my stand,
The people are my comrades and Freedom is my land.

WO-CHI-CA ANTHEM

Wo-Chi-Ca is the dream of Freedom's people,
A hope built high on nature's slopes,
Where the singing of the children is our music,
Making marching songs of human hopes.

Wo-Chi-Ca is the comradeship of children,
An inspiration for a world our own,
Where noisy laughter has a peaceful echo
Giving courage to a future we will own.

**An extensive Wo-Chi-Ca Wordbook of over 120 songs can be
obtained by order from
AVON SPRINGS PRESS.**

The third component making up the magic of Wo-Chi-Ca might be called education. This was an all-embracing element, ranging from dance and drama to democracy, from arts and crafts to unionism.

Although 'only' a summer camp, Wo-Chi-Ca was an educational institution in the true meaning of the word. Education: the drawing out of the child's natural abilities. Camp was a place where you could try your hand at painting, photography, acting, or mounting a collection of leaves. Numerous activities gave every child a place to shine, whether in sports, library work, or on the Campers' Council.

Kids learned by doing. One of the most important lessons was the satisfaction derived from shared labor and cooperation.

I remember fondly raising the roof of the Nature Cabin. With slogans, posters and songs we marched together and literally raised that old leaky roof and replaced it with a new one. I truly loved this cooperative action which produced such a positive and concrete result.

MILI KLEIN

Always, the emphasis was on cooperation and teamwork while maintaining respect for the individual. Leadership was encouraged. Not every camper became a leader, yet every child was special. Even a shy quiet camper might acquire a certain distinction from something as simple as a nickname. "Prof" and "Rooster" and "Meatballs" were current, but names such "Fatso," or "Dopey," or "Four-Eyes" would not be tolerated. A child might wear glasses or be 'different' in some way, but every child was accepted and cherished. All received generous praise for hard work and a job well done.

When the Paul Robeson Playhouse went up, I had a part of putting the roof on it. My job was to put waterproofing "stickum" on the edges and send the pieces up to be put in place. Butch used to come around and make me feel that I was the best worker there was. At Camp I felt like a valuable person in a loving community. I found out that adults could be really nice non-bossy people. I felt noticed, appreciated, valued for the kind of personality I had.

BARBARA LERNER HIKEN

Throughout the spring, long before the start of the camp season, Wo-Chi-Ca staff members met in the city weekly to discuss child psychology, health and safety, even bedwetting.

I was most impressed with the counselor training and orientation that we had for many weeks before Camp opened. The effort that Dick Crosscup and others put into that was exceptional. I took away from those sessions a profound feeling for the camp.

I was a counselor for junior boys, ostensibly nine or ten years old. Turns out a couple of seven-year-olds were in the bunk. Chief problem: bedwetters – especially when it was raining and we had to take them to the 'White House,' our camp bathroom. Ronnie Gilbert, who went on to fame as one of the Weavers, collaborated with us on "Eneuresis," sung to the tune of the title song from "Oklahoma."

JACK BROITMAN

Sometimes it was the children themselves who provided the counselor training. Bunny Rosen was in charge of a bunk of teenage girls:

Rest hour was supposed to be spent on discussions about anything the group thought important. On the second day of Camp one of the girls said she thought we were a nice group of people: we got along well, liked each other, but something was missing – our relationship was very superficial.

My first thought was "What do you expect after two days? Intimacy?" Fortunately, I kept my mouth shut. What followed was an outpouring of feelings, hopes, worries, and what each hoped to get out of Camp.

The honesty and openness of the discussion was extraordinary considering that none of us knew each other at the outset. By the end of the two-week period, despite differences of background, experience and color, we were a closely-knit group, profoundly bound together.

Yes, counseling was quite a challenge. Still, many a camper looked forward to the day he or she would become a counselor. Then again, if you weren't quite ready to take on that much responsibility, you could wait on tables, scour pots, clean toilets, or drive the camp truck. Cutting grass, scrubbing the infirmary – all staff work was considered equally vital to Camp welfare. In the year 1949 alone eighty-nine people worked on staff. A good number were former campers who were elated to remain at Wo-Chi-Ca after they turned sixteen.

The valuable training and experience more than compensated for the minuscule salaries. In 1949, a first year counselor received seventy-five dollars for an entire ten-week season. Back in the Thirties, staff had worked for room and board plus 'cigarette money.'

Why such love and loyalty to the Workers' Children's Camp? Sy Rosen credits Wo-Chi-Ca's idealism.

Wo-Chi-Ca strengthened my beliefs that a communal and cooperative society is a more advanced form of civilization than the dog-eat-dog society we live in.

Ed Smith expresses this idealism in concrete terms:

Coming from the East Side I was always on the defensive and was constantly involved with fights. Going to Wo-Chi-Ca allowed me to be with people who didn't solve their problems with their fists but were able to discuss their differences and come to a logical conclusion minus the fighting.

The recollections of Dave Greenwood illuminate the troika of our theme – integration, music and education. Dave permeates his memoir with love and laughter, but at the same time he honestly raises all the difficult questions.

Wo-Chi-Ca was my first encounter with a community of left-wingers. I lived in a middle-class neighborhood in Brooklyn, and always felt like an outsider politically. In 1940, I remember being the only kid in my class to defend the Soviet invasion of Finland.

During the Second World War, we used to collect foil from cigarette packs, candy bars, and cream cheese wrappers, roll it into balls, and take it to a collection center 'for the war effort.' One day, while I was rolling my stash of foil on the front stoop of our house, Smiley Kaplan, a boy a year or two older than me, passed by and asked with a smirk whether I was sending it to Stalin.

My parents were schoolteachers. The Rapp-Coudert Committee, a New York State 'Un-American Activities Committee,' had caused the firing of a number of leftist teachers. My parents had cautioned me and my brother to be discreet about our political opinions. Now, at Camp, I was suddenly immersed in a sea of left-wingers. My secret thoughts and dreams were shared by this little universe. I could speak freely, and no one thought I was crazy or unpatriotic. I felt liberated. The revolution had already triumphed in 120 acres of Warren County, New Jersey!

The only African American I had ever talked to before Wo-Chi-Ca was a part-time housekeeper employed by my mother. Despite my ideology, I had been slightly apprehensive about going to an integrated camp; I didn't know what it would be like. The drama of discovery was in how undramatic it was. What do you know – people! Kids or counselors...people who looked different and in some cases sounded different from the people I was used to, but otherwise – people.

I worked on the Daily Wo-Chi-Can with Dick Willing; Irwin Silber was the counselor in charge. I helped strip and clean the mimeograph machine. When we reassembled it, there were a couple of parts left over but the machine seemed to work just fine without them.

A few years later I was the compositor for the newsletter of the Labor Youth League chapter at Cornell. For this, I later had the honor of being named before the Jenner Committee, which during the McCarthy era investigated 'un-American activities' in the colleges.

One evening at Camp in 1944, there was a campfire with the theme of the Underground Railroad. The conceit was that we were runaway slaves. We listened to stories and sang freedom songs around the campfire.

Suddenly we heard terrible shouts. The senior boys, wearing bandanna masks, crashed onto the scene as a gang of slave-catchers. The first few moments of the 'raid' – till we realized who the raiders were – were terrifying, and left an impression that surfaced twenty-seven years later.

In 1971 I served as a juror in a federal trial. David Poindexter was accused of harboring Angela Davis when she fled after being accused of providing weapons to jailed militants. By the time of the trial, I was no longer a Marxist, and was strongly opposed to political violence. But I thought it quite possible that Davis had been framed, and entirely plausible that she had fled because she did not believe she would get justice.

The government's case against Poindexter was very strong. But my thought process went like this: "What would I have done if Angela Davis had come to my door and asked for help?" I knew in my gut, instantly, that I would have tried to help her. And, if I would have helped her, could I send someone to jail for doing exactly what I would have done?

I mused over why my emotional reaction was so clear and so swift. And of course what rose to the surface was the Underground Railroad campfire, which I had not consciously thought about for years. So as soon as the door to the jury deliberation room closed, I started talking about 'beyond a reasonable doubt.'

I found allies in the two Black members of the jury and a trade union business agent. The upshot was a 'not guilty' verdict in about two hours. The prosecutors looked stunned and the judge was furious. Score one for Wo-Chi-Ca.

But getting back to Camp: In 1948 Henry Wallace ran for president on the Progressive Party ticket. Some of us attended the Party convention and were very excited. We sang Wallace campaign songs: "The Donkey and Elephant Bob Up and Down on the Same Merry-Go Round."

Enthusiasm sometimes got the better of reality. People talked about the presidential race being between Dewey and Wallace, with Truman in third place. Paul Robeson visited Camp, and was sitting in the canteen chatting, when a staff member asked him in perfect seriousness, "If Wallace is elected, will you be his Secretary of State?" Paul was slightly taken aback, but did not laugh. Instead he said, "No, I don't think so. I'm an artist, and I think the best contribution I can make is as an artist."

I had graduated from high school in June of 1948, and entered Cornell in late September. My best friend in high school was a dedicated left-wing Zionist, whose group was preparing to emigrate to a kibbutz in the new state of Israel. He invited me to spend a week at the group's camp in New York State. I found it quite reminiscent of Wo-Chi-Ca, except that the songs were in Hebrew. Their description of kibbutz life sounded like, well – Wo-Chi-Ca twelve months a year. It seemed possible to live in a socialist environment without waiting for the revolution! I was converted, and though I started college, I intended to join the Zionists when they were ready to emigrate.

I suffered severe culture shock when I got to Cornell. Suddenly I was surrounded by upstate Republicans. I sought refuge in Cornell's small left community, and even joined the Communist Party early in 1949. But I did not give up my intention of going to Israel.

My Communist comrades warned me I could be expelled for the bourgeois-nationalist deviation of Zionism, and my Zionist comrades warned me that I could be thrown off the kibbutz if I supported the Israeli Communist Party once I got to Israel. But by the time the group was ready to leave in 1950, the Korean War was on, and I needed permission from my draft board to leave the country. I applied for permission to visit Israel, but my father squealed to the draft board my intention of staying there, so they refused to let me go. I felt that my father had betrayed me. He and I papered over this conflict, but, sadly, we had never really resolved it before his death in 1959.

In 1949 I started the Wo-Chi-Ca season as a counselor. Dave Glaser was my group leader. I was very conscientious but found the work difficult and exhausting. I dealt a lot better with things, ideas, and abstractions than with people in general or intermediate boys in particular. One of my campers even told me "You'd rather argue with Artie Komar about Tito and Yugoslavia than be with us."

Late in the summer, Camp leadership asked for a counselor to volunteer to switch to maintenance. The 'party line' held that counselors and maintenance workers were entirely equal contributors to Wo-Chi-Ca. I was very young, very naïve, and very ideological and bought the party line without reservation. After all, our working-class ideology would hardly permit a class structure, or looking down on manual workers. All staff members belonged to the Staff Union, and switches from maintenance to counselor were not unusual. However, transfers in the other direction were rare, and tended to be thought of, unofficially, as demotions. In short, counselors were more equal than others.

Exhausted and discouraged by counseloring, I leaped at the opportunity to shed some responsibility. To my surprise, I was the only volunteer. I was praised for my exemplary Wo-Chi-Ca spirit. I explained that it was a selfish personal choice, but my comment was dismissed as modesty.

When I reported to work as a pot-scrubber, I asked Ada B. Jackson what my duties were. She gave me an appraising look and a half smile and said, "I want clean pots!"

We fighters against the established order had some orthodoxies of our own. Roz Katz and I led a writing workshop for the intermediate campers. A very bright boy named Paul proudly submitted an anti-racist poem which unhappily included the 'N' word. The left was in the midst of a 'struggle against white chauvinism,' and the 'N' word was verboten, regardless of context. We explained to Paul that we could not print his poem. He was crestfallen.

Back in 1947, when I was a fifteen-and-a-half-year-old senior boy, I got a crush on a very cute fourteen-year-old senior girl – short, slender, with olive skin and brown hair and eyes, named Marion Samson. I tried to hang out with her, but I was so tongue-tied by my crush that I couldn't talk, which made her uncomfortable. So she tried to avoid me.

One night, there was a concert in the Music Room. When I got there, I looked around for Marion, hoping to sit with her. Didn't see her. But, being a persistent and methodical sort, I kept looking until I located her underneath the big picnic table, whereupon I crawled in beside her. When the event was over and people started walking back to the Lower Campus, I wanted to walk with Marion, but found her surrounded by a flying squad of her bunkmates. Even I had to get the message that my company was unwelcome. My heart was broken. Further, I felt humiliated that her bunkmates had been made aware of my undesirability. What happened five years later? Well, I married her. We had three children and were together for thirty-three years.

MEMORIES

The smell of Pine-Glo when the bunks and tent platforms were scrubbed...

Square dancing in the Barn...

Rena Gluck's spectacular leaps in her modern dance numbers...

Tommy Warner, naked, standing at the front of his tent platform, displaying attitude (among other things) to passersby.

Eddie Klein inveigling me into my first and last basketball game, two-on-two. Though I scored no goals I had a grand time. But I was wearing moccasins and my ankles hurt for days afterward.

Paul Robeson on the ball field, semi-crouched with catcher's mask and mitt...

The quotations from Abraham Lincoln and Carl Sandburg in the Mess Hall...

Stopping dead in my tracks outside the Barn to the sounds of the Chorus rehearsing...

Standing up when we sang "Lift Every Voice and Sing" and the Soviet National Anthem as well as the "Star Spangled Banner."

Co-op: each camper kicking in some money: theoretically according to their means, but in practice usually the same amount – and everyone getting one candy bar.

Carl, an out-of-control twelve-year-old, restrained by a Black counselor, Cyril Tyson. Carl, livid with fury, calling him every obscenity imaginable, not one of them racist.

A World War II map of Europe on the wall in the Daily Wo-Chi-Can shack, with pins marking the Eastern and Western Fronts.

Whitey Gootzeit telling us how when he hid from the Nazis in the mountains of Italy his only food was grass and olive oil.

Morris Salz earnestly explaining the significance of the Teheran Big Three meeting...

Howard Fast earnestly explaining that Titoism was latter-day Trotskyism...

The shudder down my spine the first time I heard "Wo-Chi-Ca Is the Dream of Freedom's People, A Hope Built High On Nature's Slopes..." Damn song still chokes me up.

People crying as the buses pulled out to take them home...

I fear that in trying to recall particular incidents and images, I have not sufficiently conveyed the ordinary happiness of daily life at Wo-Chi-Ca. We were busy; we were doing constructive things, creative things, physically invigorating things, all day long. And we felt that we were part of a world movement, something bigger than us as individuals, something bigger than Camp, a movement that would make a better, far better, world. No, no, you can't take that away from me.

But simultaneous with being a nostalgic romantic, I'm also an analytical, skeptical, realistic, unsentimental, post-ideological grinch. So I have to recognize some of what was wrong while I recall with delight some of what was right. And in doing that, I can't always separate Wo-Chi-Ca from the 'progressive movement,' as we called it, of which it was a part. Today I would call it the Stalinist left.

In retrospect, I feel that I grew up as a member of a cult. We had no use for conventional religion, but in fact practiced our own brand of idolatry. We cherished the totally irrational belief that the Soviet Union was a wonderful place, ignoring or denying the widely available contradictory evidence. At Camp we sang a song of the Jewish settlement in Zhankoye years after it had been uprooted by Stalin, and of Birobidjan long after it had failed as a center of Jewish life.

Our own beloved Paul Robeson suppressed his first-hand knowledge of the arrest and persecution of the Jewish writers in the Soviet Union, including Itzik Feffer, who once visited Camp.

We paid lip service to democracy, but our leading organization, the Communist Party, was led by a self-perpetuating clique, with occasional string pulling from Moscow, and our practices in unions and non-Communist 'mass organizations' were frequently manipulative.

We believed that victories of Communist parties would somehow magically erase human conflicts over power and wealth. So we were fueled by illusion.

Some fraction of that wonderful energy of the Wo-Chi-Ca spirit was based on nonsense! And that energy was addictive, so that it was very hard to give it up in the face of nasty old reality. For myself, it took Mr. Khrushchev's rubbing my nose in a fraction of Stalin's crimes to get me to bathe in the cold waters of the truth.

And yet, and yet. We recognized the danger of fascism and Nazism. We were remarkably clear-sighted in our understanding of capitalism and of racism. Our sympathies were with the oppressed (at least those outside the Soviet Union, China, and the Eastern Bloc). We walked the walk of racial equality long before it was fashionable. We rejected the notions of dog-eat-dog and devil-take-the-hindmost. Our ideals of justice, equality, and brotherhood are still wonderful ideals.

So am I glad I went to Wo-Chi-Ca? To me, that's like asking whether I'm glad that I was born in 1931, glad that I had my particular parents, glad that I grew up in Brooklyn, and so forth. It's just my life. Wo-Chi-Ca was a big, big part of my life. And like any other part of my past life, I celebrate what was joyful, learn from what was painful, and laugh at what was foolish. Wo-Chi-Ca provided more than its share of the joyful.

THE CURTAIN DESCENDS

In the summer of 1945, children tumbled out of the blue Wo-Chi-Ca buses with more than their usual excitement. Just a few weeks previously, on May 8, they had run out of their houses clutching their mothers' pots and pans to join the elated multitudes in the streets. Clanging and banging, singing and shouting, the kids paraded up and down, reveling in V-E Day. The Nazis had surrendered! Hitler had killed himself.

And yet all was not euphoria, for in April, just weeks before the great victory celebration, President Franklin Delano Roosevelt had died. Boys and girls arriving at Camp in July still felt – almost as much as their parents – the enormous loss. The children had grown up listening to the radio 'fireside chats' of the popular leader. Roosevelt was the only president they had ever known.

That summer of '45 often found campers and staff in the Whitey Meltzer Music Room, in spirited assembly.

As sure as the sun greets the morning,
And rivers run down to the sea,
A new day for mankind is dawning,
Our children shall live proud and free.

New lyrics by Harold Rome set to an old Russian melody arranged by Shostakovitch – youthful voices raised in unison. The building itself – roused from its two hundred-year-old dream of the American Revolution – seemed to stir, its ancient stones resounding to the impassioned song.

United Nations on the march,
With flags unfurled.
Together fight for victory,
A free new world.

A brave new world! Months before the German surrender, Roosevelt met with Churchill and Stalin in Teheran and in Yalta to create a new international organization that would guarantee world peace. Even as their armies advanced on Berlin, delegates from fifty nations worked two full months in San Francisco drawing up a founding agreement. On June 25, 1945 the one hundred eleven articles of the United Nations Charter were adopted unanimously. World War II would be the last in history: such was the great hope.

A golden sun crowned the San Francisco sky, but in the far Pacific the sun dripped red. Fierce combat persisted in Asia. U.S. Marines had recently captured Iwo Jima at a terrible cost in lives. In the bloody spring campaign to seize Okinawa, the U.S. lost 48,000 men. The mainland itself loomed next: the invasion of the Japanese home islands. There, loss of life would be incalculable.

Ralph Wardlow, Mendy Mendelsohn, Whitey Meltzer, Jerry Feifer... – all killed fighting fascism in Europe! How many more Wo-Chi-Cans would perish in the Pacific?

> **What were their names,**
> **Tell me what were their names,**
> **Did you have a friend**
> **On the good Reuben James?**

Even as the campers sang, their brothers, uncles and friends manned battle stations on warships steaming toward the enemy. Lucian Kaminsky, for example, was aboard one of the first ships to sail into Japanese waters. Observing the landing site with its grim fortifications, Lucian feared he and his comrades would never survive.

But on a morning early in August, Wo-Chi-Cans at breakfast heard a stunning announcement: a new and unbelievably powerful weapon – an atomic bomb – had been dropped on Japan. The city of Hiroshima was reduced to rubble with 130,000 people wounded and killed. Three days later another massive atomic bomb exploded over Nagasaki with 75,000 more casualties. In a week Emperor Hirohito agreed to total surrender. Japan was crushed. World War II was over!

How relieved Wo-Chi-Cans were that Allied soldiers would no longer storm beaches and engage in hand-to-hand combat! In spite of all we know now about the horrors of those atomic blasts, Lucian and others who were with him feel to this day that they are alive thanks to the bomb.

The war was finally over. What if that summer of '45 was exceptionally rainy, and the trail to the swimming hole so ankle-deep in mud that swim instructor Bunny Malkin was the 'no-swimming counselor?' What if the ferocious Jersey mosquitoes were more multitudinous than ever, and if the kids suffering from poison ivy – wrapped head to foot in bandages – were so numerous that the camp infirmary resembled an army field hospital? The war was over!

Camp Wo-Chi-Ca celebrated with the hour-long radio drama "On a Note of Triumph." Norman Corwin's powerful war documentary had been broadcast across the country on V-E Day. With lyrical dialogue, brilliant music, and innovative sound effects, it was immediately hailed as the finest radio program ever – an "all-time great American poem." On a splintery stage in the ramshackle barn, the Wo-Chi-Ca children gave Corwin's play a performance so stirring that the cheers surpassed the acclaim for the earlier coast to coast broadcast.

Victory has risen like a sun and moves west...

A sign that peace will come for longer than posterity can see ahead,

That man unto his fellow man shall be a friend forever...

Wo-Chi-Cans bubbled with optimism about the post-war world. Sy Friedman remembers the excitement over nuclear fission: he and his bunkmates imagined that atomic energy would provide free electricity to the whole world. Poverty and war would be obsolete under the rule of the United Nations. Everyone would live in racial harmony and peaceful labor. Campers would grow up to be counselors and counselors would marry and raise a new crop of campers. Life in the city would be just like Camp in the summer – the whole world would be a Wo-Chi-Ca.

The weed of fascism has been killed at the root...

There is no plot on earth that will ever nourish it again.

Freedom flourishes...

This is our future.

This is the future we will attain!

In the post-war Forties, Wo-Chi-Ca did indeed flourish. The camp received grants from such groups as the Fresh Air Fund and the Greater New York Fund. Wo-Chi-Ca won the affection of public figures and prominent philanthropists. Jay Schiefflin, head of a large pharmaceutical company and president of the American Mission to Lepers, served on Wo-Chi-Ca's Board of Trustees. The camp was awarded tax-exempt status by the U. S. Treasury Department.

Official endorsement came also from the state of New Jersey. Its Department of Health granted Wo-Chi-Ca a Certificate of Approval: the camp met all the state sanitation requirements in food storage, in water and milk supply, dish washing, garbage and refuse disposal, septic system, and so forth...

The campers found great acceptance in New York City. The Wo-Chi-Ca Chorus sang at rallies for war relief, as well as in union halls and public schools. In winter, at the Schomburg Library, the Chorus would lead children of Harlem in Christmas carols. Performing as the American Youth Chorus, Wo-Chi-Cans sang "The House I Live In" at Madison Square Garden. Moreover, the chorus was invited to participate in the memorial for President Roosevelt in the grand ballroom of the Waldorf-Astoria Hotel. The children wrote their own narrative, weaving folk and classical songs together. They were thrilled to share the platform with singers from the Metropolitan Opera. But perhaps Wo-Chi-Ca's proudest moment came as its chorus filed onto the stage of elegant Town Hall to sing the cantata "Ballad for Americans" with soloist Paul Robeson.

Wo-Chi-Ca's hero had likewise reached the height of achievement. Each year the National Association for the Advancement of Colored People bestowed an award on "the man or woman of African descent and American citizenship who shall have made the highest achievement during the preceding year or years in any honorable field of human endeavor." In 1945 the winner of that prestigious Spingarn Medal was Paul Robeson.

The previous year, twelve thousand New Yorkers had crowded inside the Park Avenue Armory to celebrate Robeson's forty-sixth birthday. Another four thousand were turned away for lack of space. The Duke Ellington and Count Basie orchestras performed, as well as artists Mary Lou Williams, Mildred Baily and Jimmy Durante. Congratulatory telegrams arrived from Andrei Gromyko, Vice President Henry Wallace, Theodore Dreiser, Pearl Buck, Rockwell Kent, Eugene Ormandy, Charles Boyer, Edward G. Robinson, Lillian Hellman, Oscar Hammerstein II, Babe Ruth... In her telegram, Mary McLeod Bethune called Paul Robeson "the tallest tree in our forest."

The audience would not allow Robeson to sing. "Save your voice, Paul!" they chanted, for well they knew that he played seven shows a week on Broadway. Setting a record for a Shakespeare play on the Great White Way, the Robeson *Othello* ran for 296 performances. When at last it closed, Robeson took *Othello* on a nine-month tour of the country, appearing in forty-five cities in seventeen states. So bright did Robeson's star shine in the mid-Forties that The American Magazine entitled its feature on Paul, "America's No. 1 Negro."

During this period Robeson took an active part in the struggle to desegregate major league baseball. Additionally, he toiled almost to exhaustion to re-elect President Roosevelt. Paul also campaigned strenuously for his close friend Ben Davis, Jr., a Black Communist who ran for the New York City Council in 1944. Two weeks before the election, pianist Teddy Wilson organized a Victory Rally at which Robeson contributed a scene from *Othello*. He shared the stage with other Black notables such as Coleman Hawkins, Hazel Scott, Billie Holiday, Ella

Fitzgerald, and Wo-Chi-Ca dance instructor Pearl Primus. Two weeks later they celebrated the Davis election with an all-night party in Harlem. It looked as if progressive ideas were really finding a foothold in America.

Wo-Chi-Cans too felt a great deal of confidence during this period. The camp was so popular that its list of children awaiting spaces often equaled the number of kids already bouncing on their cots. To house more children, Vaino Hill, Finnish carpenter and winter caretaker had constructed – with the help of many campers and counselors – a splendid new bunkhouse for juniors. This three-room log cabin eased the housing shortage somewhat.

The Mess Hall managed to feed all the campers and numerous visitors, but only by running double shifts for every meal. When everybody gathered for social programs, however, overcrowding became acute. In the shabby old barn, children had to perch on windowsills and sit cross-legged on the splintery floor. A larger recreation hall was sorely needed.

Parents and friends of Wo-Chi-Ca organized a series of benefit concerts featuring either Paul Robeson or fine young baritone Kenneth Spencer. They raised sufficient funds to erect a shiny new Quonset hut. Its stage could hold both a chorus and dance group, and with benches pushed against the wall, the smooth wooden floor was large enough for two hundred square dancers. On July 28, 1948, in the presence of Wo-Chi-Ca's hero himself, the new recreation hall – the Paul Robeson Playhouse – was dedicated.

Paul Robeson
Playhouse Dedication July 28, 1948
Let this be a place for workers' children to dance and sing.

dedication

It stands majestic, straight and
      tall.
On firm foundations it is built.
It symbolizes big hearted Paul
Whose spirit will never wilt.

Like the courage of the Negro
      people
His great will shall never fall.
His spirit has been captured
      by
The Robeson Recreation Hall.
      Laurel Field — Age 12

A substantial milestone in the development of the beloved camp! Would Wo-Chi-Cans be justified if on that sunlit day they imagined a straight smooth road on which Progress advanced toward a boundless horizon? Yes. But unhappily, even as the last strip of galvanized steel was nailed in place on the Quonset hut, forces already in motion would – in two years' time – shake the Paul Robeson Playhouse and the entire camp to their very foundations.

Major quakes, in fact, had jolted the political landscape even prior to the war's end. At the death of Franklin Roosevelt just before VE Day, and with the ascension of Harry Truman to the presidency, the country arrived at a crucial turning point. But who, at that fork in the road, could foresee that the new path would lurch so drastically to the right? The new president did not trust the New Dealers inherited from FDR. "Crackpots and the lunatic fringe," Truman called them, and quickly replaced them with his cronies. 'Liberal' and 'progressive' were designations Truman disliked; he preferred "Reds, phonies and parlor pinks." Members of the American Communist Party he considered a "despicable minority."

On March 25, 1947, Truman declared war on the Left. His Executive Order 9835 authorized the search for "disloyal persons" in the government. A Loyalty Board would scrutinize the ideas, opinions, and associations of federal employees. Charges of disloyalty would be made in secrecy; workers would not be permitted to confront their accusers; there would be neither judge nor jury.

What's more, Executive Order 9835 established an 'Attorney General's List of Subversive Organizations.' In July of 1948, even as Wo-Chi-Cans rejoiced in the dedication of their Paul Robeson Playhouse, one hundred ten organizations had already been listed. The infamous index did not include Wo-Chi-Ca, but the placement on this 'subversive' list of an organization very close to Wo-Chi-Ca – the IWO – would in time do just as much to bring about the camp's demise.

Truman's anti-Communism abroad mirrored his malice toward the Left at home. While at the Potsdam Conference in July of 1945, he received word that the atomic bomb – under feverish construction by American scientists – could be ready to fire off in a couple of weeks. This would enable the U.S. to avoid a costly invasion of the Japanese mainland. America could defeat Japan without Soviet military aid, thus keeping the Russians out of Asia. Truman therefore assumed an aggressive stance toward Stalin, alluding to a secret and unimaginably powerful weapon. With the weight of this imminent atomic bomb as leverage, Truman forced Stalin out of reparation agreements made with Roosevelt at Yalta only four months earlier. Two weeks later, in the mushroom clouds above Hiroshima and Nagasaki, many saw not only an end to the hot war, but a blunt challenge to the Soviet Union – the beginning of a new, anti-Communist Cold War.

The initial conflict in this war was anything but cold. In Greece, to prevent the highly popular Left from taking power, Britain moved in with armed force. Its

40,000 troops seized weapons from partisans, installed a right-wing regime, and ignited a ferocious civil war.

Following Churchill's "Iron Curtain" speech in 1946 imploring Truman for aid, the U.S. Congress provided 400 million dollars. Artillery, dive-bombers, napalm – along with two hundred fifty American army 'advisors' – all poured into the Cradle of Democracy to defeat Communism in Greece. But did all of America sing the praises of the new "Truman Doctrine?" Not quite, for in outposts such as little Camp Wo-Chi-Ca in New Jersey, children chanted the refrain of the Greek partisans:

La-o-kra-ti-a kay o-hi vasilya

Power to the people and not the king!

During the war, movies sympathetic to the Soviets could be seen not only at Camp, but in the city. As long as the Soviet Union was 'our gallant ally,' the major movie houses were happy to show *Mission to Moscow, Song of Russia* and the camp favorite, *North Star*.

But the Cold War whipped a frigid wind through the back lots of Hollywood and rattled the glass doors of studio executives. The House Un-American Activities Committee blew into town with subpoena power. Refusing to answer questions about their political beliefs or those of their colleagues, the prominent directors and screenwriters known as the Hollywood Ten were charged with contempt of Congress and imprisoned. Other 'uncooperative witnesses' found themselves on an unofficial blacklist: they could no longer work in Hollywood. Already in 1948, the 'hot topic' in films, according to Variety, was anti-Communism. And before the Red Scare subsided, at least fifty-five anti-Communist films had been churned out – *The Red Menace, My Son John, I Married a Communist*....

Perhaps the best known is *I Was A Communist for the FBI*. It first appeared as a serial in the Saturday Evening Post, then as a radio series before it was made into a film in 1951. The following year John Wayne was a tough *Big Jim McClain*, breaking up – with his fists – a Communist attempt to take over the labor move-ment in Hawaii. Also popular was the saga of informer Herbert Philbrick: *I Led Three Lives* was serialized in five hundred newspapers and dramatized on televi-sion as well. Comic books in the millions left children shuddering at the prospect of a Russian conquest of the United States and the enslavement of its people.

The assault against Communist ideas in America was more than a culture war, more even than a purge of leftists from government offices and college campuses. In the fall of 1948 the war against Communism took prisoners. The Truman Administration turned to the Alien Registration Act of 1940. With this law, known as the Smith Act, it arrested and brought to trial eleven top officers of the Communist Party.

The Smith Act made it a federal crime to advocate the overthrow of the government by force and violence. The Communist leaders were charged not with overt acts, not with employing violence to take over the country, but with holding Marxist beliefs and conspiring to teach them. More than one hundred forty prominent Communists were indicted over the next nine years, quite a number of them Wo-Chi-Ca parents. In fact, of the original group of eleven Smith Act prisoners, four were parents of Wo-Chi-Ca children.

In the face of this hostility bordering on hysteria, Camp Wo-Chi-Ca stood as a bastion of safety and security. Here, children could plainly see that while their mothers, fathers and counselors were progressives and Communists, they were not evil. Here, young campers could sing "Oh, Freedom," "Joe Hill," and "Avanti

Populo." A stay at Wo-Chi-Ca was a respite from the paranoia of the city. For two precious weeks, children of progressive parents were free to be themselves: they could admire Reds and not hate and fear them as did their friends back home in their neighborhoods and schools.

During this grim period many Wo-Chi-Ca parents were active in unions, fighting the anti-Communism threatening to destroy the labor movement. The Taft-Hartley Bill passed by Congress in 1947 required that all union officers sign an affidavit affirming they were not members of the Communist Party. Militant unions such as the Furriers, Office Workers, and the Electrical Workers held firm, refusing to repudiate their radical leaders. But these were the very unions that gave the most support to Camp Wo-Chi-Ca. Unavoidably, their aid fell off as they became increasingly embroiled in legal and financial emergencies.

Also enmeshed in the sweeping net of the Red Scare was the long-time champion of Wo-Chi-Ca, the International Workers Order. The IWO was no ordinary insurance company. It did not hire salespeople, but relied on its members to enroll others. It offered low-cost insurance premiums to working class people, charging the same rates for those working behind office desks or down in coal mines. Men and women paid the same premium, and unlike other insurance companies, the color of one's skin did not matter. The IWO had its own panel of doctors who provided medical care at charges one quarter of the market rate. Members could borrow money at minimal interest, and twenty dollars would buy a burial plot in an IWO cemetery. No wonder it was the fastest growing fraternal insurance company in the country. In fact, with a membership of 160,000, the IWO was the largest left-wing organization ever in America.

In addition to its non-profit insurance activities, the IWO spoke out on political issues. It supported the rights of the foreign-born; it opposed discrimination of Negroes and fought against lynching. On these and on many other issues, the IWO took a stand similar to that of the Communist Party – why, some of its officers were members of the Party! This was sufficient, in the Truman era, to stigmatize the IWO as a seditious and treasonous organization.

IWO members over the years had raised funds for Camp Wo-Chi-Ca through rummage sales and concerts. IWO officers accepted dollars and dimes from rank-and-file members, passing them along to Camp; IWO lodges awarded scholarships to children. At least once every summer, an official IWO delegation with as many as fifty people went up to Wo-Chi-Ca to examine camp operations, visiting their own children in the bargain. Counselors helped their campers to organize IWO Junior Clubs that would meet in the City: the Wo-Chi-Ca spirit was not for a summer alone but for all year. The bond between the IWO and Wo-Chi-Ca was as intimate as parent and child. Certainly, IWO people had functioned as godparents to the infant Wo-Chi-Ca when, in the depths of the Depression, a failing farm was purchased from its left-wing owner and nurtured into a flourishing camp.

In 1932, a young man named Jerry Trauber became junior director of the IWO. He traveled to New Jersey year after year, bringing with him new staff for Camp recruited from the ranks of the IWO Juniors. As a long-time leader of the IWO, Jerry, in 1951, hurried up to the office of Vito Marcantonio, U. S. Congressman and IWO vice-president. A verdict had just been announced: Judge Greenberg ruled against the IWO – the insurance company was to be liquidated on the grounds that most of its officers were members of the Communist Party.

Previously, an insurance company could be dissolved only for fraud, insolvency, or financial hazard. In this unprecedented case, an insurance company would be dismantled on the grounds that it constituted a political hazard to its membership. The government, in the two-year trial, called a series of highly paid witnesses. Among them was Louis Budenz, a man Howard Fast dubbed the "prince of all stool pigeons, renegades, and professional witnesses... a liar." Budenz testified that IWO President Rockwell Kent was a Communist.

In sunnier days Rockwell Kent had strolled Wo-Chi-Ca's friendly grounds, talking with campers about art. Now, in a cold courtroom in Manhattan's Foley Square – opposite a hostile lawyer and judge – Kent sat and listened to testimony alleging that the IWO was run by and for the Communist Party. Truman's Executive Order 9835 had let loose a Wreck-the-Reds demolition crew that fell upon a fully solvent company, a people's house of insurance, and razed it to the ground. With the fall of the International Workers Order, the sturdiest pillar supporting Camp Wo-Chi-Ca collapsed.

Yes, on that joyous day in July of 1948 when the Paul Robeson Playhouse was dedicated, the earth trembled silently under Wo-Chi-Ca, for the little camp was precariously perched on a dangerous fault. Many frightening post-war tremors had already shaken the ground, yet no one could quite foresee Wo-Chi-Ca's rapid slide into ruin.

Wo-Chi-Ca in 1948 was still a confident, dynamic place. True, political events were unsettling. In August, Alger Hiss was accused of operating as a Communist spy in the State Department. But also in August a new people's party arose to challenge the Red Scare, the Smith Act, the Cold War, Taft-Hartley – the entire Truman Doctrine. A group of campers went down to Philadelphia to take part in the Progressive Party convention. From high in the upper seats of the auditorium, the Wo-Chi-Cans proudly beheld their hero. **"Paul, Paul!"** they called out – **"Wo-Chi-Ca, Wo-Chi-Ca!"** But their voices were drowned in the roar of **"ROBESON FOR VICE PRESIDENT!"** Robeson, as expected, declined, and the more than 3,000 cheering delegates went on to nominate Senator Glen Taylor for vice president and Henry Wallace for president.

Back to Camp the Wo-Chi-Cans came, wearing "Wallace for President" buttons and singing all the new campaign songs. The most popular songs on the radio that summer were "Mañana" and "I'm Looking Over a Four Leaf Clover." Also in the top ten was "On A Slow Boat to China," at the very time the Chinese People's Army moved swiftly to victory over Chiang Kai Chek. Leading the Wo-Chi-Ca hit parade, however, were "Chee Lai" and "The Battle Hymn of 1948."

> **There's a fresh breeze blowing**
> **All across this mighty land,**
> **And it sings of peace and progress**
> **And prosperity at hand,**
> **With security and plenty**
> **For the people to command**
> **FOR THE PEOPLE'S MARCH IS ON!**
>
> **Glory, glory, hallelujah**
> **FOR THE PEOPLE'S MARCH IS ON.**

But the peoples' march stalled as both Democrats and Republicans threw charges of Communist domination at the Progressives. Voters took fright and barely a million cast their ballots for Henry Wallace. Still, there were plenty of causes, other battles to be fought. At the top of the list was the struggle to end discrimination, to stop lynching.

Wo-Chi-Ca's stand against racism had long earned the respect of the Black community in Harlem. Camp's percentage of Black staff members remained high, and Wo-Chi-Ca's outreach programs brought more and more Black children to the New Jersey countryside. Most were street-smart kids from the big city, but the eventful summer of 1948 brought notable exceptions: children from the Deep South.

One, already seventeen years old, was Charles Ingram from Georgia. His mother, sharecropper Rosa Lee Ingram – along with two older sons Wallace and Sammy – was charged with the murder of her white landlord who had sexually assaulted her. An all-white jury condemned all three to death. In the middle of the struggle to save his mother and two brothers, Charles was invited to come up to Camp Wo-Chi-Ca. At first guarded and unsmiling, Charles soon responded to the genuine laughter and generous offers of friendship enveloping him. With counselors-in-training, he cleared ground and hauled stones for the Paul Robeson Amphitheater.

That same summer, from Mississippi, came two of the children of Willie McGee. Younger than Charles, they also had a parent sentenced to death. Their father was accused of the rape of a white woman in spite of the fact that – as proved by his lawyer Bella Abzug – the two had had a sexual relationship for three years. Racial antagonism ran so high that homes in the North were provided for the McGee children during the lengthy trial and three appeals. That summer,

Adolphus and Marjorie McGee found Wo-Chi-Ca a happy and secure shelter.

A nation-wide protest led by the Civil Rights Congress forced the Georgia Supreme Court to commute the Ingrams' sentences to life in prison. But even a worldwide protest did not win such a stay of execution for Willie McGee: he was electrocuted by the state of Mississippi. Paul Robeson, who went so far as to approach the United Nations on behalf of Willie McGee, called his execution a "legal lynching."

What of "illegal lynching" – mob action without even the fig leaf of legal sanction? Black servicemen coming home from the war expected to share in that precious democracy they had fought for overseas. Instead, they found their wartime dreams of equality shattered. Blacks trying to vote or daring to ask for equal pay were met with violence unmatched since Reconstruction days. Between June 1945 and September 1946, fifty-six Black men were lynched. A revived Ku Klux Klan terrorized Black communities and burned crosses as far north as New Jersey.

Again, Paul Robeson spoke out passionately: "This swelling wave of lynch murders and mob assaults against Negro men and women represents the ultimate limit of bestial brutality to which the enemies of democracy, be they German-Nazis or American Ku Kluxers, are ready to go in imposing their will. Are we going to give our America over to the Eastlands, Rankins and Bilbos? If not, then stop the lynchers! What about it, President Truman? Why have you failed to speak out against this evil?"

Leading a delegation to the White House, Robeson marched into Truman's office to urge the government to make lynching a federal crime. After only a few sentences, Truman interrupted Robeson's reading of a petition and asserted that the time was not right politically to pass a federal law. In anger and frustration, Robeson declared that if the government refused to defend its Black citizens against murder, Blacks would have to defend themselves. Truman abruptly terminated the meeting. Only two weeks later, the California Joint Fact-finding Committee on Un-American Activities subpoenaed Paul Robeson to inquire if he were a Communist.

Robeson now turned his back on the glittering concert hall to confront racism full-time. He risked his life in the South campaigning for Henry Wallace. For two years he toured the country, singing at union meetings and civil rights rallies, speaking at colleges, walking picket lines.

Returning to the stage, Robeson found the doors of concert halls shut against him. With eighty-five appearances canceled, Robeson decided on a four-month tour of Europe. He sang in Copenhagen and addressed a mass meeting in Oslo, both under auspices of the Communist newspapers of those countries. In Czechoslovakia the highest levels of government honored Robeson with grand receptions. Polish audiences gave him standing ovations, parading with armfuls of flowers.

In the midst of his tour, Paul Robeson attended the World Peace Congress in Paris. Distinguished delegates from fifty countries included artist Pablo Picasso, poet Louis Aragon, atomic scientist Frederic Joliet-Curie, and scholar W.E.B. DuBois. The speech Robeson made to the assembly of two thousand has been called the turning point of his career.

"It is unthinkable that American Negroes would go to war on behalf of those who have oppressed us for generations against a country [the Soviet Union] which in one generation has raised our people to the full dignity of mankind." Such were the words the Associated Press transmitted around the world. Were his remarks misquoted, distorted? The question is disputed to this day. In any case, the reaction was vehement.

"Traitor," "un-American," the papers screamed – "ungrateful and disloyal to his country." Even some Negro organizations denounced the Paris speech. The NAACP had honored Robeson with its Spingarn Medal only four years earlier; now its top officers, Roy Wilkins and Walter White, condemned him. Josh White, Mary McCleod Bethune, Adam Clayton Powell, Jr. all hastened to declare "By no stretch of the imagination can Robeson speak for all Negro people."

Others rushed to his defense: "I say Paul Robeson speaks more for the real colored people," an army veteran wrote, "than the Walter Whites and Adam Powells..." No one, it seemed, could be neutral on the subject. "Paul Robeson is recognized by the great masses of the Negro people as more nearly their ideal leader than all of the Walter Whites and Roy Wilkinses in the country...."

In the Soviet Union, celebrating the 150th anniversary of Pushkin's birth, Robeson proclaimed "I was, I am, always will be a friend of the Soviet people." But Soviet society at this time was in the throes of an anti-Zionist campaign. Did Robeson attempt to locate his Jewish friends? Did he demand to see writer Itzik Feffer? We do know that Robeson had been Feffer's host back home: in 1943 the Soviet writer toured the United States as a leader of the Jewish Anti-Fascist Committee. At that time Feffer had spent a day at Wo-Chi-Ca, where excited campers cheered "Hoo, Ha, Hoo: Itzik Feffer is schon du!"

Wo-Chi-Can Dave Greenwood, the reader will recall, spoke in his memoir of "Our own beloved Paul Robeson [who] suppressed his first-hand knowledge of the arrest and persecution of the Jewish writers in the Soviet Union, including Itzik Feffer, who once visited Camp."

Did Robeson's persistent inquiries compel Soviet authorities to at last bring Feffer forth? The poet was plucked out of prison and sent up to Robeson's hotel room. By way of signs and notes Feffer informed Robeson that Jews were purged from the Leningrad Communist Party, that Jews were arrested, and in the case of actor-director Solomon Mikhoels, murdered. Such is the account.

But whose account? All attempts to verify it lead back to Martin Duberman's comprehensive biography of Paul Robeson. The painstaking Duberman himself points out in a footnote that "There are several variant versions of the meeting between Robeson and Feffer."

At his last concert in Moscow Robeson stunned the audience with a tribute to Mikhoels and Feffer: he sang "Zog Nit Kaynmal" in their honor. This was observed and documented. But the story of Robeson's meeting with Feffer was told only to his son Paul Jr., and Junior maintains he was pledged never to repeat it while his father was alive. So we are told, and so it will have to remain for now.

Robeson returned to New York for the marriage of Paul, Jr. to Marilyn Greenberg. He was incensed at the hostile racist crowds screaming at the wedding party. "I challenge this vicious system to the death," he told 4,500 people at a four-hour "Welcome Home" rally that evening in Harlem. "I'm looking for freedom – full freedom, not an inferior brand. We do not want to die in vain any more on foreign battlefields for Wall Street and the greedy supporters of domestic fascism. If we must die let it be in Mississippi or Georgia. Let it be wherever we are lynched and deprived of our rights as human beings."

Robeson pledged to defend the eleven Communist Party leaders on trial downtown. "An undesirable citizen," the Hearst Press editorialized. "It was an accident unfortunate for America that Robeson was born here."

Now the House Un-American Activities Committee moved to discredit and isolate Paul Robeson. It summoned prominent Negroes to counter Robeson's "disloyal and unpatriotic statements." Star witness Jackie Robinson characterized Robeson's Paris remarks as "silly," and insisted that Negroes did not want any help from Communists to fight discrimination. Robeson responded to HUAC in a speech to the Civil Rights Congress. "I am a radical," he told 1,200 cheering delegates. "I am going to stay one until my people are free to walk the earth."

The political storms of 1949 lashed at Robeson violently. But on one tranquil patch of ground in his home state of New Jersey, a little camp in the Schooleys Mountains accepted Robeson absolutely. As Paul drove up the road on August 17, Wo-Chi-Cans eagerly awaited the arrival of their hero.

SICKNESS PAST CURE

O
n August 17, 1949, Paul Robeson drove up the dirt road and past the wood sign. Each year he made a sojourn to his beloved Wo-Chi-Ca; this was his tenth. The big man beamed as eager children lined up to greet him. The clouds of controversy that hung over Robeson's head in the outside world dispersed: at Wo-Chi-Ca Paul walked in pure sunlight.

When Paul Robeson came there was great excitement. Everyone was pushing and screaming. I had never seen Paul before. He was tall and friendly looking, and had a broad smile. Larry Brown was with him.

We met him in front of the infirmary. He went in front of the Main House, and there was everybody trying to see him through the windows and doors.

LIDGIE FONER and LINDA JO GOLDWAY

This year's "Paul Robeson Day" was extra special, for Paul Jr. – a former Wo-Chi-Ca camper himself – had just married a Jewish girl from Brooklyn. But the racists! How terrible the campers felt about the bigots who taunted the wedding party as it left the ceremony. A number of interracial couples worked at Camp. It was disheartening to realize that even the world famous Paul Robeson and his family still encountered the same prejudice Wo-Chi-cans suffered outside the refuge of Camp.

Paul spoke tenderly of his son's marriage, of his pride in "this union of strength, this marriage of descendants of two great peoples who had survived the worst of times." He sang favorite songs – "Old Man River," "Scandalize My Name," "Freedom Is My Land." **"More, Paul, more!"** campers screamed, and Paul responded. The longer Robeson sang, the stronger his voice grew. He drew inspiration from the adoring faces around him.

In the Playhouse named for him, Paul addressed the children.

There are just a few things I want to say. I first want to thank you again for what you have given me today: that you here also recognize that the struggle is for peace, that the struggle is for abundance, that the struggle is for a decent life.

I have seen tens of thousands of youth like you all over Western and Eastern Europe and they told me to bring back to you their love and their friendship. And if there is one thing I want to leave with you today it is the sense of that strength that is all over the world. In England and in Scandinavia, in Denmark, Sweden, Norway, and in France and Italy there are millions who are for peace and for friendship and who are anti-fascist to the core.

Now I am proud to be with you here today in Wo-Chi-Ca and I guess you sort of feel that I am a little serious. I have been astonished at people not understanding what I feel about the Soviet Union. I stood in Stalingrad and I assure you, children, that the Russian people were in a spot with the Volga at their back – and they saved the world. I saw a letter from President Roosevelt which said that here in Stalingrad civilization was saved. Ten to twenty million Russians perished in that struggle, and but for their sacrifice millions of American boys might not be walking the streets today. But for a Russian soldier who died Jackie might not be playing baseball in Brooklyn; but for a Russian who died millions of Americans would not be here and I am grateful to this people that they saved perhaps my Pauli, that they turned back Fascism in their time. Now the responsibility is with us!

I am on record about what I feel but I love this America – I love you and I will fight and I will die for you but I will have nothing to do with American Fascism – nothing to do with the Ku Klux Klan. I will rest upon my constitutional right to be friends with the Soviet Union, to be friends with the Eastern Democracies, to be friends with China. I will have nothing to do with the remains of Fascism in the world. So you give me courage, give the grownups courage. Keep this understanding that you are going to build and struggle in peace for a decent world.

We won't allow this nation of ours to take us into war. You must live because you are the future. You will build a world that will make me proud. I stood here today helping you. You will help my grandchild, my great-grandchild. You will help the Negro people to walk this American earth in full dignity with you the Jewish people, with all Americans. We will take the lead. You take the lead and show the real kind of America that we can build.

I want to thank you today from the depths of my heart.

That evening, after the youngsters went to bed (not to sleep, for they were too excited for that!), Paul joined staff members in the canteen. Cyril Tyson and other Black counselors expressed concern over Jackie Robinson's recent testimony before HUAC. How could Robinson say yes, there was still anti-Negro prejudice in America, but then add "We can win our fight without the Communists and we don't want their help."

Why, it was Communist help that integrated baseball! Didn't Lester Rodney, in his sports column for the Communist *Daily Worker*, repeatedly demand an end to Jim Crow in baseball? Had not Peter V. Cacchione, Communist Councilman from Brooklyn, introduced a resolution calling for desegregation of major league baseball? Did not Paul Robeson along with Communist William Patterson, march into the office of Baseball Commissioner Landis to argue for integration? Did Jackie Robinson know what he was talking about?

Paul answered simply that he didn't understand Jackie's position, and that he planned to talk to him about it.

As Robeson left the grounds the next morning, everyone – kids, cooks, counselors – ran to the gate to wave goodbye. "So long, Paul," they called out, "see you next summer!" As they watched him drive away no one could foresee that the sun would never again shine on Paul Robeson at Wo-Chi-Ca. A number of kids would see Paul elsewhere in just a few days. On August 27 their parents would be taking them to hear him give a concert in Peekskill, New York.

In the Hudson Valley, some forty miles north of the Bronx, Peekskill was the anti-union company town, while the surrounding countryside was where New York City progressives – many of them Jewish – spent their summers. With the Cold War, the town's resentment of these 'Communist outsiders' intensified.

The American Legion picketed the first Robeson concert in 1946, and in both '47 and '48 there had been protests and threats. The 1949 concert was to be a benefit for the Harlem chapter of the Civil Rights Congress. That militant organization had just won a new trial for the Trenton Six, Black men unjustly convicted of murdering a shopkeeper. Paul Robeson was prominent in the struggle to free the Trenton Six.

Several days before the Robeson concert, the *Peekskill Evening Star*, the Chamber of Commerce and the American Legion called for pickets and demonstrations. So alarming did the atmosphere become that eleven Peekskill residents sent telegrams to the New York State Attorney General and the County District Attorney. These officials were urged to investigate the inflammatory statements and to "take all necessary measures to guarantee that the concert, the artists, the sponsors and guests are fully protected in the peaceful enjoyment of their civil liberties."

At 6 P.M. on the evening of August 27, an organizing group of forty-two, with writer Howard Fast among them, arrived at the concert site. Approaching the main entrance, they observed a crowd of several hundred men. Many wore army uniforms or the blue hats of the American Legion. Among their forty or fifty vehicles were fire engines bedecked with American flags. Fast's group drove into the grounds and parked near the bandstand.

Very soon word arrived that "fascists" had barricaded the entrance with boulders and a Legion truck. Fascist is the term Howard Fast employs repeatedly. Judging by the words and actions of the horde, who would argue with the great writer?

"We're Hitler's boys," hundreds shouted drunkenly as they invaded the concert grounds. **"We're out to finish his job!"** Screaming obscenities, they attacked the organizers with a barrage of rocks – some as large as grapefruits. **"None of you leave here alive!"** Wielding torn-up fence rails, they smashed the stage. They grabbed pamphlets, books and music sheets, tore up wooden folding chairs and built a huge bonfire. **"We're going to get Robeson!"**

The mob overturned fourteen cars, pushing them over an embankment. At 8 P.M. the attackers, now close to a thousand, burned a twelve-foot cross near the concert grounds. Standing by and observing the entire onslaught were three local sheriffs and three agents from the Justice Department. They did nothing.

From the beginning, the defenders had made calls to the police pleading for help. In four hours no law enforcement appeared. Finally at 10 P.M. the state police arrived and dispersed the crowd. In spite of the fact that all forty-two committee members were injured – thirteen requiring medical aid – the police arrested no one. Needless to say, the concert was canceled.

Wo-Chi-Can Issar Smith was one of the forty-two in the Howard Fast group.

My family and I were visiting friends at Camp Croton, a left-wing bungalow colony in the area. I was driven to the concert venue with my cousin June early enough to get into the actual grounds.

In a short while, the grounds became completely surrounded by a mob, preventing any further entrance or exit. As the situation grew uglier by the moment, Howard Fast, who was one of the early attendees, organized a defense line with the forty-two men who were there.

We lined up in seven rows of six to block the main access road descending to the concert grounds – hopefully to protect the approximately fifty women and children who were huddled below. I, being fifteen or sixteen years old, was in the last of the seven rows. I remember being very scared at the unruly mob directly facing us and admiring the bravery of Howard Fast as he led us, and especially when he spoke to a police officer who was at the scene. Fast was holding a stone and when the policeman – there supposedly to maintain law and order – told him to drop it, Fast replied "I will when you disperse the mob and allow the trapped people to leave unharmed." Of course, no such thing happened and I then remember the line being broken and me running wildly down the road with 'patriotic Americans' running all around me. I recall the mob burning chairs around us as we pressed close together. I do not remember how we finally got out and how I got back to Camp Croton. My mother was frantic with uncertainty as to my fate. There was an article in the **New York Daily News** *a few days later and I was in the photograph taken from behind the last defense row.*

The very next day after this assault, 1,500 citizens – representing thirty nearby communities – met to form the Westchester Committee for Law and Order. They invited Paul Robeson back to Peekskill with a proclamation: "We refuse to abandon any sections of the United States to organized hoodlums. Our freedom and civil rights are at stake."

Robeson vowed to return, to sing "wherever people want me to sing." At a Harlem press conference he declared, "My people and I won't be frightened by cross burning in Peekskill or anywhere else." The Civil Rights Congress scheduled another concert for the following week, on Sunday, September 4 – the day before Labor Day. The Congress put out a call for guards to protect Robeson and prevent a recurrence of violence.

Wo-Chi-Cans were stunned by the outrage in Peekskill, even more so that such violence was meant for their friend Paul Robeson who had enjoyed so much affection at Camp just ten days earlier. What could they do? Camp would be closing for the season the very day after the September 4 concert. Wouldn't it be okay for some staff members to leave early to see what they could do in Peekskill? Would there be more trouble? Would the police do their duty this time? If not, would violence be justified in self-defense? Disturbing questions for Wo-Chi-Cans such as seventeen-year-old counselor and Political Action Director, Mark Solomon.

With such a fascist frenzy, the camp directors felt increasing vulnerability and mandated that we all stay on hand till the very end. That meant that nobody should think about going to the second concert on Sept 4. (Camp was closing on the 5th.) But Ben and a few others quietly loaded some baseball bats in a car and took off for Peekskill. We all waited tensely for their return. Butch [camp director] asked me angrily how I viewed the reckless behavior of Ben and the group. With equal anger, if not with careful thought, I responded "They should be commended!"

MARK SOLOMON

Union members, college students, civil rights workers – Black and white – poured into Peekskill. Two thousand five hundred formed a human wall around the concert grounds. One of these bodyguards was Wo-Chi-Can Sol Spector. In a tight protective circle around Robeson – pledged to defend Paul with their lives – stood workers in their union caps as well as war veterans in uniform. All knew that Robeson, only the night before, had been twice hung in effigy. Now, in the bright sun, the bodyguards could see the glint of guns on the ridge overlooking the stage. Security people had already flushed out two sniper nests of 'patriots' holding telescopic rifles.

The concert, despite great tension, proceeded without incident. Sitting in the hot sun for two hours, 25,000 men, women and children heard pianists Ray Lev and Leonid Hambro perform music of Bach, Chopin, Lizst, Mozart and Verdi. Pete Seeger followed on guitar and banjo. Paul Robeson then sang, accompanied by Larry Brown at the piano. Paul's final song, "Old Man River," brought the audience to its feet and the concert to a close.

Robeson was hurried away in a convoy of cars, their windows covered with blankets. The audience moved toward their cars and buses.

Now every departing vehicle was forced to drive through a narrow four-mile stretch of road under a vicious hail of rocks. Smashed windows, flying glass, cut and bloodied people! The attackers pushed cars over cliffs; they dragged out the occupants and beat them. **"Get going, you red bastard! Go back to Jew town!"** Jeering women shrieked **"Commies, Jew bastards!"** while enraged men yelled **"White Niggers – We'll kill you!"** Where were the police and state troopers during all this? Stopping cars, dragging people out, beating them with billyclubs – some even drunkenly throwing rocks along with the local citizens. The mob injured over two hundred people. Union leader Irving Potash suffered a skull fracture and lost the sight of one eye.

> **When the music was all over, we started to go home.**
> **We did not know the trouble and the pain that was to**
>   **come.**
> **We got into our buses and drove out through the gate,**
> **And saw the gangster police, their faces filled with**
>   **hate.**
> **And without any warning, the rocks began to come,**
> **The cops and troopers laughed to see the damage that**
>   **was done.**
> **They ran us through the gauntlet, to their everlasting**
>   **shame.**
> **And the cowards there attacked us; their nation knew**
>   **their shame.**
>   **"Hold the Line" by the Weavers**

Ronnie Gilbert and Fred Hellerman, both members of the Weavers, wrote the words to "Hold the Line" with Pete Seeger and Lee Hayes, their partners in the singing quartet. All four were witnesses to the Peekskill horrors. Ronnie and Fred had been campers and counselors at Wo-Chi-Ca. Irwin Silber and many other Wo-Chi-Cans also experienced the nightmare. Again, Issar Smith:

I went to the second concert by bus with my brother Ed, and with the Furriers Joint Council. Frankly, I was not too thrilled with going, as the preceding experience had a strong effect on me. But it was supportive having an older brother there. The concert with Paul singing while surrounded by security was thrilling and scary at the same time. Also harrowing was the gauntlet we faced as we exited the concert grounds through a narrow road surrounded by the rock-throwing mob as the cops looked on and laughed. "WAKE UP, AMERICA, PEEKSKILL DID" was the slogan on the posters held up as we passed. It was chilling to see the face of incipient fascism.

The group that had gone from Wo-Chi-Ca to Peekskill returned late that evening, their car miraculously intact. They found the counselors gathered around a radio listening to a recording made at the riot scene. Not only local hoodlums battering people but the police themselves beating Negro men. All this not in the South, but an hour from New York City! They listened in stunned silence.

I was at Camp in 1949 and I remember a girl crying. She heard about the riot and was worried about her parents who went to the concert.
SERGE KANEVSKY

Time magazine described the Peekskill riots as examples of "misguided patriotism and senseless hooliganism." The Daily Worker termed it the onset of fascism in America.

The next morning, Camp closed for the season. It was a hushed group of young Wo-Chi-Cans on the buses going into New York on Labor Day 1949. Many were returning home to parents who had been at Peekskill.

Nationwide radio broadcasts the next few days reported cross burnings in six locations in Tallahasse, Florida. Each cross bore a sign that read "We protest Paul Robeson and Communism." Fifteen unmasked Klansmen in Birmingham, Alabama burned a cross with two effigies, one labeled **"PAUL ROBESON,"** the other bearing a large question mark. In the Bronx, two hundred 'Christians' attacked a Methodist Church meeting called to protest the Peekskill violence; they stoned the buses and burned a Negro in effigy.

And what of the neighbors around Camp Wo-Chi-Ca in New Jersey – were they not very much like the Peekskill people in New York? What would they do when they found out that an honored annual guest at that 'Indian camp' outside of Califon was none other than Paul Robeson, "the Red Nigger?"

I recall riding on the back of a bobtail truck into Hackettstown and swimming in the river there. Whenever we traveled we made a mark – this wonderful mixture of kids from different ethnic and racial backgrounds, a mixture the local folks did not seem aware of before our arrival.

NED PEARLSTEIN

Yes, even before Peekskill, flabbergasted locals would stare at the Wo-Chi-Cans coming into town. If only that were all! But frequently, the reaction to these black and white campers together would run to the baleful glare and even the derisive remark.

Jack Broitman reports "There was ill-concealed hostility when we counselors went into town on our day off." His friend Irwin Watson, a Black counselor, confided to Jack that the first time he felt bigotry was on one of the excursions to Hackettstown.

African-American counselors going three miles into Califon darn well knew they would not be getting a haircut at the town barbershop. But surely they might expect to buy a beer at the roadside tavern! No, maintains Barbara Lewin Spector in a story almost legendary.

One night, a group of staffers walked to a nearby tavern not far from Camp for some beer. At least one in the group was Black. The group sensed hostility as they crowded in amongst the locals. They ordered beers and sat quietly.

When the Black staffer finished his glass, the barman angrily snatched it up and threw it into the tavern fireplace. The other staff people calmly finished their beers, and then, in unison, threw all their glasses into the fireplace.

"Hey, what's the idea?" shouted the barman. "Oh," replied the staff people, "we thought that smashing your empty glass was the custom around here." They walked out in dignified silence.

More than fifty years later a Black camper remembers with anguish his forced departure from Camp.

My last summer at camp was in 1946 when I was sixteen. We were told not to stray off camp property because some of the neighboring farmers had complained about campers going on their land.

One afternoon I strayed off the camp grounds because I saw a beautiful multicolored piece of corn lying on the ground. It was so unusual in color that I brought it back to my bunk to show what I had found.

On the following Sunday my mother came to visit me and that's when I was informed that I had to leave. I was so upset, I just couldn't believe it, that after ten years Butch and Matt, two men that I loved and admired, would do this to me. It really broke my heart.

TOMMY WARNER

For over half a century, Tommy did not know why he was expelled from Wo-Chi-Ca. He'd spent all his summers at Camp, playing the bugle for taps and reveille. True, he had been somewhat notorious at Camp; he often got away with breaking rules by flashing his winning smile and begging forgiveness. It was not until the Wo-Chi-Ca reunion in the year 2000 when Tommy learned that the corn incident had led to racist threats against his life. The camp directors had been truly frightened. The Klan was active even in New Jersey. So, six days before the season closed, Tommy Warner was sent home. His mother never told him why. No one but the directors and the camp secretary, Eve Levine (the co-author's mother) knew the true story.

When I went to Cornell in 1948, I wore the Wo-Chi-Ca T-shirt to gym class. An Arkansas good ol' boy in my class pointed to the Black figure and said, "Who's that, your brother?" I said, "What if it were?" And he said, "You been seein' too many movies." Which reminds me that camp's interracial character was extraordinary for the time, and, to many outsiders, its most disturbing characteristic.

DAVE GREENWOOD

Racism, the fatal defect in American society; anti-Communism, America's official obsession – twin evils that would combine to destroy New Jersey's little Camp Wo-Chi-Ca.

The past two summers, Wo-Chi-Ca had employed a single night watchman. Now after Peekskill, it looked as if a small army would be needed. An army was indeed deployed that season, but on the other side of the world. An American army was fighting Communism in Korea at the time Camp opened for the 1950 season. How difficult that summer would be!

The year was 1950. It was the summer I slept with a broom next to my bed in case I had to ward off intruders. Days had passed since we were awakened by loud shouts followed by the frightful sounds of crashing objects and breaking glass. Roz, our counselor, had soothed us by assuring us we were safe. In her calm manner, she had explained that some drunken men had gotten into the recreation hall but the police came and the situation was under control. On the following morning the whole camp gathered for a discussion of last night's incident.

We were informed that the Ku Klux Klan had headquarters nearby and had targeted our interracial camp. They had sent thugs to try to rip down the sign on the Paul Robeson Playhouse.

That morning I realized that hatred and prejudice were not confined to the South.

SHEILA NEWMAN

In the summer of 1950 Camp experienced attacks by right-wingers. Staff had to patrol at night. The call went out for volunteers. I used my two-week job vacation to work as a dishwasher in the staff's place.

MARGIE KATZ

On our day off, three of us borrowed the Austin Healy belonging to Ray Saunders, who later became an actor. There was myself, Bob Carey, who became a singer, and Al Leavitt, who became a well-known jazz drummer in Europe. We were chased for five miles by a car, and ended up wrecking the Austin in Hackettstown and having to call Butch Lasky to help us get back to camp.

In 1950 they had made threats to attack the Paul Robeson Playhouse, and so a group of us guys from Outside Maintenance took turns sleeping outside the playhouse with baseball bats. No one ever attacked.

We were more worried about their threats to disrupt our drinking water that relied on a system of sand filters to purify water from a nearby stream. We drove the jeep to the brow of a hill overlooking the stream and I was given a shotgun and told to fire over the heads of any intruders. Luckily, no one showed up. I had never fired a gun in my life.

AL KISSELOFF

In the summer of 1950 I was working in the city as a shipping clerk. But I heard about the attacks on Camp that summer, and that more hands were needed because some staff members had to be diverted to guard duty. Security arrangements were in place, including reinforcements (Bullyocken!) from Local 65, plus ancient walkie-talkies so the guards could communicate. Life went on, and Camp was still Camp, but the atmosphere was affected.

DAVE GREENWOOD

The atmosphere was affected to the point of terrible internal dissension. Fran Barrett White, newly married to artist Charles White, was a counselor at Camp in 1950.

My summer contract was barely a month old when serious racial and philosophical problems erupted.

Late one night, eight very drunken young men stormed the campground, demanding that the sign on the Paul Robeson playhouse be removed. They didn't want any "Nigger" signs hanging. Threatening to tear the camp apart, they said they would return the next day with help.

By the following morning, the dirt road outside the broken gate was lined with their friends' cars. The Board of Trustees met in the recreation room and, ignoring the pleas of the staff to remain firm in the face of racial injustice, voted to rename the building immediately. I knew we had no way of guarding ourselves or the children from the troublemakers, but I was convinced the Board's action was wrong. The real issue was not the sign but the social unity we taught and, in the past, practiced. It was devastating to me that the men and women I trusted and admired could be forced to abandon their beliefs and succumb to the threats of a gang. I asked to be released from my contract.

Reaches of the Heart, 1994

In a letter to his wife at Camp, Charles White expressed his outrage over the decision to remove the Robeson sign.

The basis of their demand was the fundamental basis of fascism and racism. Those hoodlums so much as said "Remove Negroes from your camp and we'll leave you alone." As you said, they weren't attacking Paul Robeson. It was much more than that.

When the Board removed the sign, they betrayed everything the Negro people risk their lives for daily. In that one gesture, they left every child in that camp unprotected. They compromised on an issue there can be no reason or excuse for compromise. They said, in an overt action, that the camp was only for Negro-white unity when it's safe...

An excruciating dilemma: on the one hand camp directors were haunted by the horrors of Peekskill – by the real possibility of a 'Peekskill' right on their own grounds. But to take down the Paul Robeson sign from the Playhouse – the enormity of that capitulation! Their Paul, their hero, and the Playhouse dedicated to him only two years ago... What terrible times were these that put people in such a painful and tragic predicament?

How were the children affected? A poignant letter from the young campers reflects their feelings.

August 21, 1950

Dear Paul,

We are having a Paul Robeson Day this year. We will miss you, Paul.

You are a symbol of what we Wo-Chi-Cans want to accomplish in our lives. You have done so much for all peoples, and yet you don't even have the right to travel here or abroad. We were even forced to remove your name from our playhouse; children are without defense from attack by vicious hoodlums. We did it so that our camp could stay alive and shout the meaning your name has for us in our program.

Our experiences in Camp Wo-Chi-Ca have helped us to understand the necessity of fighting for Negro-white unity wherever we go. If that unity is ever threatened, we campers will take a firm stand. We will not retreat.

We are having a Paul Robeson Day at camp without you this time. But we are going to have a Paul Robeson Olympics. We are going to sing your songs and play your records just as though you were with us.

If you could spare the time, would you send a recording of your message to us? If you can't spare the time, we will understand.

We know you are leading the fight for peace. As young people, we demand the right to live in a secure world. We want to tell our children about Paul Robeson Day.

Sincerely,   Paul Robeson Day
Committee of Group D

Did the camp directors ask Robeson not to come up in the summer of 1950? Or did Robeson himself decide it would be better not to visit? In any case, uncompromising security was now of utmost importance in every Wo-Chi-Ca deliberation.

A lamentable example involved two young campers, Danny Green and his sister Josie. Attempting to board the Wo-Chi-Ca bus departing Washington Square, they were prevented. Their father Gil Green was one of the eleven Communist leaders convicted under the Smith Act. After the Court denied their appeal and ordered them to report to prison, Gil Green and three others chose to go underground, becoming 'fugitives from justice.' Camp directors, fearing the FBI might come to Wo-Chi-Ca to inquire about Gil Green, would not permit his children to attend camp.

My sister and I were barred from Camp after my Dad jumped bail and went underground in 1951. The reason given was the "safety" of the others given the hostility of the community around Camp. As I remember, the year before, Paul Robeson was prevented from coming to Camp on similar grounds.

DAN GREEN

Safety and security! So tyrannical was the time that for safety and security Wo-Chi-Cans were forced to surrender – one by one – cherished ideals and principles. The removal of the Robeson sign over the Playhouse, the cancellation of the annual Robeson visit, the prevention of two youngsters from boarding the camp bus...

The time came when even to send a post card home might endanger safety and security.

After China entered the Korean War and drove America's armies back to the 38th parallel, I sent my parents a postcard that contained a camp political joke: "The Americans are advancing in Korea. Backwards!" The postcard was intercepted by my counselor, who called me aside to lecture me. The FBI read the mail, he said, and my thoughtlessness would endanger not only my parents, but the camp itself.

DAVID HOROWITZ

Did this counselor act out of paranoia? Or did Wo-Chi-Cans have more than sufficient reason for the drastic steps they took? Drunken hoodlums did invade Camp. Threats of cross burning are remembered to this day. John Vago writes of "attacks on Wo-Chi-Ca, including serious vandalism and sabotage." David Horowitz remembers that around Camp there was "a hostility so intense that armed guards had to be stationed along its perimeter." Recalls Rima Glaser: "We had to hire off-duty prison guards to patrol the grounds at night."

And the Camp's mail: did the FBI read it? Did that agency really spy on little kids, reading the postcards they sent home to their parents? Certainly the anti-Communism of the U.S. Government had grown to monstrous proportions. In April of 1951, Julius and Ethel Rosenberg were sentenced to death for "conspiring to commit espionage." Who could doubt that the FBI would spy on a camp admitting children of Communists and which would have sheltered the Rosenberg children too, Michael and Robert, had they been old enough to attend?

Wo-Chi-Ca was still a fun-filled camp where music echoed through the tents. But clouds of caution hung over the camp all day, and armed guards came out at night. The PAUL ROBESON sign no longer adorned the Playhouse, and Paul himself did not visit. Dan and Josie Green were not in Camp, and those who were had to be careful what they wrote. How far would Wo-Chi-Ca be forced to retreat?

Safety and security demanded a still more drastic sacrifice: the cherished name Wo-Chi-Ca! With the summer of 1951, the Worker's Children's Camp changed its name to Camp Wyandot.

The name plates and signs had been removed from the Paul Robeson Recreation Hall and the Wardlaw-Mendelson pavilion. Some things were the same, but there was no longer what we called the "Wo-Chi-Ca spirit" in the same way.

JOHN VAGO

Did the Wo-Chi-Ca spirit vanish with the removal of the wooden Wo-Chi-Ca sign? Worker's Children's Camp was a noble name with a proud history, and though the new name was truly Indian, its spirit was not revolutionary. Indeed, the new name for Camp might be said to be counter-revolutionary, for in the American Revolution the Wyandot Indians had fought on the side of the British. Why then was the name Wyandot chosen? This shall remain one of the eternal mysteries surrounding the legendary camp, for every member of the Board of Directors has passed on and there is no one left who can tell us.

Dave Greenwood notes that "as part of the action plan to deflect further attacks, Camp had been renamed Wyandot. I never understood how this would protect us." In fact it did not. Even though camouflaged as Wyandot, Wo-Chi-Ca still lived in a state of siege.

I had married Dave Glaser, who was Director that year. We lived in a room in the original farmhouse with our infant son. One wall of our room was almost completely glass. Every night I would move the baby's crib as far away from that wall as I could. I slept with a baseball bat under the bed because of threats made by the local rednecks. I remember a truckload of them – somewhat inebriated – coming in one night. They didn't get very far because a bunch of us came out to greet them. Butch knew some of the from town where he would go into a bar occasionally for a little snort, and he pretty much shamed them into leaving without any serious confrontation that time. But with McCarthyism in full swing, that was the beginning of the end for a wonderful children's camp.

RIMA ROTHMAN GLASER

In the end, rumors of a determined Klan attack seemed all too real and led to the most heartbreaking retreat of all: abandonment of the grounds.

The wooden bunks, old army tents, the hand-crafted fountains of cool water, the swimming hole.... The antique stone house, the ramshackle activity shacks, the Quonset hut recreation hall once named the Paul Robeson Playhouse.... Everything – even the colorful totem pole – was left behind.

Only memories did the campers pack up to take with them. "We Welcome You to Wo-Chi-Ca, We're Mighty Glad You're Here..." "So Long, It's Been Good to Know You..." – glorious songs Wo-Chi-Cans would remember all their lives. Mouth-watering aromas from the mess hall, games with their hero on the baseball diamond, and yes, the red bandannas and flags of the early years too. The hikes into town with black and white kids side by side, the stirring films, inspiring counselors, great artists and activists who visited Camp, the classical music rest hours – even the poison ivy: every memory from those hundred twenty-seven precious acres was carefully stowed away.

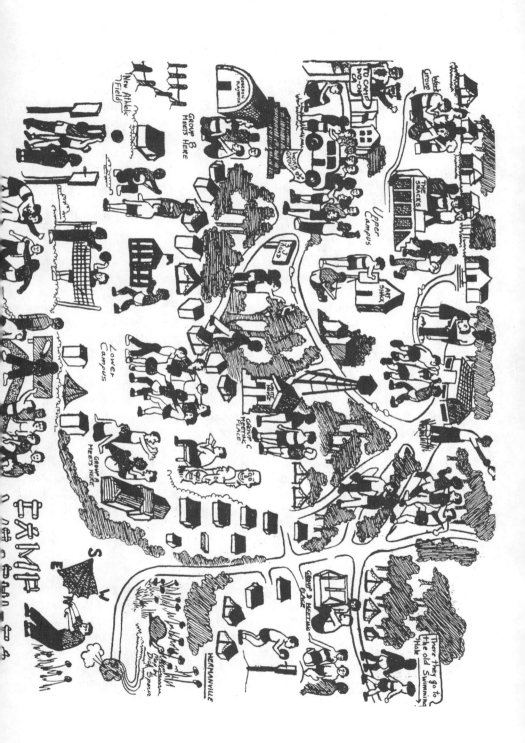

Wo-Chi-Cans, disguised as Wyandots, trudged off into exile, and the dispirited campers relocated to Mount Tremper outside of Kingston, New York.

We all knew Wyandot was still Wo-Chi-Ca with another name for security's sake. Ada B. Jackson was still the cook, and we were still interracial. But things were pretty different after the move to New York State. Wyandot was more secluded, up on a hill, with a real swimming pool, not like the old mud hole in New Jersey. There was a beautiful indoor gym, and a pretty fancy dining room. But there were major sewage problems and water shortages. And the old directors, Butch and Morris – they really personified that "Wo-Chi-Ca spirit" – were gone.

AL KISSELOF

The water and sewage problems at Wyandot come up in the memoirs of many today. "A directive from the Health Department had us digging ditches for a new sewer, a major project," Albert Lannon recalls. "I remember being outworked by Ruth Roman, marveling that a woman could do such a job!" Eugene Barufkin ("in the best physical shape of my life, before or since") also vividly remembers long sweaty hours of labor. He, John Vago and others had to build a new sewer system or the camp would be closed down.

Water, Peter Farber recalls, was in such short supply that staff members had to bring rations of drinking water to the bunks each evening. But so terrible did the stuff taste that the next summer the young camper brought with him a canteen of New York City water and made it last three weeks!

And yet the nauseating camp water was sweet compared with the odious offense committed by the U. S. Government. Only days before Wyandot opened its doors for the 1953 season – and just seventy miles from its gate – Ethel and Julius Rosenberg were strapped into electric chairs and burned to death.

"A dagger thrust in the heart of the Left," Julius Rosenberg had termed the verdict:

This death sentence is not surprising. It had to be. There had to be a Rosenberg Case because there had to be an intensification of the hysteria in America to make the Korean War acceptable to the American people. There had to be a hysteria and a fear sent through America in order to get increased war budgets. And there had to be a dagger thrust in the heart of the Left to tell them that you are no longer gonna get five years for a Smith Act prosecution or one year for contempt of Court, but we're gonna kill ya!

It certainly cut some of the heart out of Camp Wyandot. How dreadful it was for the children! How could they understand or accept that their government killed people very much like their own parents? Struggling with such questions, the campers – many as young as nine – thought about Michael and Robert, the Rosenberg children. What would happen to them? And their own parents – could they be next? Capable, sensitive counselors reassured the children as best they could, but they themselves were equally stunned by the execution of the couple they fervently believed to be guiltless.

A major event in the middle of the summer comforted Wo-Chi-Cans somewhat. On July 27, after three bitter years, the Korean War came to an end: North Korea and the United States agreed to a cease-fire.

When the Korean War truce was signed we all assembled in the recreation hall. I remember us all joining hands standing and singing "Last Night I Had the Strangest Dream." I still get choked up with the memory of that night whenever I hear that song.

ESTHER MOROZE

The end of the Korean War, however, did not bring the hoped-for end of McCarthyism. Blacklists remained in force, and anti-Communist venom still spewed forth from even highly regarded liberals. Hubert Humphrey called the Communist Party of the United States "a political cancer in our society," while Adlai Stevenson declared that Communism was worse than "cancer, tuberculosis, and heart disease combined."

In this putrescent political atmosphere, Wyandot found itself constricted and cramped. High-profile activists dared not call on Camp for fear they might draw hostile attention to it. Nearby Kingston, it turned out, was home to a chapter of the Ku Klux Klan. How tragic that the Wo-Chi-Cans, fleeing Klan activity in New Jersey, found not refuge in New York but animosity again. Kingston, after all, lay just sixty miles from Peekskill.

Many an artist, too, stayed away from Wyandot, fearing that in contracting the dread disease known as 'guilt by association,' a career would be irreparably harmed. In any case, few distinguished visitors dropped by Wyandot.

There were two notable exceptions – the first, Pete Seeger. Though some alumni assert otherwise, the great folk singer/activist never visited Wo-Chi-Ca in New Jersey. But now in its New York incarnation – and thanks to an invitation from music counselor Dave Sear – Pete did give a concert for 'Wo-Chi-Cans.' Seeger received no fee for it, though surely he needed money at the time. Famous artist though he was, Pete Seeger could barely make a living because he was blacklisted. To children in a trying time, Pete brought much comfort and cheer.

Another great artist brightened the scene at Wyandot. Anton Refregier had created murals for the Rincon Annex Post Office in San Francisco, the Grand Coulee
Dam in Washington, and the New York World's Fair. Now in 1953, 'Ref'
employed his talents to decorate the walls of the camp dining room in the
Catskills.

Anton Refregier came to Wyandot through the initiative of young camper Marian
Cuca. She had met the artist in 1951 at a tiny camp called Goat Hill. Marian
attended Wyandot for the first time in 1952, and on her return in 1953, she invited Refregier to the camp she had come to love. With other work group campers,
Marian climbed scaffolds to help Ref paint the dining room mural.

On July 27 of 1953, Marian happily joined Esther Moroze and other campers in
celebration of the Korean truce. But that evening after dinner, Marian complained of a sore throat. She was taken to the infirmary.

THE STROKE OF DEATH

Now a catastrophe would befall the little left wing camp from which it would never recover. Wo-Chi-Ca/Wyandot, since 1949, had endured a series of misfortunes. Like strokes from a wrecking ball, one devastating blow after another pounded the camp. Political blows – each assault had been political. The camp had learned to survive attacks from hysteria over 'Reds.' But now came an attack from out of the blue: not political, but medical.

Poliomyelitis: a neuromuscular disease also known as infantile paralysis, is caused by the polio virus of which there are three types. In one to two percent of the infections, the polio virus invades the nerve cells of the spinal cord. When it does, muscles connected to the damaged or destroyed nerve cells can no longer properly function, resulting in weakness or paralysis of the limbs, as well as the muscles controlling speech, swallowing, and breathing.

Polio, the 'summer scourge' dreaded by everyone! No one knew when or where it would strike – or why. Parents feared that if they allowed their children to mingle with crowds, to swim in cold water, to walk barefoot, they would catch polio. Rich or poor, famous or unknown, all were afraid. Polio could kill you, leave you crippled, or put you in an iron lung. Even the great leader of the country was not exempt: President Roosevelt walked with canes and sat in a wheelchair.

Polio hit children and young adults hardest, and no cure existed. Like other contagious diseases, it could only be prevented by quarantine and closing of public places. Today, in most of the world, polio has been essentially eradicated. But before the Salk vaccine of 1955, a diagnosis of infantile paralysis brought shudders to an entire community.

Wo-Chi-Ca always maintained a well-stocked infirmary with two nurses on duty and with recourse, if necessary, to the town doctor. Nevertheless, every cold and sore throat was viewed with alarm.

The fact is Camp had encounters with polio as early as the War years. Jack Broitman reports that "Polio scares struck in both the summers of 1944 and 1945. For some weeks Camp had to be quarantined with no visitors allowed."

A close call occurred on Memorial Day weekend of 1945. Ray Lerner and his wife had come up to help prepare Camp for its summer opening. After working all day airing mattresses, sweeping cobwebs, and repairing tent platforms, they joined others sprawled on the lawn in front of the Stone House.

Today, in a motorized wheelchair, suffering from post-polio syndrome, Ray Lerner describes his encounter with the disease.

We were sitting on the ground, listening to Howard Fast talk. I took a drink of my Coke and found I was unable to swallow. The camp doctor recognized my symptoms as polio. Seems I had contracted it in the city. I was sent home by ambulance. I came back at the end of the season for camp closing, having lost seventy pounds during my hospitalization. How surprised was the camp doctor who blurted out "You are supposed to be dead!"

In all its years in New Jersey, Wo-Chi-Ca had been lucky: only one positive case of polio, and that person evacuated before the crowds of campers arrived. But now at Mount Tremper in New York, in the middle of the season, three people were rushed from the camp infirmary to the local hospital with a definite diagnosis of polio. A male counselor and a young girl had fairly mild cases and were expected to recover. But an older camper had a more severe case. She was Marian Cuca.

Dear Diary,   *July 3, 1952*

This morning I received a letter from Camp Wyandot. It is a wonderful place to go because there are giant mountains and tall trees all around the camp. I'm going to take old clothes I'm not afraid to spoil, some comics and other necessities. In camp there are so many activities: from square dancing to telling stories of Jack London around the campfire. I especially look forward to the good old camp spirit that goes with everything you do.

Love,
Marian

Marian lived in Chelsea, a poor crowded section of Manhattan. Her father Tom, born in Yugoslavia, and mother Esther, of Polish-Jewish descent, were both active in their union and community, both class-conscious workers. They had little money to spare, but Marian was their only child and so they were able to send her to camp. Like many girls her age, Marian kept a diary.

Dear Diary,   *August 28, 1952*

The camp is really very interracial. But the campers, I'm afraid, talk a lot but are not interracial enough. In my bunk there are some very intellectual kids, and we have discussions on religion, politics and male and white supremacy.

On visiting day my parents didn't come. I took care of other parentless youngsters – eight or nine years – and had a wonderful, wonderful time. I felt very independent. I love my parents, but to be frank, I don't miss them at camp.

The other morning I got up at five and went for a walk. It's wonderful to walk at that hour!

I still can't swim, but I'm learning. I'm clean, healthy and happy.

Love,
Marian

What an exceptional girl this diary reveals! Or was Marian just a typical Wo-Chi-Ca/Wyandot camper?

Dear Diary,   *January 3, 1951*

The Korean situation is getting much worse. I hate war and wish it would stop.

Dear Diary,   *January 31, 1951*

I met a nice young girl who asked me if I wanted to go to a Harlem club for Negro and white. I could take modern dance and dramatics. It sounds good.

Dear Diary,   *February 2, 1951*

Four of the Martinsville Seven were executed today. The other three are supposed to die on Monday. It's a shame, a horrible shame.

Dear Diary,   *February 4, 1951*

I saw the movie "Red Shoes" today. It left a very high thought in my mind. I felt very emotional when I saw it. It's about a girl who is torn between her love for dancing and the man she loves. In the end she jumps in front of a train and kills herself.

Dear Diary,   *February 5, 1951*

Today I went to the dentist. I have to get a permanent tooth pulled out. I felt very bad and sorry for myself.

What is a tooth compared to life, the life of seven young Negro boys who only saw twenty-one summers?

> **Why should I cry for a tooth?**
> **You only cry when your dear ones are gone,**
> **You only cry when your life is torn to bits.**
> **What is a tooth compared to life?**
> **Nothing can compare to life except love,**
> **And nothing can compare to love except life.**
> **So why do you cry, you silly Marian?**

I need a friend to hold my hand and tell me
That seven young boys were not killed this morn.
And then you get a heartache all over again
And you know that they were killed.
You mustn't stop living because of a tooth.
You mustn't weep because of a tooth,
You must smile and laugh and say to yourself,
"What is a tooth compared with life and love?"
And then your heart will answer softly and gently,
"Nothing at all."

(I dedicate these thoughts to the Martinsville
Seven and "Red Shoes.")

Dear Diary,   *March 25, 1951*

Today I did a painting of a picket line dedicated to Lisa, who's in
Mommy's shop, because she's such a good union worker and she spent so
much of her time in her life on picket lines to do away with the sweat-
shop conditions and to better the life of workers in the dress shop. I also
wrote a letter to Albert Einstein telling him
about my ambition to be a scientist, and to
discover a cure for cancer. I plan to write him
every month. Wouldn't it be wonderful if,
just once, he should answer me!

Drawing by Anton Refregier

Dear Diary,   *April 19, 1951*

Today was Janey's birthday party. I like Adam now. At the party we played Post Office and Spin the Bottle. Adam and I kissed each other about ten times.

Love,
Marian

A typical girl in every way – ordinary, and yet so wonderfully extraordinary!

Dear Diary,   *February 4, 1952*

Today in school a bunch of "toughies" beat up a Negro kid. It seems "They" only get enjoyment out of bloodshed. These things really make me very mad. Why do men have to hate each other so? Won't we ever live in coordination? My god, Hitler Germany started like this. What is the world coming to? Are we all so stupid and ignorant? I shall never tolerate such things. Believe me my blood boils to 212F. Well, goodnight. I'm sorry to only tell you of my madness. Love – does it still exist?

Marian

Dear Diary,   *March 16, 1952*

We have finally organized a Peace Club in school after much tireless work. I am resolved to hold it together.

Last Friday I was at a dance and a movie. There I met Bob, a terrific guy who goes to Bronx Science; Freddy who is very cute and a personality out of this world; and last, but certainly not least, Peter, another terrific guy. I found out they are all working for a peaceful world. True, honest, strong, loving people. The kind the world needs.

Dear Diary,   *May 1, 1952*

Today is May Day, the day that belongs to the Youth. Since I belong to the Youth for Peace I marched with them. This was my first year marching with the Youth. It was very beautiful to see their faces in the sun. Once a great poet said all troubles, prejudices, and hate will someday evaporate under the sun's rays. And, indeed, as we marched along and shouted. "Youth unite, the future is ours!" "Youth unite, fight for peace!" "Books not bombs!" "Jim Crow Must Go!" all of us felt the same joy and happiness.

I was next to Bob. On 17th Street he put his arm around me for a moment, as he put me back in line. There are so many things to say which I just can't.

I can't write all night so I'll stop. Wishing you a happy May Day. We'll have many more! This is only the beginning.

Love, Marian

Dear Diary,   *February 3, 1953*

We had a debate in class about the Rosenbergs and whether they read anything about the case and just heard all around that they were spies and take it for granted that they are guilty. But there are many like myself who believe that Ethel and Julius Rosenberg are the innocent victims of a frame-up. We voted against their execution. It's horrible to think they might die!

Dear Diary,   *March 15, 1953*

While at camp I made friends with a Negro boy of fifteen, whose name is Don. As I write now, in March, when I see Don and a whole lot of other kids, I think back to that wonderful summer.

Don is a splendid person who is very generous, unselfish, intelligent, sweet and kind. Don and I are only good friends, but I shall always remember that summer where youth lived, worked and played together in a music-like harmony.

Here is a brief summary of all that happened since last summer:

1. Took Bronx Science exam
2. Stalin died
3. Eisenhower elected U.S. president
4. Joined the teenage Peace Club
5. Joined Science Clubs of America
6. Started art classes with Charles White
7. Met Ref during summer at Woodstock

8. *Met Ref in New York at his art exhibit*
9. *Rosenberg frame-up*
10. *Flunked French*
11. *Started wearing bra in camp*
12. *Met Donald at camp*
13. *Started doing photography*
14. *And lots more...*
    Love, Marian
    (a growing up one)

A girl not quite fourteen immersed in an incredible number of interests. She studies Yugoslav language and folk dance, takes guitar lessons, and toys with the idea of becoming a traveling folk singer. She grows dozens of plants, and cares for two canaries, a turtle, and twenty fish. She is an avid Dodger fan ("who isn't?"). She loves doing photography, working with tools, and hiking. She draws up a plan for her family to operate as a 'co-op.' She goes often to the Stanley Theater to see Soviet films. She collects poetry, listens to classical music, and reads and reads and reads....

But of all, she is most passionate about science and math. "Of course it is understood that my greatest enjoyment is mathematics, no matter what else I do." *The Star Finder*, *The Sun and Its Family*, and a life of Copernicus entitled *Sun Stand Thou Still* are some of the books Marian reads, while at the same time she takes a course in astronomy at the planetarium. The Museum of Natural History is her "second home." She conducts experiments with her chemistry set. She is "just swimming in thoughts" about going to the Bronx High School of Science. She dreams of starting a People for Science Club. Her number one favorite book is *Madame Curie*, a biography of the woman she reveres as "the greatest scientist of the times." Marian's ambition is "to find the cause and cure for cancer."

"I must tell Mommy and Daddy to read *The Microbe Hunters*. It's a most wonderful book," Marian writes. She records that she has read the book "all the way through four times already and given it as a present to as many friends."

Perhaps the most remarkable entry in the diary of the girl who dreams of becoming a scientist is the one she writes on March 18, 1952.

Dear Diary,

Today in school we had nothing to do during Social Science so I composed this crazy letter. Don't take me seriously. It's supposed to be about twenty years from now and I'm a scientist. It sounds like Marie Curie, but it's supposed to be me.

Go on read it! The blank spaces are for my husband's name. Naturally I don't know who he will be right now. It's written to a friend, but I don't know who the friend will be, either, right now.

Dearest _____ ,

We are working very hard now in the lab. So hard that many times we work far into the night. But indeed it is worth it. We have gone as far as isolating the cancerous growth from the tissues, which alone took us ten months.

We are fine except for constant fatigue. Battling that is a continuous fight. But imagine what good it will do when we have come to the end. It shall cure humanity of its most heartless killer: CANCER.

The children are fine and growing as big as giants, play-ing hour after hour in the spring sun. As you can well imagine, Paris is at its prettiest. People are as happy and gay as ever. We took a short visit to Sceaux for a week, since we have not been there for over a year. The garden is starting to flower with magnolias and goldenrods; birds are always singing. Really, we are as happy as ever.

Right now I am reading two books when time allows. Euclid's Plane Geometry in German and Huxley's works in French. They are both extremely interesting.

Of course _____ is still working on the problem of iso-lating carbonic crystals. It is quite hard to find time in which to do mathematics, but when we find time it brings us unlimited enjoyment.

I shall close now, as time does not permit me to write long letters.

I end with the best of love from the two of us.

This astonishing letter in which Marian imagines herself to be an adult – a scientist with husband and children – was written when she was not yet thirteen. No wonder that she could write home to her parents, "I'm in a bunk with some lovely kids. I'm not conceited, but we had a bunk evaluation and the conclusion of the bunk was that I'm exceptionally mature and intelligent."

And yet it WAS terribly true: polio cared not whom it destroyed. It respected not maturity nor intelligence, not beauty and certainly not youth. Marian was taken from the camp infirmary to the local hospital where she grew sicker every day.

Marian's bunkmates wrote letters, sent flowers, begged the doctors for reports on her condition. They could not believe that Marian – so lively, so vibrant – would fail to fight her way out of this nightmare.

Her artist friend Anton Refregier sent her a new drawing every day. To the girl he admired so much he wrote:

It's at times like these, when illness is so great and we are apt to feel discouraged and alone, that we have to know how much other people in the outside world think of us... You are talented, lovely, a swell kid. You got a break no human being should be put to endure, but I believe you will have the courage to pull yourself through these hard days and I promise you a lot of attention.

But no amount of courage could conquer those terrible microbes that had so fascinated the budding scientist. Marian Cuca died on August 12, 1953. With her death, Wyandot also collapsed. Midway through the summer, all – children, counselors, staff – abandoned camp.

AND THERE'S AN END

Marian Cuca was my bunkmate and dearest friend in the summer of '53. At night we would cuddle in her bed or mine when the counselor told the bunk to be quiet. We whispered about boys and what we wanted to be when we grew up. She told me about the Yugoslav Hall and I told her about living in Hungary for a year. She was one of the smartest, most mature and least judgmental girls I'd ever known. She wasn't great at softball, but tried anyway. We sang together and talked about books we loved. She was interested in science and I was going to be in the theater.

Marian's large eyes and soft voice are fixed in my memory, as are the days when my father and I visited her in the camp infirmary before she was moved to Kingston Hospital. On the day Marian died, I saw my father cry for the first time ever. At the funeral, it was impossible to look at her loveliness without realizing how mortal we all are.

SUSAN WEINSTOCK GOULD

Sue was herself fourteen as she beheld Marian in the coffin.

That day we all pledged to live her life as well as our own.

Marian was a beautiful person who impacted my life. For me, the memory of Wo-Chi-Ca and Wyandot has never been spoiled by her tragedy. Camp brought us together. I cherish the copy of her diary that I received from her parents. They were beautiful and loving to me for many years after the loss of their only child.

Camp was such a joy to Marian. It enabled her and so many of us to live the better world we believed in – not in theoretical terms but at bunk meetings and through artistic expression. It sure seemed simple then!

Marian in Greenwich Village

What a terrible year was 1953! In mid-June the Rosenbergs electrocuted, two months later young Marian Cuca buried and Camp Wyandot forsaken... Did Marian's friends and family gaze into her casket and see, in the death of the spirited left-wing girl, the general doom of the progressive movement in America?

Not quite! In spite of everything, the young people at Marian's funeral were confident about the future. Fred Jerome, also fourteen, spoke for them in his eulogy:

I want to speak of dear comrade Marian. I do not know of a single person who had anything but the greatest respect and highest admiration for her. Marian loved life ever so intensely. And when a call went out to courageous people the world over to save two innocent lives, Marian was among the first to answer the call. She gave endlessly of her time and energy. And although the murderers succeeded in stamping out those two lives, Marian continued on with her head higher than ever, determined to work all the harder to reach the goal that no amount of murders can block.

This morning I sat and watched the dawn break. It is a beautiful sight – the light of a new day. Yet how much sadness it brings to know that one so dear has not seen it. Then as I watched I realized that a new day was dawning for the entire world, and that it was for this new day that Marian had given her tireless energy. And for which we shall all now redouble our work in the memory of her shining example.

Although she may not see this new day in all its glory, she has seen the dawn. She has seen the opening of a world of peace, of happiness, of bread and roses, a world without polio!

Though Wyandot closed in mid-August, its Parents Association remained active in the city. Mothers and fathers of children who had been sent home early from the country rallied around the issue of polio protection.

When the polio epidemic hit us at Wyandot, the Board of Health provided gamma globulin sufficient only for the children in the Infirmary. My father Mark Straus rushed up to Camp to give the kids the injections.

But he cautioned that gamma globulin should be administered to everyone at Camp. The Board of Health refused. My father was a doctor who had served with the Abraham Lincoln Brigade in Spain. His concern was public health, and he wanted everyone who had been at Camp to go into quarantine to make sure the epidemic didn't spread. (My sister and I were kept at home the rest of the summer.) My father was furious at "those scoundrels" who refused to supply enough serum for the entire camp population.

ALICE STRAUS

Wyandot parents refused to take no for an answer. They organized a large demonstration in front of the Board of Health. Cameras were on hand and the story made headlines – not only in the press, but also on the new medium, television. Joan Fanshen and Peter Farber were two of many campers watching the 'Six O'clock News,' thrilled to distinguish their own parents. "I remember seeing them on TV," recalls Joan today. "All the parents were marching up and down, holding signs and singing."

The Board of Health relented and agreed to inoculate everyone. But the three hundred Wyandot campers lived in all five boroughs. With another great organizing effort, the parents got everyone down to the Board of Health on one day. Campers and staff waited in line for their shots, some carrying the new portable radios tuned to a Yankee or a Dodger game: it looked like another Subway Series coming up in the Fall. But as needles penetrated arms, many a camper winced and wondered: "Do these shots really work, or will polio get me too? Will I be back on the baseball diamond at camp next summer? Will there be a Camp Wyandot next summer?"

Before these questions could be answered, the campers would live through a brief but momentous period – the interval between summer camp of '53 and that of '54.

Imagine the wonder of young Wyandot campers (many of whom, like Marian Cuca, aspired to be scientists) at the announcement that biologists had delved deep into infinitesimal nature, down to the DNA molecules, the 'twisted ladders' that control all life. And this at the same time that other explorers had climbed 29,000 feet to the highest point on the planet, Mount Everest, almost six miles high in the stratosphere!

Consider the campers' dismay over their government's treatment of that mountain of a man, Paul Robeson. Their hero was prohibited from leaving the United States because of his "Communist sympathies." Another outspoken artist, Charlie Chaplin – also for "Communist sympathies" – was barred from entering the United States.

Picture the Wyandot kids in school, along with all other American children, diving under their desks to 'duck and cover,' practicing to survive a thermonuclear attack. (The Soviet Union had just detonated its first hydrogen bomb.) Simultaneously, the kids had to recite an altered Pledge of Allegiance. The Knights of Columbus, in a campaign against "Godless Communism," had pressured Congress into violating the separation-of-church-and-state provision of the Constitution. Patriotism and religion were now officially bound together: school children, hands over hearts, chanted "one nation under God," uttering a public prayer while swearing a patriotic oath.

A daily pledge of loyalty to God and country was insufficient in Florida. Boys of sixteen applying for summer jobs with the Dade County Parks Department – to pick up trash and dog droppings – had to sign a sworn statement that they were not members of the Communist Party!

Who were members of the Party? According to those who professed to know, they were abstract painters, university professors, rock and roll musicians, teenagers and juvenile delinquents, librarians and patrons of the library, Alfred Kinsey and his sex researchers, and those who would put fluoride in the drinking water.

A scientist who developed the atomic bomb also fell under suspicion. The distinguished nuclear physicist J. Robert Oppenheimer, Director of Los Alamos National Laboratory, was accused of being disloyal and termed a security risk. The government maintained that his association with Communist friends went "far beyond the tolerable limits of prudence and self-restraint." Oppenheimer's security clearance was revoked and he was forced off the Atomic Energy Commission.

The House Un-American Activities Committee heard testimony alleging that 600 Protestant clergymen were secret members of the Communist Party. Senator Hubert Humphrey proposed the establishment of what could only be called concentration camps for Communists – "detention centers" where, in the event of an "internal security emergency," "suspected subversives" would be held without trial. The camps were actually constructed and only awaited prisoners.

How could the government be sure to know whom to round up and place in these camps? The actor Adolph Menjou provided a simple solution: "One of the best ways to spot a Communist is if that person is seen applauding at a Paul Robeson concert or owns a Paul Robeson recording."

Such was the tenor of the time in which the left-wing kids lived while waiting for Wyandot to open next season. In the White House sat Eisenhower, a 'Father Knows Best' figure, while Americans – safe and secure in their 'cookie cutter' houses – watched "Lassie," "I Love Lucy," "The Honeymooners," and "The Adventures of Ozzie and Harriet." Hit songs of the period included "Scatterbrain," "Oh Mein Papa," "Vaya Con Dios," "I Saw Mommy Kissing Santa Claus," "How Much is That Doggie in the Window..." *The Holy Bible* and *The Power of Positive Thinking* topped the best seller list for 1954. It was the "bland leading the bland."

A revolution of sorts did break out at this time – the rock and roll revolution. Chuck Berry, Elvis Presley, Little Richard, Buddy Holly, Bill Haley and His Comets were leaders of this rebellion. Many Wyandot campers were enthusiastic followers.

In 1953 the glittering lights of Broadway proclaimed a great new play: *The Crucible* by Arthur Miller. Ostensibly about witch-hunts in colonial America, its pointed allusion to the climate of fear in present-day America did not escape the notice of HUAC – they subpoenaed the playwright. When Miller refused to identify other Communists, HUAC convicted him of contempt of Congress. The government denied him a passport. When the left-wing writer later married Marilyn

Monroe, the FBI put her under surveillance and kept a file on the actress.

In '53 and '54, Marilyn Monroe, playing a ditzy gold-digger, starred in *Gentlemen Prefer Blondes* and *How to Marry a Millionaire*. Best Picture award of 1954 went to *On the Waterfront*. Its director, Elia Kazan, also won an Oscar for this disturbing depiction of corrupt labor union bosses. Kazan's trophy, however, was tarnished, for only two years earlier he had turned informer before HUAC. After first refusing to name names, Kazan succumbed to the Un-American Committee and put the finger on eight members of the Group Theater who had been his comrades in the Communist Party back in the Thirties.

On the Waterfront played in thousands of movie houses while another film – also released in 1954 – was screened in only thirteen theaters in the entire United States. *Salt of the Earth* was the true story of a bitterly fought strike of zinc miners in Silver City, New Mexico. Only two professional actors were employed; the striking workers and their families made up the rest of the cast. Blacklisted technicians and artists produced this film – Paul Jarrico, Herbert J. Biberman, Michael Wilson, Sol Kaplan, Will Geer...

Hollywood studios, the American Legion, the FBI and anti-Communist groups mounted a ferocious campaign to suppress *Salt of the Earth*. Distributors would not touch the film; newspapers shunned it, refusing to publish ads or reviews. Yet today, *Salt of the Earth* is in a select group of only one hundred movies preserved for posterity by the Library of Congress – one of the most significant films of the 20th century.

World events at this time could not have been more unstable. At the Four-Power Meeting in Berlin, the ministers of the United States, the Soviet Union, France and Great Britain wrangled for three weeks without budging an inch. The Cold War had frozen into a vast ominous iceberg.

But the glaciers of imperialism did melt somewhat, for nationalistic fervor burned on all continents. In North Africa, Algerians took up arms against their French rulers. The people of Iran, striving to benefit from their vast oil reserves, nationalized British and American petroleum companies. But their popular government was overthrown, the despotic monarchy restored, and the oil repossessed. In Guatemala, peasants hoping to farm 200,000 undeveloped acres held by United Fruit Company saw their democratic government fall to an armed attack. The U. S. Central Intelligence Agency organized both these coups. Washington – the capital of America itself – felt the sting of passionate and violent nationalism when four Puerto Rican patriots fired guns from the gallery of the House of Representatives, wounding five Congressmen.

The Korean War wound down to a cease-fire that left troops of a divided country facing off at the 38th parallel. But America wasted no time embroiling itself in another Asian war. Supporting the French in their attempt to maintain their grip on Indochina, the United States gave France 385 million dollars. After the French met final defeat at Dien Bien Phu, America began its own abysmal involvement in Vietnam.

At home – and especially meaningful to Wo-Chi-Cans – Pittsburgh schoolchildren, in a mass inoculation, received the first anti-polio serum developed Dr. Jonas Salk. So passed the short period from the premature closing of Camp in 1953 to the scheduled reopening of the following season. But would Wyandot really open in 1954?

Wyandot campers sure hoped so. They couldn't wait to run out onto that Mount Tremper baseball diamond, even though they still grumbled over the 1953 World Series. The Yankees and Dodgers did play that year, and the Bronx defeated Brooklyn once again! Five times these two teams had battled in the World Series, and every darn time the Damn Yankees beat the beloved Bums. Campers – their hearts riding on every pitch – desperately rooted for the underdog Dodgers. After all, with Jackie Robinson, Roy Campanella, Joe Black, Don Newcombe, Jim Gilliam, Sandy Amoros... the integrated team at Ebbets Field looked so much like their dear interracial camp up in the country, while the Yankees... – oh the damn, wealthy pin-striped Yankees. What could you say but "Wait till next year!"

Wyandot did reopen the next year. And on a note of triumph, for just before the 1954 summer season, the anti-Communists suffered a tremendous setback. For four years in the U.S. Senate, Joseph McCarthy had conducted a vicious and ruthless crusade of lies, innuendo, slander, mudslinging, and baseless accusations. In order to promote himself, McCarthy destroyed the careers, reputations and lives of hundreds of guiltless men and women.

McCarthy began his political life in Wisconsin as a supporter of Roosevelt's New Deal. But unable to win the Democratic candidacy for district attorney, he opportunistically switched parties and ran for circuit court judge as a Republican.

McCarthy fought dirty to win this office. He printed campaign literature falsely claiming his opponent was seventy-three years old instead of only sixty-six. Insinuating mental infirmity and financial corruption, McCarthy defeated Edgar Werner.

"McCarthy not only drove my father to his grave," wrote Dr. A. J. Werner in October, 1951, "but turned long-standing friends against our whole family. It was amazing how one man could wreck the reputation of another man so loved and honored in his community."

McCarthy then challenged Robert La Follette in the Wisconsin Republican primary for the U.S. Senate. "Tail Gunner Joe" circulated posters of himself wearing a Marine uniform with bandoleers of ammunition, while he attacked La Follette for sitting out the war. While he was off fighting for his country,

McCarthy charged, La Follette stayed home amassing enormous sums as a war profiteer.

In the first place, McCarthy exaggerated his service record. Secondly, La Follette was forty-six when World War II began, too old to serve in the armed forces. As for war profiteering, La Follette's investments were in nothing more than a radio station. Nonetheless, with these dishonest allegations, McCarthy won the election. Deeply hurt, La Follette retired from politics and – during the height of McCarthyite madness – put a gun to his head and killed himself.

On his very first day as senator, during the 1946 nation-wide coal strike, McCarthy called a press conference. His solution to the crisis? Draft the striking miners into the Army. Workers refusing to mine coal could then be court-martialed and shot!

In spite of such an outrageous kickoff, the junior Senator from Wisconsin remained obscure for several years. But in Wheeling, West Virginia in February 1950, McCarthy gave a speech that catapulted him to notoriety. He declared that the State Department was "infested" with Reds. "I have here in my hand," he announced, dramatically waving a sheet of paper, "a list of 205, a list of names made known to the Secretary of State as being members of the Communist Party and who nevertheless are still working and shaping policy in the State Department."

The next day in Salt Lake City, he amended the number: now fifty-seven "card-carrying Communists" worked in the State Department. In the Senate, McCarthy held the floor for six-hours – this time claiming eighty-one Communists could be found in the Department of State. Fifty-seven, eighty-one, two hundred and five... Skeptical senators challenged him to identify just one! But McCarthy refused.

A special Senate committee investigated the charges, finding them "groundless" and concluded "the Senate and the American people had been deceived." The truth is, McCarthy never presented evidence for a single one of his allegations, nor was he ever able to prove one person he accused of Communism guilty of breaking the law.

In spite of this, McCarthy persisted with his slurs and smears. "Soft on Communism" he characterized Dean Acheson, Adlai Stevenson, General George Marshall... McCarthy accused Truman himself of employing and shielding known Communists. He called Owen Lattimore, China scholar at The Johns Hopkins University, "the top Soviet espionage agent in the U.S."

Yes, McCarthy attacked those in the highest positions. Even the President of the United States was intimidated. Dwight Eisenhower, who detested Joe McCarthy, was afraid to challenge him publicly and suffered much criticism as a result.

Time magazine, which usually supported Eisenhower, chastised the President's "disgraceful...appeasement" of McCarthy. But Eisenhower simply said, "I will not get into the gutter with this guy."

In colonial Massachusetts or medieval Europe, if one was accused of witchcraft, her friends dared not contradict for fear they too would be accused of being witches. In McCarthy's America, if one heard his friend called a Communist and dared to object, he himself was accused of Communism. If the President of the United States feared McCarthy, where would an ordinary citizen find courage?

And so for four years, the man with the fleshy, baneful countenance, the heavy drinker devoted to horse racing and poker – the "pathological liar" and "consummate demagogue" – terrorized the American people. In his biography of the Senator, Richard Rovere wrote that McCarthy was "like Hitler, a screamer, a political thug, a master of the mob...

"As far as I know," remarked an old acquaintance of McCarthy from Wisconsin days, "Joe looked at only one book in his life. That was Mein Kampf... When he looked at Mein Kampf, it was like one politician comparing notes with another."

Europeans, of course, knew a Hitler when they saw one, and in Joseph McCarthy they recognized an incipient fuehrer. Philip Reed, head of General Electric, observed Europe's fears during a 1953 tour. "I urge you to take issue with McCarthy and make it stick," he wrote to Eisenhower. "People in high and low places see in him a potential Hitler seeking the presidency of the United States."

At long last, the media mustered the forces to attack "America's most hated senator." Authors I. F. Stone and George Seldes, cartoonists Daniel Fitzpatrick and Herb Block, and newspaperman Drew Pearson had fought McCarthy for some time. Now, others such as Jack Anderson and Walter Lippmann stepped up their criticism. Edward R. Murrow on his TV program "See It Now," exposed McCarthy's abusive methods.

Finally, McCarthy over-reached himself: he accused the U.S. Army of "coddling Communists." From April through June of 1954, the country followed the Army-McCarthy hearings – 188 hours of gavel-to-gavel coverage. Twenty million Americans watched as the boorish junior senator from Wisconsin rudely and repeatedly interrupted witnesses with his nasal "Point of order!" McCarthy's Waterloo occurred when he ascribed Communist sympathies to a young legal assistant to Joseph N. Welch who was chief counsel for the Army. Welch's masterful response effectively ended McCarthy's career: "Until this moment, Senator, I think I never gauged your cruelty or recklessness. Let us not assassinate this lad further, Senator. Have you no sense of decency, sir, at long last? Have you left no sense of decency?"

Senator Stuart Symington of Missouri spoke for his colleagues. "The American people have had a look at you for six weeks. You are not fooling anyone." By a vote of 67-22, the U.S. Senate censured Joseph McCarthy for "conduct that tends to bring the Senate into dishonor and disrepute."

The *Louisville Courier-Journal* stated "...McCarthy has shown himself to be evil and unmatched in malice."

In disgrace, often drunk for days on end, frequently hospitalized, Joseph Raymond McCarthy died in May 1957. The newspapers reported that he drank himself to death.

The sigh of relief at McCarthy's demise was heard even in Europe. "America was the cleaner by his fall," an English newspaper editorialized, "and is cleaner by his death." Such was the epitaph for the "single most despised man in American political memory."

Yes, Camp Wyandot did open on a note of triumph, for in addition to McCarthy's fall, fighters for racial equality – in May of 1954 – won a significant victory. The U.S. Supreme Court handed down a unanimous decision in the case of Brown vs. Board of Education. All nine judges ruled that "separate but equal" schools were unconstitutional and therefore illegal. It would not be long before the demand for civil rights would expand to buses, restaurants and public facilities all across the land.

The Wo-Chi-Ca folks had long practiced the equality that was now the law of the land. As Camp Wyandot, they struggled to remain faithful to that ideal. Funds, however, were scarce, for six months before Camp opened, the International Workers Order had been dissolved. The IWO of course, had been the long-time sustainer of Wo-Chi-Ca/Wyandot. The courts did rule that the Workers Order did not actually own the camp, and therefore the State of New York could not seize Wyandot's assets. Still, Camp finances – always uncertain and usually in the red – would not receive the customary boost from IWO fundraising. Unions, struggling to survive right-wing attacks, had to reduce or eliminate financial support. And many social agencies, yielding to the nationwide anti-Communist hysteria, withdrew their assistance. Not since the early years of Wo-Chi-Ca did Camp directors worry so about providing even such a basic necessity as food.

In previous years, word of mouth was sufficient to fill every bunk, with a long waiting list to boot. Now, half-filled buses and vacant beds called for an exceptional solution. Promotion and advertising! New director Ken Friedman and his staff printed a small booklet: the Guide to Camp Wyandot. The illustrated brochure depicted a camp with 280 acres of open woodland, with boating and fishing on a small lake fed by a mountain stream. With an eye no doubt to polio fears, the brochure assured parents that Wyandot had a "constantly filtered pool, well-ventilated fully-screened bunks," and an infirmary with heat, isolation room, doctor plus two nurses on staff, and proximity to a large hospital in Kingston.

With its "four story chateau...two large ball fields, beautiful indoor basketball court, fully equipped arts and crafts building, small indoor theater," the Guide presented the picture of an idyllic camp for children. Eleven photographs showed campers and staff – Negro and white – happily engaged in various activities.

Those reading the brochure would at once recognize in Wyandot a camp attempting to perpetuate the spirit of the Left. Its objective was to "bring respect for all people... in one world where freedom and equality exist for all."

"Respect for work and working people...is another aim of our camp. An understanding of the labor movement is given to the children by having them join craft unions when they are engaged in work projects."

The cherished 'co-op,' so well remembered by alumni from Wo-Chi-Ca days, remained a feature at Wyandot. In the brochure, we read that "The camp's cooperative is so planned that each child, regardless of the amount of money he contributes, can receive the same amount of candy, ice cream, etc. as the next child."

Cooperation extended to sports as well: "The camp's athletic program is geared for group play, with a minimum of individual competition. The aim is to develop the feeling that through united group activity the greatest joy can be realized."

Chief among the values to be taught, of course, was the unity of peoples. "Our aim is to include in our staff all racial, national and religious groups...so that the children can see full equality in practice in all the leadership levels of camp. We strive to get a similar representation in each bunk, so that the camper can learn by the experience of bunk life the equality of all people."

No question but that Wyandot's heart – even in the difficult year of 1954 – was smack in the center of the Left. "In music they will learn songs of the Jewish, Negro, Irish, Italian peoples, as well as many American folk and labor songs. In dramatics they will produce plays and skits about events in labor history or respect for the various people who make up America."

Certainly working-class Wyandot was unlike most camps of its day. Wyandot strove mightily to keep alive the soul of the progressive movement. And yet even its most ardent alumni agree that Wyandot never quite captured the spirit of Wo-Chi-Ca.

Try as it might, Wyandot was not another Wo-Chi-Ca. Though much larger and more luxurious than its predecessor, it was nevertheless plagued with sewage problems and water shortages. Most serious of all, low morale could not be overcome. The misery of McCarthyism still hovered like a mournful cloud that nothing could dispel. The execution of Julius and Ethel Rosenberg and then the death of Marian Cuca "...finally," as Al Kisselof laments, "nailed the coffin down for Camp." At the end of the '54 season, Wo-Chi-Ca/Wyandot closed its doors. Never again would they open.

HOLD FAST TO DREAMS

A shroud of silence stifled the left-wing camp – a blanket of fear so heavy it would not lift for near a quarter century. "It is impossible to convey properly the fears that marked that period," recounts playwright Arthur Miller. "Nobody was shot, to be sure. Rather than physical fear, it was the sense of impotence, which seemed to deepen with each week." Impotence – inability to act. Fear froze people's tongues: they could not voice a left-wing thought.

In his book *Naming Names*, Victor Navasky – publisher and editor of *Nation* magazine – tells of "worry and depression" in the populace of the Fifties. He quotes a friend who speaks of "...fatigue, fear, insomnia, drinking, headaches, indigestion, failure to function well, worsening of relations to colleagues, suspicion, distrust, loss of self-respect."

Navasky cites Sylvia Jarrico who, during the days of the blacklist, was married to Paul Jarrico, producer of the film *Salt of the Earth*. For refusing to sign the University of California loyalty oath, Mrs. Jarrico was fired from her editorial position with *Hollywood Quarterly*. "We lived," reports Sylvia, "with the constant sense of being hunted."

In this frightening atmosphere – which Supreme Court Justice William O. Douglas termed "The Black Silence of Fear" – Wo-Chi-Ca children dared not whisper even the name of the summer camp so precious to them. Bob Bookchin's mother destroyed his Wo-Chi-Ca Yearbook, "for fear that McCarthy-stimulated agents (FBI and whatnot) would persecute anyone who ever went to Wo-Chi-Ca." Judy Tarail reports that one of her friends was so affected by the times that she moved to another country. "For some of us it wasn't a great thing to say 'I went to Wo-Chi-Ca.' It was actually unsafe to say it at the time and for a long time after."

The kids departing Wyandot as it closed forever in '54 would be middle-aged before they would unite again. Not until 1976, when shocked and saddened at the death their hero Paul Robeson, did the campers rouse themselves to come together in a great reunion.

In the year following Wyandot's demise – on December first of 1955 – a white bus driver in Montgomery, Alabama ordered an African American woman to give up her seat to a white passenger. She refused. "Well, I'm going to have you arrested," he warned. "You may go on and do so," forty-two-year old seamstress Rosa Parks replied. These simple and courageous words began the Montgomery Bus Boycott.

In spite of harassment, threats, arrests – even bombs – Southern Negroes, under the leadership of Dr. Martin Luther King, Jr., stayed off the buses for more than a year until victory came in a Supreme Court decision declaring segregation on all buses unconstitutional.

Also in 1955, the AFL and CIO merged. Their union was weakened, however, by their shared anti-Communism. "We must insist," declared the Seafarers International Union of North America, "that this fight [an "unrelenting war against Communist influence"] shall not have been in vain, and that our memberships must continue to be protected against any influence from this vicious element. What we specifically refer to is the question of fellow travelers, former travelers, and former Communists who today give lip-service to American institutions but are still suspect, and the sincerity of their motives doubtful." Joe McCarthy had been kicked out of the Senate, but his witch-hunting ways found welcome in the house of labor.

The first McDonald's restaurant opened that year in Des Plains, Illinois. Americans began to devour what would amount to billions and billions of hamburgers. But with baseball fans it was still hot dogs. The 1955 World Series again pitted Brooklyn against the formidable 'Bombers' from the Bronx. 'Da' Bums' lost the first two games. Wo-Chi-Cans and Dodger lovers everywhere despaired. Not once in seven tries had the Dodgers won a World Series: the last five times they were beaten by these same damn Yankees. Here it was happening again.

But on October 5th, on the seventh and deciding game, Johnny Podres pitched a shutout! The Dodgers won the Series! Brooklyn was bedlam: a week later people were still dancing in the streets.

The Brooklyn Dodgers – first team in major league baseball to break the color line! After half a century they were champions of the world. Throughout St. Thomas in the Virgin Islands 5,000 people rejoiced in a four-hour parade. Their banners read "AT LAST - BROOKLYN WINS" and "SNIDER, DUKE OF BEDFORD AVENUE." In the Dominican Republic, where once the Dodgers held spring training, a new baby was named Podres Garcia in honor of Johnny Podres.

So ended the myth of Yankee invincibility. Alas, the very next year the Dodgers once again lost the World Series to the Yankees. After that, the Bums abandoned Brooklyn altogether for the greener grass of Southern California.

Two events in 1956 profoundly affected Wo-Chi-Cans. Nikita Khrushchev's speech on the crimes of Joseph Stalin is shocking even today. Khrushchev told the Communist Party Congress of a "cult of the individual" which [did] "elevate one person to...a superman possessing supernatural characteristics, akin to those of a god." The "sickly suspicious" Stalin, revealed Khrushchev, "practiced brutal violence" and "mass terror." Stalin obtained false confessions of guilt "with the help of cruel and inhuman tortures." Stalin generated "mass deportations...of whole nations." [His] "persecution mania reached unbelievable dimensions."

The disclosures of Khrushchev impelled Howard Fast to leave the Communist Party. Did other Wo-Chi-Cans leave as well? Dave Greenwood, for one, has already stated that he did so, and we have an anecdote from Ray Lerner to the same effect.

After my recovery from polio in 1945, I finished college at Columbia. I got my BA and MA in Sociology. I even wrote a term paper on Camp Wo-Chi-Ca! But I switched to epidemiology – got a PHD, and traveled all over working for the World Health Organization of the UN. I taught at Columbia, the State University of New York, and also Albert Einstein College. I even wrote a treatise on the medical effects of abortion that is still used as a textbook.

I joined the Party in the late 40's, and in the 50's I was one of the contacts for the CP leaders who went into hiding from the Smith Act. Bob Thompson, Henry Winston and Gil Green stayed in my apartment part of that time. In fact, when they decided to turn themselves in, they wrote an open letter to the New York Times on my typewriter. I still have that typewriter! I was the one who drove Winston to the courthouse in Foley Square the next day, where he surrendered to the Feds.

Wo-Chi-Ca? I think about it all the time. I only spent one summer there, in 1946, but it had a lot to do with shaping the rest of my life.

Even though I dropped out of the Party after Khrushchev's speech, I still believe in the principles of Marxism and Socialism. I saw them working at Wo-Chi-Ca.

RAY LERNER

A number of Wo-Chi-Cans undoubtedly left with Ray at this time, though it is important to note the interesting observation of Martin Duberman, author of the definitive biography of Paul Robeson: "In contrast to the many white Communists who went to pieces over the Khrushchev report, deserting the CPUSA in droves, few black members left the Party, preferring to read Khrushchev's revelations as a sign of renewed hope, an indication that the U.S.S.R. was about to return to the purity of its earlier revolutionary goals."

And we must also note that a number of white Wo-Chi-Cans chose to remain in the Party, maintaining their membership to this day. Foremost would be Julia Davis. Yes, the very same woman who back in the 1930's gave Wo-Chi-Ca its name, lives today in Florida, now in her nineties and a lifelong member of the CPUSA.

How many more Wo-Chi-Cans of Julia's generation share her political commitment? It would be difficult to say. But when the authors placed an appeal for Wo-Chi-Ca memoirs in the People's Weekly World, sons and daughters around the country received phone calls from their elderly parents with the urgent notification that "Wo-Chi-Ca is looking for you."

The current treasurer of the Communist Party USA, Esther Moroze, was a camper at Wo-Chi-Ca. Another alumnus, John Vago, writes that...

...my wife and I are both active in the Communist Party in Philadelphia, and in our respective unions. Our kids are both participants in the Young Communist League.

Michele Artt of Detroit, the "third-generation Communist" who recently lost her mother (the legendary Helen Winter), is a former camper. One more Wo-Chi-Can still in the Party is the granddaughter of another Communist legend, Mother Bloor. This is Carla Smith:

I am proud to be the next-to-youngest granddaughter of Mother Ella Reeve Bloor Omholt, and am happy to have spent time with Gram at Camp Wo-Chi-Ca. It was there that I met the courageous genius, Mr. Paul Robeson. He and my grandmother were good friends and comrades. Paul was over six feet tall; in contrast my grandmother was about four feet.

What inspired me at Wo-Chi-Ca was the profound sense of collectivism and humanism that prevailed at the Camp. Everyone was there to teach the campers how to share and live together.

It was no wonder that I joined the Communist Party at the age of seventeen. I had already been a member of The Young Workers Liberation League.

Yes, I chose to remain in the Party. I think it was my grandmother who instilled in me the profound sense of struggle, the deep compassion for the miners, farmers – all the struggling poor.

My father was also a very courageous comrade. He was beaten up in hunger strikes. He was a scholar and had a profound knowledge of Marxism-Leninism. My mother was Jewish. She came from a poor working-class family. Her mother, my other grandmother, was extremely kind and loved Mother Bloor. They were good friends.

My mother and father were very poor. My father was a functionary, and my mother worked as a secretary. Together they wrote **The Life & Times of James Connelly in the United States.** *My father also wrote a book on the life of Daniel DeLeon. Henry Winston described my parents as two jewels in the movement.*

I remained in the Party because I saw the need for a Communist Party in this country, based on the conditions of this country. I was disappointed to learn that Howard Fast left the Party. I always felt the class struggle still exists. Imperialism is at its highest form and we are living in the belly of the beast.

My husband and I have taken an active role in the peace movement. The danger of war has never been greater. It is our responsibility to make sure that many innocent civilians are not killed again. The terrorists only help the right-wing agenda. They should be punished. But let us not let the warmongers utilize war for military profit and greed at the expense of the poor.

I will never forget the wonderful time I had at Wo-Chi-Ca. The camp gave me roots and a foundation to stand up for what I believe. I will always be grateful to my Gram for sending me there. Yes, I am proud to be her granddaughter. I am proud to be a Communist.

Actually, Carla and these other comrades may have been a bit too young to be affected by Khrushchev's speech, or by the other serious event of 1956 – the insurrection in Hungary. Khrushchev's denunciation of Stalin whipped up violent storms in the Soviet Union's eastern neighbor. Citizens demanded independence from the USSR, and a revolt broke out in Budapest. Reform Communist Imry Nagy, announcing that Hungary would drop out of the Warsaw Pact, went on the radio: "Soviet troops attacked our capital with the obvious purpose to overthrow the legitimate Hungarian democratic government. Our troops are fighting. The government is in its place." Thousands of Hungarians were killed. How many Wo-Chi-Cans were disillusioned?

But let us return to the Fifties. The year 1957 saw soldiers deployed in Arkansas against mobs protesting the new desegregation laws. In September, the federal government dispatched paratroopers to Little Rock, where a defiant Governor Orval Faubus refused to let Negro pupils enter Central High School. Integration was enforced with bayonets, and the Constitution upheld.

In 1957 *Time* magazine chose for its Man of the Year "Russia's stubby and bald, garrulous and brilliant ruler: Nikita Khrushchev." Not only had he presided over the launching of Sputnik, but Khrushchev "had furnished the Moscow metro with the world's best subway toilets." *Time* noted that in 1957 "Russia graduated three times as many engineers as the U.S. and published five times as many book titles."

'Hula Hoops' and the 'Cha Cha' both become national crazes in 1958. In that year rehearsals began for Lorraine Hansberry's first play, *Raisin in the Sun*. On opening night the Broadway audience refused to stop applauding until Hansberry came on stage. No one cheered louder than her proud husband, poet Robert Nemiroff, Wo-Chi-Ca alumnus. The two had met at a picket line protesting the exclusion of Black athletes from sporting events.

On the first day of 1959, general jubilation broke out in Cuba. Thirty-two-year old Fidel Castro, leader of the victorious revolution, drove across the entire island on the road towards Havana. Every village along the way held a fiesta, and girls proudly put on a new revolutionary uniform – red sweater and black skirt, both worn very tight.

But the revolutionary events of the Sixties! What reader who lived through that decade does not skip a heartbeat at the thought of the assassination of President Kennedy? Or stir with emotion remembering the quarter-million-strong civil rights march in Washington where Martin Luther King proclaimed "I have a dream?"

Who can forget the flight of Maj. Yuri A. Gagarin, first man in orbit around the earth, or American astronauts walking on the moon? What of the trial and execution of Adolf Eichmann, who had carried out Hitler's 'Final Solution' to kill the Jews? Who didn't cry at the Cuban missile crisis – and even call family and friends to say goodbye, fearing it was the end of the world?

The very dawn of the Sixties began dramatically, with a tremendous blow against the House Un-American Activities Committee. Hundreds of Berkeley students crossed the Bay to San Francisco to protest the HUAC hearings. Thousands witnessed the police turn high-power fire hoses on the demonstrators, then drag them by their feet down marble city hall steps. But the next day the students came back in force to chant "Sieg Heil!" "Sieg Heil!" Never before had such a challenge been hurled at the Red Hunters and Red Haters.

Back on campus, the students set up tables in Sproul Plaza to sign up members and collect money for 'off-campus causes,' for civil rights groups such as SNCC and CORE, as well as SDS, the Du Bois Club, and others. Campus administrators tried to remove the tables and met with determined resistance. With Bettina Aptheker organizing and Joan Baez singing, the Free Speech Movement at the University of California was in full swing.

A leader of the FSM was arrested and placed in a police car, but hundreds of protesters, singing "We Shall Overcome," encircled the car, blocking its way for thirty-two hours. One speaker after another climbed to the roof of the police car.

The University had hundreds of students carted off to county jail and suspended others from school.

Also in Berkeley, a furious conflict broke out over a patch of land. Again the might of the University of California is pitted against the people: on one side, bulldozers demolish homes while on the other citizens plant grass, flowers and trees... Chain link fences here, a playground with free food there. Huge protest marches, tear gas canisters, rocks and bottles... Sheriff deputies firing buckshot blind one man and kill another; Governor Ronald Reagan calls out the National Guard; a helicopter sprays the campus with tear gas – the struggle over People's Park! Involved in it all: former Wo-Chi-Ca camper Art Goldberg.

Art, who worked on Ramparts magazine, was also active in a group founded in Oakland that patrolled Black neighborhoods, defending people from the brutality of the police. The Black Panthers developed into an anti-capitalist party, a socialist, a revolutionary – some would say Marxist – organization.

In addition, Art Goldberg participated in the anti-war demonstrations at the Chicago Democratic Convention. There, peace marchers were attacked so savagely by the police that Senator Abraham Ribicoff, in his speech nominating George McGovern, was moved to denounce (on TV!) the "Gestapo tactics on the streets of Chicago."

What a decade! Malcolm X shot to death at a rally in Harlem...Senator Robert F. Kennedy gunned down in Los Angeles...Martin Luther King Jr. shot and killed in Memphis...Schwerner, Goodman, and Cheney – three civil rights workers — murdered in Mississippi. Fearful events, terrible times!

Paradoxically, the Sixties also gave us 'Love-Ins,' 'Be-Ins,' and 'Flower Power.' In February of '64 the Beatles appeared on the Ed Sullivan Show. In the summer of '67, the youth of America basked in a 'Summer of Love.' But Wo-Chi-Cans were a bit older than this generation, and for the most part bypassed the 'Psychedelic Sixties.' Did they smoke grass? Perhaps. But it is unlikely that many 'dropped acid' with Ken Kesey and Timothy Leary. The typical Wo-Chi-Can, about thirty-five at this time, did not 'Turn On, Tune In, and Drop Out.'

I went as a volunteer with CORE in the Mississippi Summer of 1964.
While there, I became friends with John O'Neal, a founder of the Free
Southern Theater. We went to Jackson, Mississippi together. There I was
introduced to two white students who were preparing to integrate a
Black junior high school in the fall.

GABE KAIMOWITZ

Yes, Wo-Chi-Cans were deeply involved in the civil rights movement. Alvin

Poussaint, after becoming a psychiatrist, devoted two years – 1965 to 1967 – to the struggle in Mississippi. Grace Horowitz Chawes, once the Camp nurse, went to Mississippi in 1964 to work on a medical team.

Rick Reno Neff relates his involvement:

I was in Alabama, at the tail end of the walk from Selma to Montgomery, and spent some time in Birmingham afterward. I had been before, and then was active afterward, in the civil rights and anti-war movements in Chicago and then the San Francisco Bay Area. I was also very involved with the United Farm Workers organizing efforts in California and then Michigan.

But at least one Wo-Chi-Can – "Rooster" was his Camp nickname – involved himself deeply in the 'Sixties scene.' Gene Gordon (not the co-author) was in a way the most revolutionary Wo-Chi-Can of all. For Gene was a member of The Living Theater.

These actors were "among the boldest and most innovative experimenters of the 1960's. Their performances included rituals of love, affirmation, nonviolence, and communality drawn from various mystical and contemporary sources: Artaud, the Kabbalah, the continuous use of drugs. The thirty members of the Living Theater frequently tripped together and often performed while high on LSD."

So we are informed by Martin A. Lee and Bruce Shlain in their book *Acid Dreams: The Complete Social History of LSD: The CIA, the Sixties and Beyond.* "The Living Theater," they report, "was already heavily into drugs when the police chased them out of New York City in the early 1960's." Escaping to Europe, they remained there for twenty years, Gene with them a good part of that time.

Revolutionary was their nudity, their practice of leading people from the street to the theater and audiences from the theater to the street. They used drama as a means of advancing social change. The Living Theater, still under the leadership of Judith Malina, performs to this day in New York while Gene Gordon now lives quietly in San Francisco.

Through most of the Sixties a folk music revival swept the States, and it was folk, rather than rock music, that captivated most Wo-Chi-Cans. They admired Phil Ochs, Tom Paxton, Bob Dylan, Joan Baez, Peter, Paul and Mary, and, of course, Pete Seeger. These were the ones who put themselves on the line, singing to protest racism and the war in Vietnam. In 1964, Pete Seeger, Phil Ochs and others gave concerts in Mississippi to help with the voter registration drive.

The Animals, the Monkees, the Byrds, the Beatles...? It is difficult to imagine Wo-Chi-Ca musicians Ronnie Gilbert, Fred Hellerman, Ernie Lieberman, Jerry Silverman or Dave Sear ecstatic over the Jefferson Airplane or even the Grateful Dead. Wo-Chi-Cans marched to a different drum; their idol was a singer and writer of over a thousand political folk songs. Woody Guthrie died of Huntington's Chorea on October 3, 1967, at the very height of the Psychedelic Sixties.

By 1968 more than half a million American soldiers were in Vietnam; 57,000 would be killed. At the close of the decade, Americans read in their newspapers that troops of the US Army, in one small Vietnamese village, had massacred as many as three hundred men, women, and children. With this outrage in My Lai, revulsion and outright opposition to the war spread widely.

Struggles for the environment, for women's rights, gay liberation – the tumultuous Sixties came to an end. Its farewell party in upstate New York was the greatest rock-concert ever: the Woodstock "Festival of Life." Three days of Richie Havens, Ravi Shankar and heavy rain... Arlo Guthrie, Joe Cocker, Jimi Hendrix, Janis Joplin and six hundred acres of mud... Five hundred thousand people and Santana, The Who, Blood Sweat and Tears, Sly and the Family Stone... Traffic Jams up to twenty miles long and Crosby, Stills, Nash and Young... the Paul Butterfield Blues Band, Country Joe and the Fish, The Creedence Clearwater Revival... And so good-bye to the Sixties!

The first year of the new decade saw American troops storm into Cambodia, while at Kent State University in Ohio, those protesting the invasion were fired upon: National Guardsmen killed four students. On May 3 of the following year, demonstrators in Washington demanding an immediate end to the war in Vietnam were met with 5,100 city police, 500 park police and 1,500 National Guardsmen. Ten thousand Federal troops stood by, just in case. Tens of thousands of protesters, calling themselves the "Mayday Tribe," attempted to shut down the nation's capital. Certainly the District was disrupted, as police used tear gas extensively; it wafted over the Washington Monument and Lincoln Memorial. The police also wielded billy clubs, injuring 150 demonstrators and arresting 7,000.

Beginning in 1970, the CIA – under secret orders from President Nixon – set out to destroy the government of Chile. The country's democratically elected president, Dr. Salvador Allende, was a Marxist. A military junta seized power and murdered Allende. Death squads killed over 3,000 people, and thousands more were jailed and tortured.

The year 1972 gave our nation the Watergate burglaries, the scandal in which Nixon was involved; he resigned from office in 1974, the first time an American president was forced to step down.

An unprecedented event occurred in 1975: American and Soviet spacecraft – Apollo and Soyuz – joined together in space. Astronauts and Cosmonauts in orbit shook hands, swapped flags, and exchanged gifts such as tree seeds to be planted in each other's countries. And finally in that same year, a helicopter lifted the last Americans in Vietnam from the roof of the U.S. Embassy building in Saigon. The city was renamed after Ho Chi Minh.

A turbulent period, to say the least, from the time Camp closed in '54. Twenty-two stormy years! What else could possibly happen? The unthinkable happened. At the beginning of 1976 – on January 23 – Wo-Chi-Cans heard that the gentle giant was dead.

Most campers had no idea that Paul Robeson was sick, or how he died, or even where. How did it come to pass that so many Wo-Chi-Cans lost touch with their hero? What had happened to their Paul in the twenty-two years after Camp closed? Actually, it had been more than twenty-two years since Wo-Chi-Cans last saw Paul at Camp, for his final visit took place in 1949, when Camp was still back in New Jersey. Paul never did visit Wyandot in upstate New York.

The press reported that Robeson died in Philadelphia where his last years were passed in sickness and seclusion. But the papers did not disclose how a man of such stamina and spirit came to die a forlorn death. Were Wo-Chi-Cans aware of the ceaseless harassment and outright persecution Paul Robeson endured? Even Wo-Chi-Cans could not conceive the full extent of his torment, nor could they imagine that it would break the health of such a giant.

Did Wo-Chi-Cans know that already in 1941 the FBI scrutinized Robeson's every move? Did they realize that FBI agents followed Paul everywhere – yes, even to Camp Wo-Chi-Ca? An undercover agent, writing to his superiors, reports that he...

...attended a party and banquet given in honor of Paul Robeson at Camp Wo-Chi-Ca. There were banners on all of the buildings and tents which read "Welcome Paul Robeson" and "Paul Robeson Freedom Fighter." When Paul Robeson arrived at the camp, the Campers gathered around him and sang a song of welcome specially written for this occasion.

He then was escorted to the Administration Building where there were more cheers for him and presented with a scroll from the children of the camp. During the presentation of the scroll by a young girl, he became so emotional that tears rolled down his cheeks. When the older folks saw this, many of the women were affected likewise.

There was a football game played by the campers in which Paul Robeson took part. At the banquet which followed he presented some of the children with medals for their achievements while at camp.

After the banquet, there was a show put on by the children in which they sang songs that were written by Paul Robeson. To show his appreciation, Paul Robeson then sang several songs requested by the campers.

Among the guests present were...

The FBI spy concludes his report with names of notable people present: an official of the Harlem branch of the YMCA, various IWO officers, etc.

That the FBI for thirty years opened Robeson's mail and listened in on his phone conversations was bad enough. But that there would be outright attempts to kill Paul is abominable. On four separate occasions, his car's front wheel somehow worked loose and flew off.

Who can imagine what an arduous ordeal was Robeson's struggle to regain his passport, seized by the Department of State? An eight-year battle – legal, financial, political and emotional. The State Department decreed that "Robeson's travel abroad...would be contrary to the best interests of the United States." An attorney of that agency labeled Robeson "one of the most dangerous men in the world."

What effect on his health and peace of mind did loss of income have – a drop from $104,000 in 1947 to $2,000 in 1950? His records removed from music store shelves and his dates at concert halls canceled? What effect when friends crossed the street to avoid him and even Blacks turned against him? "A great whisper and a greater silence in Black America" – this, asserts Professor of History Sterling Stuckey, was Paul Robeson. "Stay away from me," Paul had to warn Sidney Poitier. "Being seen with me will ruin your career."

In 1955 Paul underwent prostate surgery, while at the same time his wife Essie had a radical mastectomy. Khrushchev's revelations in '56 distressed Robeson so – according to his biographer Martin Duberman – that he suffered emotional collapse. Arteriosclerosis, early senility, deep depression... – such were the diagnoses of his doctors at this time.

Wo-Chi-Cans may have been unaware of Paul's severe health problems, but certainly they knew that he was subpoenaed in 1956 to appear before HUAC. Paul, "in deep trouble" psychologically according to his doctor, nevertheless prevailed over his tormentors.

The Committee demanded to know whether Robeson had written "Only here, in the Soviet Union, did I feel that I was a real man with a capital M."

"I would say in Russia I felt for the first time like a full human being," Paul answered, "and no colored prejudice like in Mississippi and no colored prejudice like in Washington, and it was the first time I felt like a human being, where I did not feel the pressure of color as I feel in this committee today."

"Why do you not stay in Russia?" demanded Rep. Scherer. "Because my father was a slave," retorted Robeson, "and my people died to build this country, and I am going to stay here and have a part of it just like you. And no Fascist-minded people will drive me from it. Is that clear?"

"The reason you are here," insisted Scherer, "is because you are promoting the Communist cause in this country." Robeson shot back: "I am here because I am opposing the neo-Fascist cause which I see arising in this committee. You are the true un-Americans, and you should be ashamed of yourselves."

In spite of illness, Robeson would enjoy other triumphs in the Fifties. 1958 was especially auspicious. His autobiography *Here I Stand* was published. A Supreme Court decision compelled the State Department to restore his passport. In that year people around the world celebrated Paul's 60th birthday: the entire nation of India honored him with a "Paul Robeson Day." A warm welcome in London, a frenzied reception in Moscow, an exultant appearance at Carnegie Hall!

Were Wo-Chi-Cans members of that sold-out New York audience? Did they yell – as they had at the Progressive Party Convention back in 1948 – "PAUL! PAUL! WO-CHI-CA!" Once again they would not have been heard. For just as in the convention hall in Philadelphia, so now in the concert hall in New York, the auditorium rang with whistles, shouts and cheers.

In 1959 Paul starred, for the third time in his career, in *Othello* – this time in Shakespeare's birthplace, Stratford-upon-Avon. But the Sixties brought emotional collapse, chronic depression, months of hospitalization, a diagnosis of Paget's disease. In 1963 his wife Essie was told she had terminal cancer; she died in 1965.

That same year Paul almost died of double pneumonia. By 1966 he was "an invalid" living in seclusion in the home of his sister Marian. So sick was he that in 1974 the FBI said of Paul Robeson – once "one of the most dangerous men in the world" - that "no further investigation is warranted." All too well had the government done its job. "What they have done to Paul has been the most cruel thing I have ever seen," cried W.E.B. DuBois: "The persecution of Paul Robeson by the Government...has been one of the most contemptible happenings in modern history." Bishop J. Clinton Hoggard, a friend from Paul's boyhood, said of Robeson "This was a man who bore on his body the marks of Jesus...marks of vengeance."

Paul lived with his sister for the better part of thirteen years. Marian and Paul Jr. strictly controlled access to him, allowing only the closest of friends to enter the house. There was a time when the magic word 'Wo-Chi-Ca' would gain entrance to Paul's home, to his theater dressing room, to wherever... But not even the name of his beloved camp could open the door to the cloistered dwelling at 4951 Walnut Street in Philadelphia. It is doubtful that even one Wo-Chi-Can saw Paul in this period.

Paul was too ill to attend the 75th birthday celebration held for him, again at Carnegie Hall. Were Wo-Chi-Cans present at this "Salute to Paul Robeson?" At least one was, for Paul, Jr., a camper for two summers, organized the event. Coretta Scott King proclaimed to the full house that Paul had been "buried alive" because he championed human dignity and civil rights long before her husband did.

On January 23, 1976 the tallest tree in the forest fell; nearly no one was there to hear it. Days later Wo-Chi-Cans read in the newspapers that their hero Paul Robeson was dead.

At least one Wo-Chi-Can was present at Paul's funeral in Harlem on a cold rainy January 27: Bobbie Rabinowitz, her husband and two sons, squeezed into the A. M. E. Zion Church along with 5000 friends and admirers of Robeson. Other Wo-Chi-Cans attended memorial services elsewhere for Paul, and they were startled to realize that they had not gathered together as campers in over twenty years. Immediately a nucleus of New York alumni went to work on a reunion. Going through the files of Camp Secretary Eve Levine (she had died the year before), they were able to find the addresses of two hundred campers.

Up in Hyde Park, New York, a pair of Wo-Chi-Cans ran a camp for kids. When Wyandot went under in '54, Rima and Dave Glaser picked up the banner. Apart from its higher fees, Camp Trywoodie was much like Camp Wo-Chi-Ca. Even the Wo-Chi-Ca totem pole was reproduced on Trywoodie grounds. In the year of our country's bicentennial, the Glaser camp was still operating. It was here that the 1976 Reunion took place.

From as far away as Canada they came to pay respect to the memory of Robeson, to share stories of Paul's thrilling visits to Camp. Counselors and campers and bunkmates from twenty-five years in the past sang and danced and talked into the night. By '76 the Red Scare had wound down and Wo-Chi-Cans felt relaxed. Laughing, they learned that a number had sent for their FBI files, and – lo and behold – their childhood attendance at Wo-Chi-Ca was cited as a "subversive activity." But on one subject they did not laugh: they confessed they had not gone back to visit the original campsite. Loss of the 'sacred ground' was too painful even to think about.

Nevertheless, this long-delayed Wo-Chi-Ca reunion sent all away happy. Yet astonishingly, another twenty-two years would elapse before the campers would meet again. Once more it took Paul Robeson to bring Wo-Chi-Cans together –

this time not his death in 1976, but the centennial of his birth in 1998.

This subsequent twenty-two-year period included such earth-shaking events as the breakup of the Soviet Union and the entire Socialist Block of nations. We can imagine the effect of that on Wo-Chi-Cans! In any event, at this 1998 Reunion they were old enough to be the grandparents now of the campers they once had been, and needed name tags to identify each other. Some also wore buttons demanding that the U.S. Post Office issue a Paul Robeson commemorative stamp. Wo-Chi-Can Margie Goss Burroughs led this effort to honor the Renaissance man.

The organizers had provided words to the old Camp songs, but most disdained their use: "We don't need no stinkin' song sheets," they wisecracked. They remembered the lyrics as if it were yesterday. "We Welcome You To Wo-Chi-Ca," "In A Camp That's Called Wo-Chi-Ca," "Wo-Chi-Ca Mine...."

But one piece of music formed the highlight of the Reunion. No matter that an old phonograph machine and a cracked 78 record made an awful scratchy sound. The voice was booming and mellow and oh so familiar. "Ballad for Americans" flooded the room as a hundred Wo-Chi-Cans – tears in their eyes – sang along with Paul.

They joined in on "Joe Hill" as well, and as they raised their voices, they knew in their hearts that Wo-Chi-Ca – like Joe Hill and Paul Robeson – would never die. Wo-Chi-Ca would live forever.

But all too well the campers knew that they would not live forever. So many Wo-Chi-Cans gone already... They resolved not to wait another twenty-two years for the next reunion. Why not another one in just two years? And on the original grounds of Wo-Chi-Ca! The land, many were amazed to learn, had not been paved over for condos, but remained a rustic camp maintained by a Lutheran/Episcopal church. What's more, its administrators were genuinely interested in Wo-Chi-Ca's history – they would be happy to host a gathering on the 'sacred ground.'

And so, in June of 2000, one hundred fifty alumni found their way back to rural New Jersey, to their beloved childhood camp. Up the wide path they walked – yes, the same dirt road was still there. A Wo-Chi-Ca sign in wood to welcome them? No, but the Stone House – the old administration building – looked as imposing as it had when they were kids.

"There's the Quonset hut, the Paul Robeson Playhouse! And look – the amphitheater, the stone steps we built! And the Log Cabin, the Mess Hall, the old Art Shack, the baseball and soccer fields, the swimming hole... Are they all still here? Untouched by time?"

Can it be? Our lost Wo-Chi-Ca shimmering in the sun – like Brigadoon? Most miraculous of all, in the distance (is that mist over on the meadow or only in our eyes?) four wooden cabins, their window screens open to the breeze. "The bunk houses! The places where we slept! Can we go in?"

Gingerly they open a door. A curtain of spider webs brushing their faces makes them shiver. They behold a dozen bunk beds ready to cradle young bodies. "How small this room seems now!"

Along the back wall, rows of narrow wooden doors hide the shelves where once they kept their folded clothes. "What would I find if I dared to open this closet door – would I see the child that was me so long ago?" One Wo-Chi-Ca woman does swing open the door and is startled to see her own name in foot-high faded red letters. Just one more marvel on this magical day!

Back out to the sunshine and air. No heather, not quite a hill, but what a day this has been! The Wo-Chi-Ca Reunion of 2000 – isn't it almost like being in love?

In truth everything has changed. The old swimming hole has been enlarged to an impressive lake; the Log Cabin – once a bunkhouse for the littlest Wo-Chi-Cans – is an adult Christian retreat. And the Art Shack interior... – well, it is now strewn with junk. But wait! In one dusty corner lies a piece of splintered wood with peeling paint. Yes, this is the upper half of the totem pole constructed by Elizabeth Catlett and her young charges sixty years ago.

The old Paul Robeson Playhouse is now a gymnasium with the entire inside given over to a basketball court. One end of the Quonset hut, extended by a wood deck, is adorned with two large soda machines.

Behind the Playhouse, the amphitheater seems the same, but all the grass growing between the stones make it seem as ancient as an amphitheater in Greece. In
the warm afternoon the Wo-Chi-Cans sit on the steps they built with their own
hands – sweating and singing as they worked – and applaud as Bill Pickens from
the Paul Robeson Foundation places a commemorative plaque to rededicate the
Playhouse.

Black and white sing and dance in the evening – carry on as children again on
the very site where once they lived 'in a true democracy.' In the old mess hall
they eat meals seasoned with much reminiscence: "We churned out peach ice
cream by hand!" "We mopped and squeegeed these wood floors!" "Remember
how we applauded the cooks after a delicious meal?"

Long gone are the hand-carved tables, though the wagon-wheel chandelier still
hangs from the ceiling. When someone stands under that fixture with her fingers
high in a V-sign, her signal quiets the noisy room just as it did half a century ago.
But only for a moment, in respect for tradition. The call for silence is futile: so
many memories, so much to say.... Is it not, at long last, time to get the entire Wo-
Chi-Ca story down on paper? The authors immediately go about to solicit memoirs, and so begins the collection that forms the body of this book.

*I had just arrived from Norway where I had spent the war years as a
refugee from Germany. At Wo-Chi-Ca, I saw America at its best.*
                                            DOLLY ROTH HONIG

Ned Pearlstein writes of his "wonderful memories" of...

*...the swimming hole and a small wooden boat in it. I remember sleeping
in a tent on a platform under wonderful star-filled nights, the walks into
the village to get candy, the sound of a train in the distance... The mix of
people from different ethnic and racial backgrounds!*

*Evenings on the grass by the crafts building when performances were
given (Gilbert and Sullivan, a great discovery for me!), Paul Robeson
singing – not more than ten feet away –"Water Boy" and more. Shaking
his hand and being so impressed with his size and gentleness.*

*The good-byes to the young counselors who were going off to Spain to
fight Franco and the reverent feeling that we had as children seeing them
go. I feel so fortunate that I attended Wo-Chi-Ca.*

Young campers bidding farewell to their counselors going off to the Spanish Civil War. How many readers have such memories of their childhood summer camp?

I was eleven years old when I went to Wo-Chi-Ca for the first time. At that young age, I knew that the camp had changed me forever. I was quite a shy little girl, and was in fact very reluctant to leave home for an unknown experience. I didn't know anybody, I didn't know the songs or dances, and I was scared.

But somehow all of my fears faded because I was soon made to feel very safe. The counselors were extremely warm and affectionate. I blossomed in those two weeks and came back the following summer for four weeks. Later I worked as a waitress and then a counselor for two summers.

Today, more than fifty years later, I think about Camp with a renewed appreciation and fuller understanding of how unique and special Wo-Chi-Ca was. It affected so many children in a very deep and profound way. The story of Camp Wo-Chi-Ca had as its center love and understanding of all peoples, now known as diversity. We were the first Rainbow Tribe.

ADELE BROITMAN

Those who attended Wyandot too – even in the last difficult years – write fondly of their experience.

I was the camp craft counselor that last summer of Wyandot. I was sixteen. The memory of Marion's death from polio the previous summer was there. On our day off several of us went to a movie in town only to be asked when we returned, "What was the social significance of that movie?" It was, I think, a Hollywood film.

The camp director had a wonderful dog named Tippy – half-Collie, half-German Shepherd. The dog adopted me and slept in my bunkhouse. He tangled with a skunk one night and hit my bed stinking, and I ran him out while the campers went "Yuck" and hid their heads under their pillows.

I wore my jeans low and 'rocky' and sang doo-wop rock and roll rather than folk songs. I was a rebel and flaunting it, a Lower East Side hoodlum with no social graces. Teen-age tough-guy stuff. Camp was tolerant enough to let me be.

ALBERT LANNON

Eugene Barufkin's Wyandot memories include the rattlesnakes of Mt. Tremper and the gathering of fossils in Esopus Creek.

I have carried a rock embedded with fossils for forty-eight years. These experiences have remained with me all my life. Our camp had a spirit that can NEVER be duplicated. But when it was over, it was over. That sadness is still with me today.

Seldom did the authors receive a memoir or anecdote that did not feature Paul Robeson.

The two events that stand out in my Wo-Chi-Ca experience are playing softball with Paul Robeson as referee, and the time when the local veterans threatened to enter Camp and tear down the Paul Robeson sign on the Playhouse.

FRED WILSON

"My best memory," writes Shelly Kitzes,

...is being asked to accompany Paul Robeson when he sang at Camp in 1949. Rima Glaser came across campus to grab me and pull me to the Playhouse. "Paul Robeson needs an accompanist!" After a very quick rehearsal I played for Paul's performance. He sang "Water Boy," "Old Man River," and "Let My People Go." At the end he said "I want to thank Shelly Kitzes for playing so well for me on such short notice. I'll have to tell Larry (Lawrence Brown) to watch out!" This was a big highlight in my life.

Still another story about Paul Robeson, a bit longer and set in a locale far from Camp, is priceless:

In 1959 I was traveling through Europe with a friend. We actually drove a Ford station wagon from London to Moscow and back, something nobody did in those days. But before we got that far, we were in Vienna for the World Youth Festival. We still qualified as 'youths' in those days. Robeson had just gotten his passport back and had been invited to perform at an outdoor concert at the Festival. My friend and I were traveling with a tape recorder and my guitars. He was the recording guy and I was the guy who sang on street corners for gasoline money.

Anyhow, there we were on this huge outdoor square in Vienna, and there's Paul up on this two-by-four plank stage that was erected fo• the occasion. We had all our wires trailing onto the edge of the stage, and our tape recorder – a big suitcase-size thing on the cobblestones beneath the stage – was plugged into some power lines nearby because it wasn't a battery-operated recorder.

So there's Paul, singing away, and all of a sudden the lights go out and the place is in complete darkness! Everybody assumed it was some kind of sabotage. And everybody began to look at us: "Who are these guys with all these wires, coming out from under the stage – you know, dressed in peculiar blue jeans?"

The crowd turned nasty. There were all these people concerned about Robeson's security, as well they should have been. It looked like a very touchy moment for us, and I couldn't think what to do. I was actually physically afraid that something bad was gonna... – so I jumped up on stage and yelled "Paul, Paul! Wo-Chi-Ca! Jerry from Wo-Chi-Ca!"

He turned around, gave me a big smile, shook my hand and saved my ass right there and then. The magic word 'Wo-Chi-Ca.' And that was the end of our troubles in Vienna.

Jerry Silverman illustrates here not only the magical effect the word 'Wo-Chi-Ca' had on Paul, but the magic of Robeson's name to foreign soldiers half-way around the world.

A few weeks later we were crossing the Polish-Soviet border at Brest-Litovsk. The aforementioned Ford station wagon, which had been a source of great curiosity all through Eastern Europe, was really getting a close inspection by the Soviet border guards.

What really got them were the three coffin-like boxes we had built into the rear of the wagon to contain all our gear. They weren't sure what to make of all that recording equipment and the books we were carrying. Those books included copies of my **Folk Blues** *and* **Lift Every Voice**, *a song collection published by People's Artists.*

The guards were on the phone calling for instructions, when once again, inspiration struck. The Foreword to the book was written by Paul, and featured a fine drawing of his smiling face. I turned to the guard and pointing to the picture, said in my best Russian: "Vy znayete etovo cheloveka?" ("You know this person?") He immediately said "Paul Robeson." Then, pointing to my name among the list of associate editors, I proudly said, "I eto ya!" ("And that's me!") A moment later we were smilingly waved on.

"One of the most precious possessions I have," relates Helen Engelhardt, "is Paul Robeson's autograph and a brief statement which he inscribed beneath a copy of a poem that I wrote about him when I was ten years old."

Paul Robeson

**There he stands: a mountain of muscle,
A statue of hope, a salvation.
Strong, calm and confident.
The kind of person you can look up to
In respect and gratitude.
He is Paul Robeson.**

"'I shall be proud,' Paul wrote to me, 'if – a little – I have helped with many, many others to see that you grow up in a much better world - a world of Peace and Equality.'

"Though the words make me wince now – the awkward rhetoric, the clichés (Paul's as well as mine) – I am glad I grew up in a family and a community of individuals who had a vision of a 'better world' and devoted themselves to bringing it about. I am grateful that I had a real hero such as Paul to look up to.

"Camp Wo-Chi-Ca was not my first camp, nor was it the last, but it was by far the most memorable – indeed it transcends the category of 'camps' to be first in the experiences which have transformed my life.

"It was where I first heard and fell in love with folk songs, a love that endures to this day. It was where I first lived with people from different backgrounds. Wo-Chi-Ca became a way of life that we sang about and talked about. In spite of – or probably because of – the rhetoric and vision that infused it, Wo-Chi-Ca was unique."

Wo-Chi-Can Ronnie Gilbert was a member of The Weavers quartet that in the Fifties led the hit parade with "Tzena, Tzena" and "Irene, Goodnight." Ronnie went on to a career as actor and playwright as well as a lecturer on activism, performing arts, and social movements. For his TV documentary on the

Suffragettes, Ken Burns asked Ronnie to provide the voice of Elzabeth Cady Stanton. Ronnie's book and play *The Most Dangerous Woman in America* are tributes to the great labor leader Mother Jones.

Lucky summers I was sent to Wo-Chi-Ca, the Worker's Children's Camp. It's late 1930- or early 1940-something. The camp chorus is rehearsing in The Barn, a cool, dark refuge from the heat. We are learning John Latouche and Earl Robinson's "Ballad for Americans." There have been rumors... "In seventy-six the sky was red/Thunder rumbled overhead/Bad King George couldn't sleep in his bed/And on that stormy morn/Ol' Uncle Sam was born!"

The barn door swings open. Yes! There he stands, framed black in the doorway, and I swear, the light dancing on his shoulders like little flames. Then comes the deep voice, rolling into our camp, into our Barn, into our lives: "Old Sam put on a three-cornered hat/And in a Richmond church he sat/And Patrick Henry told him that/While America drew breath/It was Liberty or Death!"

I am sixteen or seventeen. Someone takes me to the theater to see Robeson as Othello. It comes near to costing me my high school diploma for refusal to participate in the senior project, a minstrel show. Put on blackface and caper – how could I?

So yes, I remember Paul Robeson, and I remember the Peekskill picnic at which I might have gotten to sing with him again if the local paramilitary patriotic types hadn't turned it into a bloody rout. I don't much go in for hero worship anymore. One tends to give that up after having been around the corner several times. But I can't give up Paul. I don't want to. He's still my hero.

Paul Robeson – certainly the foremost – was not however the only hero to visit Wo-Chi-Ca. Heroic too were Mother Bloor, Canada Lee, Rockwell Kent, Howard Fast, Larry Adler, Albert E. Kahn, Dr. Edward Barsky, and untold others.

Wo-Chi-Ca's staff too included its share of heroes – Elizabeth Catlett, Charles White, Jacob Lawrence, Gwen Bennett, Dick Crosscup... Vaino Hill who with hammer and chisel remained throughout the snowy winter at Camp carving furniture of wood.

With such role models no wonder that Wo-Chi-Ca children developed into heroes themselves. Whitey Melzer, youthful camper, later a popular children's counselor, Army radio operator, aerial gunner – shot down on his eighth mission over

Hitler Germany. For him Wo-Chi-Ca named the Whitey Melzer Music Room.

Jerry Feifer, Whitey's close buddy and classmate at Brooklyn College, student of Yiddish culture, lover of dance, athletics, but especially books – killed in France at the Battle of the Bulge. "It's Wo-Chi-Ca that made me the kind of soldier that I am today," he wrote the campers. "It's for Wo-Chi-Ca and the freedom of the children that I fight." The Wo-Chi-Ca Library was named for Jerry Feifer.

A compendium of Wo-Chi-Cans with accounts of their accomplishments would be immense indeed:

Belenky, Robert: Child psychologist. at his farm in Vermont, directed a program for at-risk inner city children. Since retirement, divides time between Haiti and Russia, working with homeless street children. His book, *Raising Nobody's Child*, will soon be published.

Bravo, Estella Siegel: Resident of Havana more than thirty years. A leading cinemaphotographer of Cuba. Recently completed film on Fidel Castro and Cuban Revolution.

Flacks, Dick: A founder of Students for a Democratic Society at Port Huron, Michigan in 1962 and a leader of SDS throughout the decade. active in university-based protests against Vietnam War. Currently teacher of sociology at University of California, Santa Barbara, author of *Making History: The American Left and the American Mind*. Host for twenty years of a weekly radio program, "The Culture of Protest."

Holland, Bert: Following discharge from the USNR in 1947 attended the University of Chicago where he participated with CORE in desegregating a public swimming pool and a 'whites-only' baseball field. Organized demonstrations to prompt University of Chicago Medical School to drop 'race' on its entrance applications.

McWilliams, Anne Epstein: Married forty years to African American attorney. Both active in civil rights movement. Anne worked in early childhood education in Washington, DC and in US Virgin Islands. Now, in 'retirement,' coordinates children's literacy program in Oakland, California.

Salerno, Eric: Grew up in Italy after father, Michele Salerno, editor of L'Unità del Popolo, Italian language newspaper of Communist Party of the United States, was deported. Eric writes for Rome's leading paper Il Messaggero, specializing in Third World and African affairs. Author of four books, including *Genocide in Libya* about Italian colonialism. Expects soon to publish an English translation of his family memoir, *Reds in Manhattan*.

Scheer, Robert: Former Vietnam correspondent, managing editor and editor-in-chief of *Ramparts* magazine. Currently syndicated columnist for the Los Angeles Times as well as contributing editor for *The Nation* magazine. Author of six books including *Thinking Tuna Fish, Talking Death: Essays on the Pornography of Power*. Host of "Left, Right and Center" on National Public Radio, Santa Monica.

Silber, Irwin: Journalist, former foreign correspondent for *The Guardian*. Producer of Folkways Records, editor of scores of folksong collections, co-founder of *Sing Out!* magazine. producer of "hootenannies all over New York City." Author of numerous books, including *Socialism: What Went Wrong?* as well as *A Patient's Guide to Knee and Hip Replacement*. In 1958 successfully defied HUAC on First Amendment grounds. Married to folk/blues/jazz singer and social activist Barbara Dane: with her edited *The Vietnam Songbook*. On honeymoon transported his wife to 'the sacred ground' in New Jersey, formerly Camp Wo-Chi-Ca.

Solomon, Mark: Retired history professor and long a leader in peace and justice movements such as U.S. Peace Council and World Peace Council. Writes extensively on U.S. foreign policy, peace issues, and anti-racism. Cofounder of Committees of Correspondence for Democracy and Socialism. Most recent book is *The Cry Was Unity: Communists and African Americans, 1917-1936*.

A sample so small barely suggests the sum that would be found in just one category of Wo-Chi-Cans – one that for convenience we might call 'political.' We would have to include Leeza Vinogradov who is with Women for Peace and also Bernie Eisenberg, so active in the fight to save Pacifica Radio.

And what of artists and actors in our compendium – doctors, dancers and singers? Here we would find Matt Borenstein, a distinguished photographer in New York City, and Crystal Field, founder and director of Theater for a New City located in the heart of Manhattan's Lower East Side. This true neighborhood theater offers tickets as low as five dollars and even free admission, while it involves the community in every possible way.

Architect Bernie Feldstein, Nobel Laureate in economic science Robert Fogel, and social worker Joy Glickman are all alumni. Joy worked in settlement houses and with the homeless for thirty years.

Dancer Rena Gluck Rena, a camper and counselor for eight years at Wo-Chi-Ca – she studied with Pearl Primus – went on to found the Batsheva Dance Company in Israel and is Chairwoman of the Jerusalem Academy of Music and Dance.

Ulric Haynes, Jr., Dean for International Relations at Hofstra University, was a Foreign Service Officer, a member of the staff of the National Security Council, and U.S. Ambassador to Algeria.

Fred Hellerman with Wo-Chi-Ca friend Ronnie Gilbert formed one half of the legendary folk song group The Weavers. Fred's life has been devoted to music – singing, playing, producing, arranging and publishing.

Fred Jerome is publishing a new book about Albert Einstein the "passionate pacifist;" it will reveal the FBI's surveillance of the great scientist.

Betty Bernstein LaDuke studied art at Wo-Chi-Ca with Charles White and Elizabeth Catlett. She travels frequently to Africa, sketching the daily life of Eritrean women, portraying their culture in vivid paintings. Betty's daughter, Winona LaDuke, has twice run for vice-president of the United States with Ralph Nader.

Lew Levinson teaches drama and directs plays at Laney Community College in Oakland, California. Ronnie Mathews, for over forty years a noted jazz musician, has played with Clark Terry, with Dexter Gordon, and with Art Blakey's Jazz Messengers.

Congressman Vito Marcantonio, representing Spanish Harlem in the late Thirties, raised money to send several Puerto Rican children to Wo-Chi-Ca. One of these young campers, Ernesto Puente, made a name for himself perhaps more recognizable than any other alumnus of the camp. He was no less than the 'Mambo King,' Tito Puente!

Bobbie Rabinowitz is a life-long union activist and founder of the New York City Labor Chorus. Teddy Reid of Jamaican heritage retired from a practice in psychiatry, but from his home in Mexico travels to Tucson to train senior therapists. Lynn Okun Scholnick, a former psychologist, pursues a second career as a sculptor, and volunteers as an AIDS therapist.

Hi Schwendinger and wife Julia (Siegal) are noted professors of criminology. Mike Stoller is in the Rock and Roll Hall of Fame.

Stephen Trachtenberg is president of George Washington University in the nation's capitol. Cyril Tyson is author of *The Unconditional War on Poverty*.

And so it goes... Alan Wilson, the son of missionaries, raised in China, heard about Wo-Chi-Ca through an army buddy in World War II and worked the summer of 1947 as a counselor. The following summer he brought his new wife back with him. "Why did I choose to spend my honeymoon at Wo-Chi-Ca? Well, I was expected back (though not with a wife). Also, the Cantwell Committee (a local HUAC in Seattle) was making moves to see whether they could force either

Suzanne or me to divulge political information about people more important than ourselves. I don't think Wo-Chi-Cans knew they were harboring refugees in addition to providing a delightful spot for a honeymoon. That second summer I scrubbed pots and pans in the kitchen and Suzanne worked in the canteen. We stayed on into the fall to help Vaino Hill build and repair tent platforms. We later moved to Berkeley and both taught at the University of California until retirement."

Richard Worrell grew up in Harlem, went on to become a surgeon and professor of orthopedics at the University of New Mexico Health Science Center. His 'Worrell Knee Replacement' is world famous, and Dr. Worrell has been named one of the top one hundred physicians in the United States.

But enough! We run the risk of transmuting *Tales of Wo-Chi-Ca* into a vanity book or an in-group chronicle. In our research we made contact with five hundred Wo-Chi-Cans. But this number is only five percent of the ten thousand campers, visitors and staff members who passed through in twenty years. Many an intriguing story we did not enlarge upon. A faded snapshot taken at Camp shows William E. Dodd, Jr., son of the Ambassador to Germany, an outspoken critic of Hitler. Another story would concern a poor Black family in the Bronx who sent their daughter Marilyn to Camp Wo-Chi-Ca. Marilyn's brother Colin rose through army ranks to become a general and finally, Secretary of State.

Would this seem to indicate that Wo-Chi-Ca was 'mainstream,' a patriotic camp? Young Beatrice Levy certainly thought so and declared it in ringing terms in her in Daily Wo-Chi-Can article:

WO-CHI-CANS ALL... AMERICANS ALL!!!

The whole camp will celebrate this day which brought independence to our country during the year 1776. We are going to greet this day with a cheer, because everyone wants to show how proud he or she is to be an American.

At Wo-Chi-Ca we have many different campers of different nationalities – in the Spirit of Americanism we all work and play together. Wo-Chi-Cans all – Americans all! HAIL TO THE 4th OF JULY!

Yes, Wo-Chi-Ca is an 'American Story.'

On Wednesday morning, instead of reveille, Paul Revere will ride on his horse and go to every bunk and wake up everybody. The dramatic group will dramatize The Trial of Peter Zenger. During rest period the town crier

will go around and announce various discussions. There will be Olympic Games on the ball field and there will be a dramatization of The Raid on Harper's Ferry. We are sure it will be a great day.

ELSA CAULLY and DICK LEVINE (in the *Daily Wo-Chi-Can*)

The former Wo-Chi-Ca site is now an interracial Christian camp that annually hosts retarded children, while the Mt. Tremper locale where once Camp Wyandot stood is occupied by the Zen Mountain Monastery, a Buddhist center. Fine institutions both, and grounds whereon efforts are made to build a better world.

Yet a number of people in these troubled times retain a vivid memory of a little utopia on those grounds. One such is Issar Smith:

It was a marvelous era when things were clearer than now. It was an era when there was no question of who were the good people of the world and who were the bad ones. Camp stood for the good things (and still stands for) peace, justice, economic equality (socialism), an end to racism, the interaction and true camaraderie between people of all races and cultures. The world has changed greatly from those days, but this children's paradise showed what life could be at its best. It was certainly a formative experience in my life.

Another alumnus, Arthur Komar, former Professor of Physics at Yeshiva University writes...

Wo-Chi-Ca, was a little world in which we learned that it was indeed possible for people of many races and backgrounds to live in a relationship. The abhorrence of competitiveness, the joy of loving one another was so evident at Wo-Chi-Ca....

From the lives of the Wo-Chi-Cans whom I have known and followed over these many years I have seen only love and kindness. Yes, there is a way. Our little world of Wo-Chi-Ca showed that it was possible...at least for some short time...until the sharks of the world had their way.

Utopia: isn't that a little too... – well, utopian? But Oscar Wilde insists that "A map of the world that does not include Utopia is not worth even glancing at, for it leaves out the one country at which Humanity is always landing."

> **Have you ever dreamed of a place**
> **Far away from it all,**
> **Where the winter winds will never blow,**

Living things have room to grow;
And the sound of guns
Doesn't pound in your ears anymore?

So we are asked in the film about Shangri-la. Moreover, R. Buckminster Fuller warns us that "The world is now too dangerous for anything less than Utopia."

The children and grandchildren of Wo-Chi-Cans never did see that 'World of Tomorrow' that their parents believed would be their heritage – an earthly paradise, life as it can and should be. But just as people of all cultures and climes hold on to a dream of a Golden Age free from disease, from greed and war – a time of social harmony, a Garden of Eden – so too does humanity persist in its dream of Utopia.

Wo-Chi-Cans think of their childhood camp as such a utopia, a Camelot, the reflection of a lost ideal.

The camaraderie, the politics, the games, the work, the culture, the songs, the profoundly healthy sense of engagement in an effort to forge a better life – all that was exceptional for a summer camp and for its time. In the present, when the culture and politics of the postwar left is often vilified and denigrated by small and uninformed minds, Wo-Chi-Ca shines ever more brightly as a testimonial to what we were really about: fidelity to the values of peace, justice, democratic practice, and fierce commitment to defend everything that is decent and human in our culture. That experience, I am sure, is in our bones.

MARK SOLOMON

Camelot – "The Once and Future King." There once was a camp. But can there ever be a future Wo-Chi-Ca; can the whole world be a Camelot someday?

Today the United States dominates the world militarily, economically, and culturally. Too often our country is seen as arrogant and disdainful: "Why do they hate us so?" we ask ourselves every day. Is the U. S. the last mighty empire in a world on the brink of ruin? Is a rapacious America the Midgard Serpent of Norse mythology circling the globe with its tail in its mouth, crushing all in its grip?

Or can America be the salvation of the world, its last best hope? Wo-Chi-Cans would answer in the affirmative for, as their hero Paul Robeson constantly reminded them, "Our greatest songs are still unsung." Let America return to its roots, say the Wo-Chi-Cans – to its radical heritage, to the America of Walt Whitman, Mother Bloor, Paul Robeson, Woody Guthrie, Pete Seeger....

Let America be America again.
Let it be the dream it used to be.
Let it be the pioneer on the plain
Seeking a home where he himself is free.

(America never was America to me.)

O, let my land be a land where Liberty
Is crowned with no false patriotic wreath,
But opportunity is real, and life is free,
Equality is in the air we breathe.

Langston Hughes objects to...

...finding only the same old stupid plan
Of dog eat dog, of mighty crush the weak.
Of profit, power, gain, of grab the land!
Of grab the gold! Of grab the ways of satisfying need!
Of work the men! Of take the pay!
Of owning everything for one's own greed!

Hughes, whose poetry was often heard at Wo-Chi-Ca, sings...

O, let America be America again –
The land that never has been yet –
And yet must be – the land where every man is free.
The land that's mine – the poor man's, Indian's, Negro's,
ME – Who made America,
Whose sweat and blood, whose faith and pain,
Whose hand at the foundry, whose plow in the rain,
Must bring back our mighty dream again.

Sure, call me any ugly name you choose –
The steel of freedom does not stain.
From those who live like leeches on the people's lives,
We must take back our land again,
America!

We, the people, must redeem
The land, the mines, the plants, the rivers.

The mountains and the endless plain –
All, all the stretch of these great green states –
And make America again!

May this story of the camp that once was and *must be again*, take wing and like an arrow point the way to a World of Tomorrow that is not an empty dream, but the only viable future for humankind. Yes, Let America be America again! And may a thousand Wo-Chi-Cas bloom.

WO·CHI·CA
DECLARATION of RIGHTS

The right to eat three good meals a day......
The right of a child to go freely to a free school...
The right of children to have camps like Wo·Chi·Ca...
The right of a child to be healthy..........
The right to have family, parents, friends
The right to take pride in calling ourselves worker's children
The right of a child to speak his mind
The right of camper and pupil to have a voice in the
     government of camp and school...
The right of a youth to choose his own life's work...
The right of all races to work and play together....

Photograph of Paul Robeson
on pg. 56, Rutgers University

Photograph of Paul Robeson (frontispiece)
used by permission of Paul Robeson, Jr.

Photos of Paul Robeson on pgs. 58 and 61 courtesy of
Schomburg Center for Research in Black Culture,
The New York Public Library,
Astor, Lenox and Tilden Foundation

CAMP PHOTOS AND MORE
CAN BE FOUND ON THE

WO-CHI-CA WEB SITE:

WWW.WO-CHI-CA.ORG/

Additional copies of
Tales of Wo-Chi-Ca
Can be ordered from

Avon Springs Press
1548 Golden Rain Rd.#12
Walnut Creek, CA 94595
(925) 934-3204
june.gene@yahoo.com